FEMINISM, SEXUALITY, AND THE RETURN OF RELIGION

Indiana Series in the Philosophy of Religion
Merold Westphal, editor

FEMINISM, SEXUALITY, AND THE RETURN OF RELIGION

Edited by Linda Martín Alcoff and John D. Caputo

Indiana University Press
Bloomington and Indianapolis

This book is a publication of

Indiana University Press
601 North Morton Street
Bloomington, Indiana 47404-3797 USA

iupress.indiana.edu

Telephone orders	800-842-6796
Fax orders	812-855-7931
Orders by e-mail	iuporder@indiana.edu

Library of Congress Cataloging-in-Publication Data

Feminism, sexuality, and the return of religion / edited by Linda Martín Alcoff and
John D. Caputo.
        p. cm. — (Indiana series in the philosophy of religion)
    Includes bibliographical references and index.
    ISBN 978-0-253-35621-5 (cloth : alk. paper) — ISBN 978-0-253-22304-3 (pbk. : alk. paper)
1. Religion—Philosophy. 2. Feminism—Religious aspects. 3. Continental philosophy.
I. Alcoff, Linda. II. Caputo, John D. III. Title. IV. Series.

BL51.F434 2011
200.82—dc22

2010046030

1 2 3 4 5 16 15 14 13 12 11

In Memoriam,
Charles Winquist (1944–2002)
Who Never Disappointed

CONTENTS

ACKNOWLEDGMENTS

The editors wish to acknowledge Cathryn R. Newton, Dean Emerita of the College of Arts and Sciences, Syracuse University, for her generous support of a conference entitled "Postmodernism, Culture and Religion, 2: Feminism, Sexuality and the Return of Religion," held at Syracuse University on April 26–28, 2007, upon which this volume is based.

We are very grateful for the grant we received from the Ray Smith Symposium of Syracuse University, which was a major contribution to the financial support of the conference.

We thank in particular Deborah Pratt and the staff of the Religion Department at Syracuse University, for the efficiency, energy, and mastery of every detail that made our work easier and provided so well for the comfort of our guests.

FEMINISM, SEXUALITY, AND THE RETURN OF RELIGION

INTRODUCTION

Feminism, Sexuality, and the Return of Religion

Linda Martín Alcoff and John D. Caputo

As Sarah Coakley bravely proposes in this volume, feminism, sexuality, and the return of religion represent three powerful forces in contemporary society that we should now attempt creatively to rejoin. Although these three are often oppositional—even in deadly opposition—with feminism and sexuality viewed as the road to perdition by those who desire the return of religion to its dominion over Man and World, the question this volume considers is whether another possible narrative of the triadic relationship is possible. Might feminist and queer theory even have something constructive to offer religion in this new era of reactive faith?

These are contested terms and contested relationships, and the political effects are far from uniform. The return of the glory of God—even the good old God of Lacanian formulation wrestled with by several of the authors herein—is at the least, one would have to admit, a mixed blessing. After all, the axiological nihilism of late capital provides succor to those who would privatize the sufferings of the poor and subcontract out mercenary wars over resources to the lowest—in all senses of that word—bidder. Religious absolutism, or strong theology, provides a rejoinder to a wealthy world that turns a blind eye to mass disasters of distribution. Commodity fetishism run amok has produced an oppositional, anti-materialist, sometimes anti-Western fetishism of religious texts and traditions. If the Cold War presented the only alternatives as capitalism versus communism, today's dialectic is often presented as secular capitalism versus traditional theocracies (a representation no more fully adequate to the real nature of the conflict). During the Cold War, a nonaligned movement based in the very countries who were generally used as pawns by the superpowers repudiated both sides and declared their determination to mark out a third course more clearly invested in the interests of the global poor. Perhaps we can follow this model, given that women and gays (an intersecting set) are again being used as today's pawns in the geopolitical debates over the meaning and value of culture, tradition, and religion.

After all, it is critically important, as Saba Mahmood demonstrates here, that feminists and queer theorists become very clear about the ways in which our agendas have become alibis for anti-Muslim exclusion and unilateral military action, in some cases used against our avowed goals but in others with willing support from movement leaders. This is nothing new, of course. The liberation of women played a critical role in justifying British control over India in the early days of colonialism so that, in the words of Gayatri Spivak, white men might save brown women from brown men. Still today this motivation of a kind of perverse gallantry continues to work for the West to cloak its campaigns—both military and political—against Muslim autonomy. But when tropes of liberalism, equality, and tolerance are used to justify invasion, we must remember Fanon's wry remark that in Europe "they are never done talking of Man, yet murder men everywhere they find them."[1] So today in the West, as Mahmood points out, overwrought memoirs by Muslim women recounting their oppression at the hands of Islam make quick bestsellers, with the result that more women are dragged from their homes, more women are "collaterally" killed, and more anti-woman, anti-gay extremism is inspired among a generation of the dispossessed. And tolerance for gay sexuality is being used as a litmus test in some European countries to determine an individual's ability to "merit" democratic rights associated with citizenship, providing cover for anti-Muslim policies of exclusion and naked ethnocentric nativism. If the advance of gay rights can be used to legitimate secular fundamentalism and enact a hierarchy of civilizations, then no liberatory agenda is free from recuperation. We must surely be aware by now that neither feminism nor gay liberation is always on the side of democracy and cultural equality, that both can and have been used as excuses for imperial incursions, and that no constituency enjoys consensus about how to draw the map of its most favored allies and most feared enemies. This complicated terrain provides more reason, not less, to look with fresh eyes at the possibility of reconfiguring the relationship between feminism, sexuality, and religion.

The recuperation of discourses of gender and sexual justice should give us pause. How can a (genuine) demand for gender and sexual justice be spoken in this overdetermined discursive terrain? How can we avoid being pawns once again, to be played by the cynical Fathers, whether secular or theocratic, for their own ends? One route out of this dilemma is to put forward our own "theological uncertainties," as Catherine Keller urges us here. Besides, as she warns, refusing the theological risk would simply put into effect Paul's dictum that "women should be silent in church."

The essays collected here seek if anything to de-substantiate our settled certainties about the opposition of religion and sex. Feminist and queer theologians have been exploring and debating the transformative potentialities of various religious traditions for some decades now. Although here too there is no consensus, the dialogue has resulted in an improved articulation of the central questions and has inspired a renewed inventiveness that has succeeded in imagining a range of provisional answers. These theologians are committed to transformation, and not simply to a posture of defensiveness, retreat, or, for that matter, deconstruction in the face of doctrinal conservatism. Faced with such a potent multiplication of all manner of faith communities, the theorists of religion find in the upsurge of debate the potential for an increased intensity in critical reflection and serious exchange. Crises, as Naomi Klein has pointed out, bring opportunities.

One challenge to transformation, though, is the dense weight of the sacred texts themselves, saddled as they are with an enormous interpretive history that often enacts more force on institutional action and policy than the originary documents. As Keller notes, for example, changing the gender of the pronoun for God is hardly sufficient when "God" always brings along its "archive: the historical trove of scriptures, prayers, creeds, songs, theologies . . . punctuated percussively, in relentless elegance, with its He's, Lords, and Fathers." If this legacy has obscured the true Word, how can the latter ever be made manifest? Should God be given a sex change, so to speak, or should we simply reduce the magnitude and forcefulness of the powers we accord him (or her)? Or should we retreat from the naming process itself, as Cixous might prefer, given that God as a concept retreats in power just as we attempt to confer it with representation? Or still, as Coakley suggests, mightn't we rather focus first on transforming ourselves, our manner of relating to each other, as well as our practices of devotion?

Perhaps the most critical challenge to transformation lies not with how divinity is metaphysically articulated but with the valuation of its purported opposite: the carnal or embodied character of human existence. Women, St. Augustine declared, are closer to the beasts of the field, less close to God. Women's association with a passively construed nature and distance from rational transcendence was considered so extreme to Hegel that he likened the distinction between men and women as analogous to the distinction between animals and plants. Women are, after all, it seems, merely tomatoes. Gays and lesbians are similarly associated today with uncontrollable appetites and with a carnality that is beyond redemption. Their attempt to marry is said to sully the ritual itself, demolishing its sanctified state for all who enter it, gay or straight. Arguably, at root here for both anti-woman and anti-gay ideologies is a symbolic order that is anti-flesh, anti-material, anti-sexual, and perhaps as necrophiliac as Mary Daly once charged in its love for the puerile purity of a fleshless existence, the imagined life after embodiment that we can have only in an imagined afterlife, precisely after life—bios—is no more.

Feminist theologians have long been concerned with the denigration of embodied and sexual existence found in numerous traditions. Yet neither feminist theologians nor cultural analysts of religion agree that a simple celebration of pleasure, or promotion of sex-positive moralities, would actually constitute an effective alternative to the vilification of the flesh. If a misguided denigration of bodily natures has played a role in the subordination of women and queers, it is likewise far from clear, as Nietzsche understood, that the intensifications of bodily experience offered by many ascetic religious traditions truly works to subvert the valuing of the body—or at least any more so than secularist rationalisms that have likewise pitted computational models of the mind against messy, emotional, embodied identities. Ascetic inspired prostrations of the flesh only remind us more vividly of our fleshly existence, rendering it more, not less, acutely felt. Moreover, if Coakley is right, the very ascetic and sacrificial turn away from a certain manner of sensuality—an emptying out of the self, or kenosis—may not be the disempowering move some feminists take it to be if the ascetic practice results in an enhancement of one's concrete, or material, self-regard. For Coakley, the problem seems to be not asceticism as much as it is the pursuit and adoration of purity: purity of purpose, of intention, of moral valence. It is this aspiration to purity and to clarity of boundaries that conspires against a recognition of the always-compromised reality of human relationships. Thus it is not the body per se that is the crux of the issue but the way the body is considered an obstacle to purity rather than, as the early Christians imagined it, the very road to transcendence. Mahmood has similarly challenged Western feminist shibboleths about the political meaning of women's willingness to sacrifice their lives, including their freedom of dress and of movement, to God. Her careful ethnography of women in the Islamic Mosque movement in Egypt gives evidence of their clear agential action and the ability to use their devotional practices to resist—and critique—their husband's hegemony, even from within a version of patriarchal absolutism.[2] By invoking God's will, devout wives can trump their husband's attachment to habits that turn them away from familial duties.

If feminism were to make a flat-footed repudiation of the religiously inspired practices of modesty, self-sacrifice, and devotion followed by millions of women worldwide, it would render them mere dupes, falsely conscious of their true selves and thus unworthy of self-determination under any discursive regime. Coakley and Mahmood, using theology and anthropology respectively, effect a necessary complication on Daly's earlier characterization of all forms of religious asceticism and devotion as intrinsically misogynist and death-loving. Both also find themselves in opposition to versions of secular liberalism that imagine the possibility of culturally neutral public spaces and that assume freedom's ideal is an unencumbered self, a self who chooses its religious commitments and obligations. Coakley urges us to rethink the relationship of freedom to sacrifice and purgation, and to see the latter as a means to overcoming the false desires—the falseness of desire itself—which is the real obstacle to achieving autonomy. Mahmood points to all the ways that women's religious devotion trumps the requirement of obedience to the master/ husband, providing both means and motivation for oppositional behavior.

Queer theory from Foucault forward has also helped trouble the assumed concordance between increased sexual activity—"the more the better"—and liberation. In this way it too helps open a space for a different debate over the possibilities that religious traditions represent for more sexually egalitarian futures. As Mark Jordan reminds us, the disciplinary regime of Christendom is the forerunner, not the opposition, to today's disciplinary regime of sex, where modern subjects are led to believe that they must explore, and manage, every tiny tremor of erotic affect if they want to be sufficiently free. Extrapolating from this Foucaultian premise, Jordan suggests that the death of the Christian God with the rise of secularism resulted only in better-managed sex, which is not to be equated with better sex. But Jordan also complicates for us the Christian tradition's relationship to the erotic and asks, provocatively, "whether some Christian speech might still afford other possibilities for contesting the regime of sexuality," specifically, whether it might even help to "disrupt the regime"?

Here Jordan develops two interesting suggestions. The first is that the current evangelical fervor for familial, heterosexual, married, reproductive sexuality needs to be reminded that Christianity has viewed reproductive sex as only a second-best alternative—far second—to celibacy. In championing a doctrine of the "imperative of fertility," these newcomers have to stretch the text to make Jesus a committed heterosexual. Thus Jordan suggests that acknowledging the reality of Jesus' silence about sex might provide a more effective rejoinder to the modern regime of King Sex if it is read as an acknowledgement of the inadequacy of speech in the realm of desire. Secondly, Jordan offers a rumination on the erotics of the sacred and the possibility of imagining an erotic theophany, with the help of Nietzsche and Bataille. The point here again is to work toward a real alternative to the degraded commodity of sexualization that modern society defines as freedom. In so doing we will realize the need to resist the usual hierarchies of sex-positive modernities set in opposition to sex-negative premodern Christianities.

Thus it is far from clear where the interests of feminism and queer liberation lie, even in regard to what may seem to be the most settled

questions about the valuation of embodiment, sexuality, or the resources of our varied traditions. Religious controversies have brought home
one point about which there is some indication of a growing awareness
among feminist theorists: that liberation is a word with multiple referents.
Whether one wears the veil—a symbol, some say, of female inferiority—
or whether one strives for the stylish sexual display demanded by patriar-
chies of a different sort, women remain subject, and subjected, to cultures
not of their own making. Just as oppression can take dissimilar, even
opposite forms—from required concealment to mandatory exposure—so
too might liberation, autonomy, and freedom (whatever these are) take
highly distinct and varied forms. The Western liberal metanarrative
that gender equality will advance best through a state-protected, secular
public space—what Mahmood calls "normative secularism"—is slowly
giving way to the recognition that feminist narratives of progress can be
no less imperial and hegemonic than any other over-glorified trope put
forward as transcultural, from freedom, to democracy, to development.
Feminism needs to get out of the business of debating the terms of the
universal metanarrative altogether in favor of the project of cross-cultural
dialogue and horizontally conceived coalitions that accept irreducible differences of ends.

The irreducible particularity of women's oppression is nicely fore-
grounded here in Kelly Brown Douglas's focus, which is not on women
in the imagined abstract but on black women, and not on religion but on
the specific traditions of North American Christianity into which African
Americans were inculcated under conditions of enslavement. Thus the
question for her is historically and contextually bound: how can a black
womanist/feminist be Christian? Douglas argues that the Platonized version of Protestant Christianity in North America made common cause
with a derogation of black women as overly sexualized, and thus we need
to understand the strong traditions of church-going women in African
American communities as a strategy of defense: the practice of a "hyper-
proper sexuality" against the hyper-sexuality imputed to the whole community. Nonetheless, Brown Douglas is critical of the focus on propriety
as a final position. Against this she invokes blues women, who signified
their protest very differently through frank revelations of desire, in all its
divergent forms, including non-heterosexual ones. But she also invokes
here the idea that sexuality is endemically divine, affirming our relation to

God by drawing us out of ourselves and into relations with others. This notion retains elements of both universal and particularist approaches to liberation through a common (or universal) divinity of relationality but one that is attentive to the historical obstacles faced by a very particular group of women.

Religious hermeneutics provides a model for how to think the universality-in-particularity that Brown Douglas's essay manifests. As Vattimo has argued, if we are to understand Christianity as the actual antiauthoritarian, "unmasking" force it originally was, then we have to come to see literalist dogmatism as heterodoxy. The project then becomes to try "and understand the meaning of the evangelical text for me, here, now . . . reading the signs of the times with no other provision than the commandment of love."[3] Like any categorical imperative, the imperative to love requires interpretive applications to have any reality, any manifestation, and such applications cannot be clarified in textual prescriptions. Such a hermeneutic approach dissolves the opposition of universal and particular and even mandates variation and difference as a necessary outcome to the following of divine law.

Vattimo also usefully suggests in this volume that the real obstacle for gender and sexual equality is not theistic faith but a naturalism that would enshrine papal interpretations of God's will with the authority of Natural Law. Here he is once again aligned with Cixous, for whom the interruptions of belief—the challenges to faith—come out of naturalist approaches that would fix the reference of terms. Feminism and gay sexualities are most often and most widely condemned via the use of naturalistic arguments that inevitably predict the demise of civilization as we know it if hetero-normative familial relationships are not enforced by law on all. This contradiction—the need for Natural Law to have a codified legal enforcement if it is to survive—symbolizes the contradiction of the Enlightenment itself, which understands its mission as the conquest of myth even while it enshrines the myth of its own omnipotence and omniscience. The genius of the contemporary Catholic Church has been to mimic this move in reverse: to lay a claim to naturalism at the very heart of its mythic narratives through equating papal encyclicals with defenses of the natural order. This parallels the move of Enlightenment skeptics who claimed a mythic world-historical providence in the very guise of their narrative and axiological agnosticism. In both cases, adding naturalist pretensions to one's prescriptions works only to keep Christianity and Enlightenment rationality in unenlightened opposition.

We might read much of the discussions among these papers as sharing Vattimo's claim that the obstacle to gender and sex equality is less religion than it is naturalism, or perhaps perversions of naturalism that mistake the nature of Nature as a terrain of metaphysical absolutes and ahistorical covering laws. If this is so, then secularism is not the solution, nor is a secular public space that tries to sequester any substance of belief behind closed doors. Such public spaces are never value-empty or culturally noncommittal, given that their very organization—their distributions of rights and responsibilities, not to mention resources—are implicated in and justified by evaluative systems with substantive doxastic commitments about the nature of human life. Rather than obscuring our doxastic commitments under a guise of secular neutrality or trying to settle differences through a scientistic discourse of naturalism, it is surely better to put it all out on the table, in public, for the open and messy discussion it will inevitably engender, to ask: what is freedom? what is equality? what is autonomy? what is sacred?

In "Promised Belief," Hélène Cixous continues the work of complicating the relationship between feminism, sexuality, and the return of religion undertaken in the previous papers. For her, as for the other contributors, there is no simple and straightforward way to liberate women and sexuality from religion, nor is it straightforwardly obvious that religion cannot play a role in this liberation. Her essay, while more personal than political and more literary than theological, may be viewed as a contribution to the constitution of a third way that eschews both secular capitalism and theocracy, that rejects both instrumental reason and a fanatical faith, that eludes both secular fathers and the fathers of faith. Cixous searches for a deeper and more nuanced sense of worldliness that does not insulate itself from a certain faith even as she pursues a sense of faith that is faith in the promise of this world, a faith in life. She questions the opposition of the genders, as if there were just two, inscribed in nature and underwritten by an Eternal Father who, as the author of nature, patrols the borders between the two. She crosses genders by engaging in a feminine writing, but this means an archi-feminine hospitality to the multiplicity of voices, masculine and feminine and unclassifiable voices still to come, which resists the policing of women and of sexuality that transpires in and under the name of nature and of God. To that extent, her paper is a profound meditation upon the name of God and upon religion itself, albeit of a more unorthodox, vigilant and radical sort. For while the papers of the other contributors are vigilant about the damage to woman and sexuality done by the "good old God," which means by men who have authorized themselves to speak in the name of God—theology as ventriloquy—Cixous stakes out a new terrain in which the prospect opens for a new sense of religion. Such a religion would turn on a faith in life, an affirmation of life, an amen to life, in which the affirmation of the multiplicity of sexual and gendered existence engenders multiple forms of life, multiple ways to say yes to life, even and especially in the face of death.

But by offering an evocative meditation upon belief rather than religion, and upon the mortality of our carnal being rather than the politics of gendered and sexual bodies, Cixous's essay is deeply if indirectly involved in the debate conducted in the other papers. Her text, like Vattimo's, belongs to the growing genre of what might be called secular or atheistic theology, meaning what theology will have become once the fleshless life of an imaginary afterlife has been deconstructed and life is reimagined in rigorously and vigorously carnal terms. Her discourse has nothing to do with biblical literalism but a great deal to do with literature, nothing to do with naturalism but everything to do with bodily life, nothing to do with a neutral public space but everything to do with a certain constitutive faith that undercuts theocratic power, nothing to do with a purist faith but everything to do with how belief is mingled with unbelief.

The text, the latest installment in the lifelong conversation that she conducted with Jacques Derrida in personal meetings, over the telephone, and in a series of brilliant published exchanges, is about nothing less than life and death, faith and resurrection. In *H. C.—for Life, That Is to Say . . .* (1998), Jacques Derrida describes the "sides" in this "singular, almost interminable argument" between these friends "for life."[4] "We the two French, Judeo-marrano halfJews":[5]

As for me, I keep forever reminding her each time, on my side, that we die in the end, too quickly. And I always have to begin again.

For she "because she loves to live" does not believe me. She, on her side, knows well that one dies in the end, too quickly; she knows it and writes about it better than anyone, she has the knowledge of it but she believes none of it . . .

And I say to myself, on my side: "Would that I might [*puissé-je*] believe her, I wish I might [*puisse*], yes, I wish I might believe her . . ."
(*HC*, 2; cf. p. 36)

This debate, become all the more poignant after Derrida's death in October 2004, amounts to another discourse on "faith and knowledge," she for faith, and he for knowledge; she for dreams, being a dreamer par excellence, a "nightfilmmaker," while he has his doubts.

To be sure, H. C. knows what Derrida is saying is true, but her belief and love and dreams are not defeated by the known fact of death. Just so, Derrida wants to be on her side, even though he is right about what he knows. She is "for life," but he is hardly against it. So each one is also on the side of the other; he is also a man of faith and a dreamer, and she is also a woman of knowledge. These sides are porous; these genders do not hold up. Knowing as they both do about death, believing as they both do in life, they are nonetheless stationed strategically on different sides of this debate, and each must play his or her assigned part. She "promises" him belief—hence the title of the piece—promises him that she believes what she believes, promises that like Socrates she will stay at her post. But as belief comes mixed with nonbelief, her belief is also a promise she makes to herself to repeat belief, especially in the face of the incredible. The two cross sides, faiths, dreams, loves, and genders; they both affirm many genders and many sides, and they do not want to be trapped inside just one or two.

When Derrida says he wishes he "might" (*puisse*) believe H. C., he links belief with what it is in our power (*pouvoir*) to believe. For Derrida, to believe what it is "possible" (*posse*) to believe is barely believing at all; it is mostly just a reliable calculation.

If one hears the full might of meaning this word has, to believe should then lie and only reside in this impossible faith in the impossible. Then one could believe only in miracles. And to believe would be the miracle, the magical power of the miracle.
(*HC*, 4)

Would that he, like she, might miraculously believe the unbelievable. It would take all his might to match her almost almighty faith, her "omnipotence" (*HC,* 20). Her belief in life proceeds from loving life with all her might. As Cixous points out, the root of the English "belief," the archaic *lief,* is a cognate of the German *lieben,* to love. "I would as lief go south as north" means I would be just as glad to. Belief means what I like or love to think, what love wants me to think. Belief, she says, loves to believe. He would like to love and believe in life, as she does. Would that he might.

The exchange takes place between two parties or two sides (*côtés*) (*HC,* 37), like messages from shore to shore (*côte*), like the conversations over the telephone, which he said is pure hearing without sight, like tuning an instrument with your eyes closed, or like faith itself. He must not go over to her side, for to receive from her requires her distance; still he is finally "too much on her side." In the end, he has no surety about what a "side" would really mean (*HC,* 21). For Cixous, life is not even a true "side," but a whole, because life does not know death. She is not proposing a Stoic conundrum but the "grace of the finite instant," the graciousness of life, the vivacity, in which death makes no appearance until life has departed the scene (*HC,* 81). In *Being and Time,* Heidegger says that "my death" has no phenomenality as such, that death is "given" only in being-unto-death, which is a more authentic mode of being-in-the-world and hence of what Heidegger will not deign to call "life."

Cixous here makes public the first text that Derrida ever wrote about her, an unpublished 1965 commentary on her first book, *The First Name of God* (*Le Prénom de dieu*),[6] which bears witness to their shared preoccupation with the unpronounceable name of God. Cixous's "objection" to the employment of this name, Derrida comments, is not the one we find in negative theology, where this name's unnameability is a function of being primordial and originary. On the contrary, he says, for Cixous this name is precisely not originary, is only one among many first names, having been preceded by writing, by literature, which is, Cixous adds, her true religion and true faith.

Her subject here will not be "religion" or any specific religion but faith (*foi*) and "belief" (*croyance*), especially in the English. Her point of departure is the story of Moses striking the rock at Meribah, where the Lord God, whom she cannot understand—that she finds understandable—asked Moses to believe the unbelievable:[7]

> The great believers are unbelievers who believe. Believe and not
> believe *in a split second*. Believe and not believe mingled in the
> chink of a second. (PB, 137–38)

The faith of Moses is cut, split between the two times he strikes the rock;
but that's what faith is, a promise, a promised promise, but without any
guarantees. Cixous places Derrida in the position of Moses and belief in
life in the position of the "promised land": he looks on her (promised)
belief the way Moses looks on the promised land, believing in it, but not
believing he will get there himself.

For forty years, the same storm rages. "We never stop talking of God
who doesn't exist stopping and starting, stopping beginning starting up
again." She is not sure if he wants her to come to his side, or if he wants
to go to hers, she who is sure that she casts mortality over anyone she
loves, starting with her father. But she must put on a brave face and not
show any weakness about all this. She was assigned to be his ally against
himself, and he was praying like mad, to her, to himself, to believe her. "If
only he might believe her"—this prayer is directed to himself in whom
he does not believe, a prayer for belief, without belief, which is why it is
fitting that we so often pray in a language we don't understand (like Latin
or Hebrew), where the signifier is cut off from the signified.

The faith he places in the belief she promises him (that she promises
herself) is based on the fact that she is a dreamer, a seer of apparitions and
ghosts, incredible things you're not supposed to see or believe—miracles,
really. Above all, the dead come back to her in dreams, where they are
given a special "leave" from death. So this atheistic theology of "resurrection" is set out under the name of the "leave," as if Jesus were granted a
leave from death by the disciples, allowed to spend some time with them
"without forgetting death."

> —Do you think we'll still be around in ten years? he says.
> —Do you think we'll still be around? Afterwards? he says. He
> waits for my response.
> —I, in any case, don't think so. He says. But I wish it could hap-
> pen, I wish I could believe differently he says. (PB, 147)

Once Derrida says, almost as if speaking to himself, something like "I
ought perhaps to convert." Does he mean that he ought to come over to

her side? One day he stops by to say he has an appointment in Paris, that he will be back later. She is filled with anxiety, and we are thus introduced to the time that Derrida was diagnosed with pancreatic cancer, a well-known "death sentence" (Blanchot).

That brings us to resurrection, which means "eternity on leave," a leave from death, like Derrida now "on leave" from the hospital (ominous cousin of "hospitality"), the disease having been detected early enough that he would live for fifteen months after the diagnosis:

> The only limit to the resurrection is its leave status. . . . It is not the resurrection of a past. Not at all. It is the resurrection of the present. . . .
>
> A few hours, all the forces of life after death gathered together to substantiate a return to reality will keep you going for a few hours. (PB, 154)

Resurrection means coming back to life within life, a happiness in the face of certain death, when there is still time, before death makes its final call. We are freed, not from time's ineluctable order, but from the order of death, if only for a moment—a few months, more or less—a brief lifting of the latch, a suspension, remission, hesitation, a chance. The weakness of the flesh overwhelms them with its force, the impotence on her side but a "pale imitation" of the impotence on his side. But if he seemed a ghost to her, that was her fault, her failure to dream, to believe in life, while there is still time for "happiness in tears." Just as when he was off on one his many travels she was nourished by the thought of his return, so now, at the onset of "the Long Voyage," she must not fail to nourish the image of a return, impossible though it seems.

Resurrection is an "extra-mortal joy" that does not deny the death sentence; it is a pause in the horror, but not a "reconciliation" with death or fate. Resurrection grants us patience, tolerance, without denying the truth, without pretending there is no death. No hollow chest-thumping "death where is thy triumph?" after which one is never heard from again. Hold on to the dread, for the "monsters" are also "benevolent guardians of the presence of the survivor within me." She is sustained by the "tiny glowworm of the Leave event blinking," by the thought that they might meet up again, in her dreams perhaps, waiting without a definite date:

There's a chance that someone-I-don't-know-who—or who-knows-what—may come back. You can't keep from dying. Afterwards there's no longer *anything* at all keeps you from returning. (PB, 158)

Life will not always be so lifeless; she will do what she needs to do: "Nothing is more mysterious than belief, except for death." She writes "there may be leaves" on a post-it, the writing insuring that belief lasts in those moments when she stops believing. At least for a few hours a day she will be able to "taste the richness of life." We are immortal mortals, at least for a few hours, in our dreams and memories. Belief requires that we promise to believe the unbelievable, to believe even when belief has dried up. You have to promise to believe in leaves in order to be granted them. He would have liked to believe, to be on her side, a blind Moses listening to someone describe the promised land, wanting to believe what she was promising.

In the view that Cixous strikes here, and this is her provocative contribution to the present discussion, the return of religion in the sense of the resurgence of the patriarchy and homophobia, of the dogmatism and neo-tribalism of the various fundamentalist movements, is undone, not by reasserting the fiction of a supposedly neutral secular Enlightened space, but by an affirmation of faith. But faith here means a more archi-faith in carnal life, a joy in life that demands faith without forgetting death, a faith whose inspired texts are supplied by literary spirits, where the name of "God" is one of many first names. The faith she puts forward here means an underlying and constitutive faith that is distorted if it is contracted into the competing creeds of theists and atheists that feed the wars, both cultural and blood-stained, between what today passes for the "religious" and the "secular."

NOTES

1. Frantz Fanon, *The Wretched of the Earth*, trans. Constance Farrington (New York: Grove Press, 1963), 9.

2. See her *Politics of Piety: The Islamic Revival and the Feminist Subject* (Princeton: Princeton University Press, 2005).

3. Gianni Vattimo, *Belief*, trans. Luca D'Isanto and David Webb (Stanford: Stanford University Press, 1999), 6.

4. Jacques Derrida, *H. C.—for Life, That Is to Say . . .*, trans. Laurent Milesi and Stefan Herbrechter (Stanford: Stanford University Press, 1998), 21. Hereafter HC.

5. Hélène Cixous, *Insister of Jacques Derrida*, trans. Peggy Kamuf (Stanford: Stanford University Press, 2007), 179.

6. Hélène Cixous, *Le Prénom de dieu* (Paris: Edition Bernard Grasset, 1967).

7. Hélène Cixous, "Promised Belief," in this volume. Hereafter PB.

ONE

In Defense of Sacrifice: Gender, Selfhood, and the Binding of Isaac

Sarah Coakley

INTRODUCTION: WHERE THREE ROADS MEET

This paper is positioned where three roads meet. When we speak of three such roads, we recall immediately the fateful encounter of Oedipus and his father, Laius, whom he was to strike down and kill in dreadful ignorance that it was his own father that he assaulted. But the three roads of which I am going to speak in this paper do not intersect at the place where the son kills the father, as in the Oedipal myth, but rather at the place where the father nearly—or perhaps actually—kills the son.[1]

I refer, of course, to the biblical narrative of the sacrifice, or "binding," of Isaac (Gen. 22:1–14). This was a biblical topic on which Freud himself was entirely but revealingly (one might say repressively) silent.[2] And to this Freudian silence we shall return, briefly, later; for arguably this lacuna tells us something significant about another silence—a silence about the *divine*—in Freud's system. Yet it is to the "binding of Isaac," the *akedath*

Yiẓhaak, that I want to turn our attention in this presentation. This story might initially appear to have nothing whatever to do with our conference themes of feminism, sexuality, and the return of religion—those three contemporary roads that we seek now in some way creatively to recon-join. For is not the *akedah* the archetypal *male* myth, the utter inverse of anything feminist? Is it not, after all, precisely the *exclusion* of the "femi-nine" that is the distinctive characteristic of the cultic act of sacrifice, an intentional supplanting, perhaps, of the primal "feminine" sacrificial power of childbirth?[3] Is it not the necessary violence of such sacrifice that condones, justifies, and even glorifies the abuse of the powerless (includ-ing, of course, women and children)?[4] Is it not precisely the establishment of "patriarchal" religion that is the *telos* of this story, with its adulation of unthinking male obedience, even unto death, and its promise thereby of future generations of sons as yet unborn?[5]

My answer to these classic feminist charges against sacrifice will be both Yes and No. It would be foolhardy to resort to the familiar tactic of denial; the story of the "binding" of Isaac is as dense and multifaceted as anyone may care to make it. Such is the irreducible complexity of a found-ing myth of this sort of power, and I am not in the business of attempting to sanitize it from the historic taints of patriarchal interpretation. Indeed, as I shall shortly show, its very earliest interpretation, already lodged in the biblical text itself, might be called a classically "patriarchal" one, and its original roots may lie in an all-too-vivid acquaintance with the prac-tice of infanticide.[6] And yet where deep truth lies, the more densely do distractions and perversions from such truth congregate; and it is such a deeper level that I seek to probe in this paper.

At this deeper level of truth, I suggest, our first focus must be not on Abraham, the powerful and obedient one who has so mightily exercised the modern and postmodern imagination as to whether his action was "ethical" or beyond it, but rather on Isaac, the ostensibly powerless one, who emerges from his ordeal—I shall argue—unscathed, re-enlivened, and utterly transformed.[7] Isaac, in short, is the type of the one who tri-umphs over human powerlessness, not by a false, compensatory will-to-power and further patriarchal violence, but through the subtler power of a transformative, divine *interruption.* Here is the surprise, then: for the purposes of my playful feminist midrash,[8] Isaac can be read as gender-labile, the "type" of feminist selfhood transformed. Isaac's experience, that is, can be the paradoxical test case for feminist freedom.

So let me then make the bold assertion of my thesis at the outset. I seek to demonstrate that only sacrifice, *rightly understood,* can account for a feminist transformation of the self that is radically "theonomous," rooted and sustained in God. Only thus is the self rendered authentically "free," and so propelled both beyond the idolatry of false desire for that-which-is-not-God and beyond the restrictions of the gender binary that so exercises current secular gender theory.

Consider, in this regard, the three roads that I claim now meet at the *akedah.* The first is the modern feminist road that seeks to empower woman, to endow her with "freedom," or perhaps now in postmodernity to bestow upon her that more elusive possession of "agency." The second road is the road of "sexuality" (as we have come to call it in modernity), the road that seeks to understand the riddle of psychophysical desire and its final satisfaction. The third road is the road that leads us back to "good old God," as Jacques Lacan would call him. How shall these three roads meet? My claim is that *the contemporary secular difficulties of the first two roads cannot successfully be traversed without converging on the third;* my more specific thesis is that it is only in the crisis of a divine "sacrifice" (a term to be defined with care), and an accompanying divine interruption of the normal human workings of power and violence, that a theonomous self is formed that can overcome the secular feminist *impasses* of the first two roads.

Clearly, these are bold claims. I can only make initial headway with them in the space of one short presentation. Yet I shall attempt to instantiate them here by making three basic moves. First, I shall position my argument in the context of the current postmodern debate about "sacrifice" and "gift," a debate that has also educed intriguing new interpretations of the *akedah.* Here I shall argue that the tendency in this debate toward a disjunctive choice between "gift" and "sacrifice" has obfuscated the possibility of a third and deeper alternative in which such a disjunctive choice is not demanded; yet the same disjunctive choice has—in these recent debates—simultaneously pressed the language of the "feminine" into positions either of occluded powerlessness or of eschatological "excess." Only a careful reconstrual of the inner logic and meaning of "sacrifice" can address these false dilemmas and probe to the mysterious level of a divine undergirding of human agency. Second, I shall—in the most complex and dense portion of the paper—return to the Genesis text itself and to some of the more intriguing details of interpretation discoursed upon in later rabbinic exegesis. On the basis of these rabbinic hints and guesses, I shall construct my own feminist midrash in which Isaac becomes the type of feminist selfhood, caught, it initially seems, in a web of patriarchal narcissism and threatened violence, but eluding them precisely by means of consent to divine intervention—a divine interruption that resists a *false* sacrificial logic. Thirdly, I shall return in closing to consider what all this may mean for current feminist theory and for our reconsideration of the first two "roads" of gender and sexuality. Here I shall contrast my own theological proposal both with some notable seeming impasses in contemporary gender theory and with one heroic attempt, in the spirit of Freud, to bring the *akedah* into complementary psychoanalytic relation to the undertakings of the Oedipal crisis. I shall conclude, as you may suppose, that "good old God" is far from dead, but not a mere commodity either, for any instant amelioration of our current gender-theoretical dilemmas. The "sacrificial" ordeal of our feminist hero Isaac nonetheless remains on offer; its transformations are undeniably costly, but they are the price of freedom in the richest sense. And oddly, this lesson can at the end even be turned back on Abraham: his ordeal too, though not one of powerlessness, is equally one of purgation and transformation—the giving up of a falsely idolatrous desire in aid of proper detachment, proper submission to God. "Theonomy," in short, is not a given but a lifetime's undertaking—an ascetical task in response to primary divine gift. It changes everything—not least, as we shall see, the relation of sexual desire to gender.

THE POSTMODERN PROBLEM OF SACRIFICE

The problem of sacrifice in the modern and postmodern period can scarcely be described simply. Nonetheless, here I shall attempt some broad brushstrokes in order to set up my own alternative for consideration.

It is actually two problems in the contemporary discourses of sacrifice that I seek to highlight, although in practice they do interrelate and mutually entangle with one another. The first is the issue that currently dominates the continental discussion of "the Gift": How is gift-giving possible, if at all, without manipulative intent—*do ut des?* And if such manipulation always lurks in gift-giving, can there be such a thing as "pure gift," which would somehow escape the supposedly tainted economy of exchange? Since sacrifice, at least according to many of its modern theorizations, falls squarely into the *do ut des* category, "pure gift" and "sacrifice" are seemingly disjunct—unless, that is, death itself becomes the means of their intersection. So the problem here is that of the apparent *disjunction* of gift and sacrifice, except in the potentially violent finality of death. Gift is insidiously manipulative, unless also necrophiliac.

The second problem[9] is obviously related but nonetheless distinct. It is the problem of whether sacrifice itself can ever be anything *other* than violent—or, as the backside of this difficulty, whether the well-meaning "liberal" attempt to sanitize sacrifice into some form of moralism may cause it to lose its power and distinctiveness altogether. Let me say a few words about each of these dilemmas in turn. In doing this we need also to attend to their gender associations.

It is a notable feature of the debate spawned originally by Marcel Mauss's *The Gift*,[10] that the "feminine" is seemingly occluded by the "economy of exchange," yet—as more than one feminist has pointed out[11]—it is actually crucial to that economy. In a society glued together by ritualized patterns of barter, the "bride-price" (or alternatively, the sexual favors of the prostitute), figure large, but they are given little explicit emphasis in Mauss's highly romanticized account of "primitive" social cohesion. What then is the alternative to *do ut des,* or gift as manipulation, which is so easily elided with an equally manipulative "sacrificial" approach to relations with the divine? In reaction to Mauss's adulation of gift exchange, Derrida famously reasserts the remaining possibility of a "pure gift" that escapes the economy of exchange but that by definition can only be offered by the "absolute other" (the *tout autre*).[12] Reading the story of the *akedah* in this way, in quest for a "pure gift," Derrida can see Abraham's offering as the one example of sacrifice that *escapes* the taint of exchange precisely in turning Isaac over to death. For here Abraham "renounces all sense and all property"[13] in his willingness to kill his son. Death, then, is the one place where "pure gift" and sacrifice can meet: in "gift *as sacrifice*,"[14] that is, in the sacrifice of the economy of sacrifice itself. If we ask where "femininity" resides in *this* account of gift, the answer is more elusive than in the case of Mauss's model but is nonetheless still revealing. Whereas Derrida himself remarks on the "exclusion or sacrifice of woman" in the logic of sacrifice[15] and leaves the question "in suspense" whether the inclusion of woman as a ritual actor would alter that logic, it is striking that his own talk of "excess" or "pure gift" can itself occasionally garner the association of the "feminine," for it stands altogether outside the masculine economy of exchange.[16]

The alternatives, then, seem to be these: *either* gift as manipulation, in which woman is occluded and subordinate but an object of barter necessary to the whole system; *or* sacrifice as the "gift" of death, from which any actual woman is ritually excluded, yet "femininity" vaguely adulated as a figure for "pure gift's" "excess." The options are scarcely looking promising from a feminist perspective.[17]

Yet are these really the only alternatives? Before we dare to suggest an answer to that question, let us superimpose on it the second problem in the contemporary debates on sacrifice: the problem of whether sacrifice is *intrinsically* violent and thus in need of reduction to the ethical. We are reminded here of Kant's famous insistence that Abraham should, from the outset, and on clear ethical grounds, have *resisted* the demands of "God" to "butcher[] and burn[]" his son: "Abraham should have replied," says Kant, "to this supposedly divine voice: 'That I ought not to kill my good son is quite certain. But that you, his apparition, are God—of that I am not certain.'"[18] Yet this Kantian approach is, of course, most memorably rejected in Kierkegaard's *Fear and Trembling,* in which Abraham, the "knight of faith," finds himself inexorably engaged in a "teleological suspension of the ethical."[19] The seemingly impossible paradoxicality of Kierkegaard's position is, as John D. Caputo illuminatingly indicates in *The Prayers and Tears of Jacques Derrida,* remarkably close to the paradoxes of Derrida's knife-edge account of "pure gift" in death: both Kierkegaard and Derrida resist to the end a *transactional* account of faith, and so also resist reading the *akedah* as straightforwardly restoring the ethical. Yet if sacrifice is not constrainable in some sense by ethics, is it not merely released into a dangerous realm of non-accountability in which—as Derrida, ironically, sees more clearly than most—close imitations of sacrificial "purity" can pass into the opposite and become monstrous instantiations of violence and abuse?[20]

In these modern and postmodern stories of sacrifice, then, gift and sacrifice, morality and the suspension of morality, are seemingly set as alternatives; and "woman," one way or another, is figured out of center stage. Is there any other, feminist, way through and beyond these dilemmas that does not simply declare "sacrifice" a male problem in need of *disposal*?

The chief problem—as Derrida himself indicates—seems to reside in the absence of any feminist presence in the sacrificial site itself. Yet to place a woman in the position of *Abraham* would be, not to transform the fundamental logic of the operation, but to conjure up the specter of a Medea slaughtering her children. In contrast, both rabbinical and contemporary feminist exegesis make much of the role of Sarah, whose almost instantaneous death in Genesis 23 is taken to be the result of maternal shock and grief.[21] Yet her position in the story, excluded as she is from the vital sacrificial action, presents us with little that can be done by way of its inner transformation. It is only Isaac, I submit, who, in crucial relation to the interruptive and saving action of the angel, can give us the key to a new feminist reading of the logic of the *akedah* that maintains the irreducible significance of the sacrificial in relation to the moral and yet—*without death*!—refuse also the disjunction of divine gift and sacrifice. This refusal of mine to disjoin gift and sacrifice resides in my own Christian theological insistence that *divine* gift (the constant lure and invitation of grace) inevitably presses on us a particular form of "sacrifice" as it intersects with the timeline of human sin. In these conditions divine gift inevitably invites human sacrifice if it is to draw us more deeply into participation in that gift. More accurately, we should say that this divine gift is itself reflexive (a ceaseless interaction between "God" [the Source] and "God" [the Spirit], into which humanity is invited as participator, through a purgation that joins that humanity, sacrificially, with the perfect God/Man).[22] *This* "sacrifice" is neither blind obedience nor condoned assault, nor yet, exactly, is it Derrida's "gift of death"; for the participation in this reflexivity-in-God involves purgation into life rather than sacrifice-as-death. Nor again, finally, can this "sacrifice" be *reduced* to the moral, for it is more truly the mysterious *ground* of the moral—the making of a theonomous self which is authentically free because authentically submitted to God.

My Christian theological commitments are now on the table, and they explain, I hope, my insistence on a "deeper magic" for sacrifice, beyond the seemingly false alternatives of the current debates. But these Christian theological commitments have deep rabbinical roots, as we shall now show: the typological connection of Christ with Isaac that is already found in the theology of Paul (Gal. 4:28–31; Rom. 8:32) indicates the extent of the overlap to come. But to this overlap I now add my contemporary justification for "kidnapping" Isaac for feminist reflection. Only Isaac, I suggest, can represent the position of the modern and postmodern feminist woman, who, no longer and inevitably tied to the home (like Sarah), yet thrust into the world of patriarchy in a position of relative powerlessness (under, of course, the superficial guise of a supposed modern "equality"), is yet further endangered by the false logic of a distorted, patriarchal sacrifice. To read Isaac's role thus will be, as we shall see, to select a particular track through myriad and fascinating rabbinical alternatives and to insist, as did an important strand in that rabbinical tradition, that Isaac was not an innocent and defenseless child but already a person of maturity and discernment.[23] He was, however, a person whose relationships were about to be "interrupted." To Isaac as an honorary woman, then, we now turn.

WHY IS ISAAC A "WOMAN"? RABBINICAL EXEGESIS AND THE INTERRUPTION OF PATRIARCHAL VIOLENCE

So far in this presentation, I have allowed our gaze to be dominated by that most famous of pictorial representations of the *akedah*, Rembrandt's 1655 etching of *Abraham's Sacrifice*. Yet the more or less subliminal messages of this etching are, it seems to me, significantly different from the oil painting undertaken twenty years earlier by Rembrandt.[24] Here the exposed body of a nearly grown son is curiously hairless—androgynous, we might say, or even feminine, just as the interruptive angel in this painting also appears more feminine than obviously masculine in gender-stereotypical terms. As we pass into this second section, then, let us take stock of various chosen textual themes by comparing them with some striking and unexpected visual representations in which gender codings undeniably play an extra part. The combination of textual and iconographic messages undeniably complicates but also enriches our quest for exegetical clarification.

My interest in casting Isaac as an "honorary woman" lies in his perilous negotiation of the line, well known to feminist women in the contemporary workplace, I suggest, between submission to the logic of a *false* patriarchal sacrifice (in which male violence and scapegoating dominate), and the choice of an authentic and discerning "sacrificial" posture of another sort, on the other hand (in which genuine consent is given to the *divine* call to purge and purify one's own desires in order to align them with God's). These traits involve fine and important distinctions to be made, and there is no denying the slipperiness with which interpretations of the *akedah* ever threaten to slide back to what I have termed false patriarchal sacrifice, even as a subtler alternative is displayed and sought. It is striking, however, how certain strands in the rabbinical reflection on the *akedah* regard distinctions of this sort as vitally important. Let us consider a number of rabbinical traces of this kind.[25]

One of the most touching, first, is the tradition in the (relatively late) ninth-century CE *Midrash Tanhuma*[26] that, after his sacrificial ordeal and his mother's death, Isaac went to look for Hagar to bring her back for Abraham to marry. What occasions this suggestion in the text is the renewed mention of a place name (*Beer-Lahai-Roi*)[27] that was earlier linked to Hagar; but implicitly—one might surmise—it involves a striking sense of identification, in the Isaac who has lately come through the ordeal of sacrifice, with the rejected and despised bond-woman with whom he now apparently seeks some sort of reconciliation.[28] A further rabbinical "trace" of interest—as already noted—is the emergence by the third century CE (as evidenced in *Sifre Deuteronomy*) of the tradition that Isaac was himself fully *consenting* to a sacrificial intention, to the extent of even "binding himself" upon the altar (a move that Jon Levenson describes as a "sublimation").[29] Here is no instance of child abuse, then, but an adult caught in a nexus of potential violence but fully intentional about his own actions. This exegetical feature is consonant with the tradition enshrined in the fifth-century *Midrash Rabbah* that Isaac was of a mature mentality (either 26 or 37 years old) at the time of the *akedah*, and therefore could not have been bound without his explicit consent.[30] Whilst later, medieval traditions about the *akedah* (as Spiegel's *The Last Trial* so memorably traces) tend, paradoxically, to follow the third-century *Mekilta De Rabbi Ishmael* in insisting that Isaac actually *did* have his blood spilt by Abraham[31] (despite all that Genesis says to deny this[32]), what rapidly emerges from this martyrological line of thought is an equal insistence that Isaac then rose again, triumphantly from the ashes. Indeed, in some medieval narratives the *akedah* of Isaac becomes a sort of proof text for the very possibility of the resurrection of the dead.[33] We have at this point, then, met an important convergence of Jewish and Christian thought about the typological significance of Isaac's ordeal, one that links it to the *purposive* suffering of others, including Christ's; and this is seen as ultimately transformative and life-giving in virtue of the resurrection and of the salvific intentionality Isaac purposefully embraces.[34]

So there is a significant divergence in the available meanings of the *akedah* that we have unearthed at this point that cannot go without further remark. Again, what is at stake for us is the crucial distinction between a form of sacrifice tending to patriarchal violence and abuse and a form that is voluntarily purgative but aimed at the fullness of life. It would seem that the earliest-known interpretation of the *akedah* of all, however, is that enshrined in the Genesis text itself, in 22:15–18,[35] and it is this text that invites quite justifiable feminist suspicion. It looks, in any case, like an interpolation, since, rather oddly, it involves the angel calling to Abraham a *second time*, in order to tell him that his suitable obedience has earned him the reward of many male descendants: "Because you have done this, and have not withheld your son, your only son, I will indeed bless you."[36]

We are struck here afresh, in this fateful first intra-biblical interpretation, by the ambiguous and suspicious closeness of blind moral obedience on the one hand, and abusive and violent possibilities on the other. This is why it is worth contrasting this most early *akedah* interpretation with that provided many generations later, in the sixteenth century, by John of the Cross,[37] supplying as he does, in his own hand, a drawing of Christ's purposive sufferings overseen from the perspective of a *loving* Father. When he writes explicitly of the *akedah* in a letter to a woman directee, Dona Juana de Pedraza (Letter 11 to Dona Juana de Pedraza, January 28, 1589), his stress is entirely on the purgation of desire and the placing of the sacrificial suffering involved in the context of divine love: "O great God of love, and Lord!" he writes. "How many riches do you place in the soul that neither loves nor is satisfied save in you alone, for you give yourself to it and become one with it through love. And consequently you give us its enjoyment and love what it most desires in you and what brings it most profit. But because it behooves us not to go without the cross, just as our Beloved [Christ] did not go without it. . . . God ordains our sufferings that we may love what we most desire . . . But everything is brief, for it lasts only until the knife is raised; and then Isaac remains alive."[38] The difference in tone between that earliest Genesis interpretation and this one from John of the Cross is striking and instructive. For John of the Cross, the seeming threat of divine punishment is dissolved in love; moreover, he can pronounce this message of hope to a woman directee precisely through his insistence that any suffering herewith is merely for her ultimate flourishing through the redirection and purification of desire in God.

But no less instructive is the distinction between the second, misleading "interruption" by the angel, and the first (in which Abraham's hand is stayed and the ram is substituted for Isaac). I spoke earlier of the importance of this *first* angelic "interruption" in the *akedah* text for the rethinking of sacrifice and the rendering of it compatible with what I called reflexive, purgative, divine "gift." But I now suggest that we might think of this drama of the first angelic intervention at the *akedah* in the light of the earlier, equally miraculous angelic appearance in Genesis 18 [39] in which three mysterious angels are entertained by Abraham and Sarah at the Oaks of Mamre as they come to announce the birth of Isaac and the end of Sarah and Abraham's much-bemoaned childlessness. In both this case and the first angelic intervention of the *akedah*,[40] we might say that a negative duality is ambushed and transformed. In the case of Genesis 18, it is the barren sterility of the elderly couple that is interrupted by a mysterious threeness; in the case of the *akedah*, it is, we might say, the curious capacity of an intense father/son relationship to tip from mutual narcissism to violence that is equally and most decisively opened up and stopped by a third. For the rabbis, there was a great deal of lore about what sort of angel or angels were involved in this interruption,[41] but the (feminist) point for our purposes here is that an angelic third has decisively broken the spell of a patriarchal duality. Consider here (in contrast to this *decisive* turning away of Abraham's sword from his prey in the French MS representation of n. 40), the very different effect if the event is drawn *without* an angel. We may consider here a sketch by a disturbed 14-year-old Jewish boy in psychoanalytic treatment: only a dark cloud hovers above a submissive Isaac, and no angel of salvation is at hand at all.[42] Similarly,

I fear, George Segal's memorable sculptured *akedah* behind the chapel at Princeton leaves us, literally, with dagger drawn.[43] Yet in contrast, representing the angel as a mother, as one early thirteenth-century pulpit relief ostensibly does,[44] is surely not the miraculous psychoanalytic answer that Erich Wellisch, in his fascinating study *Isaac and Oedipus,* tries to hypothesize. Rightly taking Freud on for his repression of the *akedah* complex and his over-concentration on the Oedipal dilemma, Wellisch seeks to read the *akedah,* with its—in his view—return of the son to harmonious relations with father *and mother,* as the answer to which the Oedipus complex is the problem.[45] It is a heroic attempt, but it finally fails, in my view, to do justice to the profoundly *interruptive* force of the staying hand of the angel if it is merely figured as the triumphant return of the family power of the Jewish mother to a father-son relationship that has gone astray! No, something more subtle is at stake here—not reducible to the need for a comforting "feminine" presence to compensate for potential male violence or to resolve the Oedipal dilemma as such.

In my third and last section, I now want to draw out the further implications of this mysterious divine "interruption" of patriarchal sacrifice so poignantly expressed in our original Rembrandt representations. I want to relate this interruption more closely to the subtler form of sacrifice—sacrifice suffered as a purgation of desire for the sake of love—which I have already sought to defend and clarify. What can such a form of sacrifice mean for contemporary issues of "sexuality" and "gender"? What happens when the mysterious angelic threeness at the Oaks of Mamre renders the barren couple fertile? What happens, again, when an interruptive "third" complicates and disjoins the close, but tense, duality of a father and beloved son? What happens, in short, when divine thirdness interrupts classic human binaries of sexuality and familial descent?

Let me close here with a systematic, and *theological,* proposal about the relation of what we now call sexuality and gender, and how they might be related to the sacrificial nexus we have explored.

THE SACRIFICE OF SEXUALITY AND GENDER: "THREENESS" INTERRUPTS "TWONESS"

I said at the start that I sought to demonstrate that "only sacrifice, *rightly understood,* can account for a feminist transformation of the self that is radically 'theonomous,' and thus rendered authentically free, propelled beyond the idolatry of false desire and beyond the restrictions of the gender binary that so exercises current secular gender theory." That was a bold claim, but after our engagement with both text and art of the *akedah* we are now in a better position to return to it. We stressed at the outset that the modern, post-Kantian interpretation of the *akedah*, largely propelled by the well-known Kierkegaardian dilemmas, is focused almost exclusively on Abraham and primarily concerned with ethics and violence. But we now see that there is another deep vein of Jewish exegesis of the *akedah*, perhaps nowhere better expressed in the modern period than in the work of Rabbi Abraham Kook, that the *akedah* is at base—and underlying all the fascinating details of exegesis to which we have partially attended—about the problem of idolatry.[46] It is about the primal sin of the false direction of desire. Put that way, we see how well Rabbi Kook's insight accords with that of John of the Cross cited earlier: when I am brought into the reflexive circle of divine desire for me, it is that subtler sacrifice I have sought to describe and defend here—subtler than the patriarchal sacrifice of violence—that is demanded of me if I am to unite my desires with God's desires. In that place of sacrifice, and not without pain and suffering, desires are sorted and idolatry purged: my desires are gradually set in the light of divine desire—a desire *for* life and joy, not for their suppression.[47] In that place of sacrifice, deeper than any *individual* ethical decision, I am also en route to a freedom that is free precisely because it is rooted in God. This is the road back to divine union, to a perception of what it is for the wellsprings of human agency to flow unhindered in God's own prior agency.[48]

Two important things follow from this line of thought, it seems to me, about our current difficulties on the other two roads that I claimed at the start meet God at the *akedah*. And with these somewhat bold proposals about sexuality and gender, I shall bring this speculative paper to its close.

First, let me venture a reflection on sexuality: if the "sacrifice" of the purgation of desire draws all desires in its wake, then what we now call our sexuality must be drawn vitally into the divine tether of desire. There is a profound sense, then, in which sexuality is, theologically speaking, my most urgent reminder of my creatureliness and my dependence on God. This is not to be confused with a *tantric* approach to sex (there is no direct *identification* of sexual pleasure and relationship to God proposed here); rather, it is about a play within a web of desire that is ultimately God's and that through sacrifice, rightly understood, draws all my desires more truly into alignment with God's.[49] Hence, and ironically, I can agree most happily with Judith Butler when she says that "sexuality establishes us as outside of ourselves."[50] Yes, I would say, outside of ourselves and *in God*.

So secondly, and finally, then, there is the vexed matter of gender, understood, I propose, as "embodied relationship." What is the relation of this gender to "sexuality" just discussed and to the purgative play of divine desire in us? If the logic of "interruption" in sacrifice that we have examined can be allowed to guide us here, then we shall be forced to conclude that the "thirdness" of the divine interruption in sacrifice seems to disturb any fixed, or sterile, binary in gender. Divine desire, we might say, is ontologically more fundamental than gender. Gender "matters," to be sure, for it is our mode of embodied relationship—created, fallen, and en route to redemption in God. But it is made labile to the workings of divine desire as twoness is interrupted by the third.[51] Hence, when our three roads—feminism, sexuality, and God—meet at the *akedah*, there is a sacrifice, all right. But unlike patriarchal sacrifice, it is a sacrifice that I have argued feminism cannot do without; for ultimately it shows us not only where true freedom (from patriarchy and other ills) lies but also how we might rethink sexuality and gender creatively in God.

CONCLUSIONS

I have levied here an unusual argument for the feminist significance of sacrifice read through the complex traditions of the *akedah*. In so doing, I have—with the majority Jewish tradition of the premodern era—put the spotlight on Isaac rather than—with the majority Christian tradition of the modern era—on Abraham. I have argued that the Kantian and Kierkegaardian dilemma between the ethical and what "suspends" it can be sublated by attention to a rendition of sacrifice motivated by the purification and intensification of love for God. As such, the true meaning of such sacrifice—as the passage toward proper ascetical "detachment"—is ultimately as applicable to the figure of Abraham as it is to Isaac, although for Isaac it comes through a more painful and dangerous powerlessness, which I have figured as Isaac's symbolic "femininity" vis-à-vis patriarchy.

On this picture, sacrifice is the necessary *purgation* of false desire (leading to life, not death) that occurs when the divine gift hits the timeline of human sin and asks of us nothing less than complete and ecstatic commitment to the divine; it progresses ultimately to a theonomous selfhood in which freedom is constituted by right dependence on God and God alone; and it culminates in re-entry into social and community life, recharged with divine life and love.

As such, I have argued, sacrifice is as much a *feminist* mode of transformation as it is a death knell to patriarchy; yet patriarchal sacrifice, its dark mimic, ever hovers as a seductive and demonic alternative. The one, sacrifice-for-God, brings freedom, union, and peace; the other, sacrifice-for-the-world, re-establishes the law of patriarchal violence, possessiveness, and abuse. Again, the one, sacrifice-for-God, "interrupts" the fixed repressive gender binary of patriarchy; the other, sacrifice-for-the-world, re-establishes the violence of mandatory "hetero-normativity" and male dominance. The problem of continuing political vigilance, not to say of intense spiritual discernment, is clearly not to be gainsaid. But the rejection of "sacrifice," *tout court,* is too high a price to pay.

Finally, in the course of this argument I have brought minority strands within Jewish and Christian tradition about the *akedah* into a sort of mutual submission of their own: "Deep calls to deep," as the psalmist says; and we may well think this of the remarkable confluence, in particular, of strands of thought in John of the Cross and Rav Kook. If a founding myth of such ineluctable power and elusiveness as the *akedah* can bring Jew and Christian together once more rather than dividing them, it will indeed be a sign that a transformative spiritual purgation has occurred—one worthy, in the best sense, of the name of feminism.[52]

NOTES

1. During the presentation of this paper at the Syracuse conference, a set of visual images were used as backcloth to the unfolding of the argument. Figure 1 (the familiar Rembrandt van Rijn, *Abraham's Sacrifice*, 1655, etching and drypoint: http://www.nga.gov/collection/gallery/rembrandt/rembrandt-9957.html) was projected for the whole of the introduction and the first section of the paper. Note that according to one strand in rabbinic/haggadic tradition (possibly retro-influenced by Christianity), Abraham does actually carry through the sacrifice of Isaac, but Isaac is then restored dramatically to new life. For the classic modern discussion of these traditions, see Shalom Spiegel, *The Last Trial: On the Legends and*

Lore of the Command to Abraham to Offer Isaac as a Sacrifice, with introduction and preface by Judah Goldin (Woodstock, Vt.: Jewish Lights, 1993); for a more recent account of how Jewish and Christian traditions interrelated on this theme, see Edward Kessler, *Bound by the Bible* (Cambridge: Cambridge University Press, 2004), esp. ch. 5. I shall return to this theme of Isaac's near-death, or death, below.

2. The index of Freud's collected works reveals no sustained discussion of Abraham and Isaac, and nothing at all on Genesis 22. It is of course Moses, not Abraham, who most vibrantly exercises Freud's imagination: see his *Moses and Monotheism* (London: Hogarth Press, 1939).

3. This thesis has been most memorably sustained by Nancy Jay, *Throughout Your Generations for Ever: Sacrifice, Religion and Paternity* (Chicago: University of Chicago Press, 1992).

4. See Carol Delaney, *Abraham on Trial: The Social Legacy of Biblical Myth* (Princeton: Princeton University Press, 1998). Similar presumptions about the violence of sacrifice are to be found in Bruce Chilton's *Abraham's Curse: Child Sacrifice in the Legacies of the West* (New York: Doubleday, 2008); and behind both studies lurks the influential theory of René Girard on sacrifice as "primary violence": see especially *Violence and the Sacred* (London: Athlone Press, 1977), and *Things Hidden Since the Foundation of the World* (London: Athlone Press, 1987). Note immediately, however, that it remains a moot point whether sacrifice *is* intrinsically and necessarily violent: such is a specifically modern presumption, as Jon Levenson in *The Death and Resurrection of the Beloved Son* (New Haven: Yale University Press, 1993) is wont to insist, and it enshrines the modern Kantian/Kierkegaardian moral dilemma (moral law vs. its "suspension") on the assumption that sacrifice cannot be distinguished from "murder" (Kant's word). Anthropological cross-cultural treatments of sacrifice, in contrast, tend to be more careful to stress the multivalence of sacrifice—its capacity for diverse meanings, including bloodless gift and moral transformation: on this point see the still-useful collection *Sacrifice,* ed. M. F. C. Bourdillon and Meyer Fortes (London: Academic Press, 1980); and *Understanding Religious Sacrifice: A Reader,* ed. Jeffrey Carter (London: Continuum, 2003), which provides a fine recent introduction to the plethora of modern and contemporary social science theories of sacrifice. Two monographs that witness to a notable recent turn against the Girardian presumption of sacrifice-as-violence are Jonathan Klawans, *Purity, Sacrifice, and the Temple: Symbolism and Supersessionism in the Study of Ancient Judaism* (New York: Oxford University Press, 2006), and Kathryn McClymond, *Beyond Sacred Violence: A Comparative Study of Sacrifice* (Baltimore: Johns Hopkins University Press, 2008).

5. See Yvonne Sherwood's recent feminist work on the *akedah,* including: "Textual Carcasses and Isaac's Scar, or What Jewish Interpretation Makes of the Violence that Almost Takes Place on Mt. Moriah," in *Sanctified Aggression: Legacies of Biblical and Post Biblical Vocabularies of Violence,* ed. Jonneke Bekkenkamp and Yvonne Sherwood (Edinburgh: T & T Clark, 2003), 22–43; and idem, "Binding-Unbinding: Divided Responses of Judaism, Christianity, and Islam to the 'Sacrifice' of Abraham's Beloved Son," *Journal of the American Academy of Religion* 72 (2004): 821–61.

Note that in this paper I shall myself use the term "patriarchy" in a generic sense to denote any cultural arrangement furthering male authority and hegemony, and thereby implicitly undermining the possibility of women's full flourishing. A particular instance of such patriarchal arrangements is of course the insistence on the greater value of sons (especially eldest sons) over daughters for the maintenance of patrilineal descent.

6. See Levenson, *Death and Resurrection*, for a powerful statement of this thesis, already sketched by Spiegel in *Last Trial, 85–88*.

7. As we shall see further below, this "positive" rendition of the outcome of Isaac's ordeal is one strand in Jewish tradition on the *akedah* that became intensified during the appalling pogroms of medieval Europe. The primary stress at this time was on the figure of Isaac as the suffering and dying (yet victorious) one, rather than on Abraham (see Spiegel, *Last Trial, 17–27*). Kessler, *Bound by the Bible*, ch. 5, argues that even from the time of earliest Jewish exegesis of Genesis 22, it is Isaac who is the main point of interest in contrast to Christianity's primary focus on Abraham. Contemporary "liberal" Jewish preaching tends, in stark contrast to rabbinic interpretation, to take for granted the modern identification of sacrifice with violence or murder and to read Isaac as rendered psychologically damaged and ineffective as a result of his ordeal (I have this from conversations with a number of North American Conservative and Reform rabbis).

8. It may be important to stress at the outset of my own account of the *akedah* that the genre I am engaged in here is not a straightforward scholarly retrieval of rabbinic and Christian classical sources (such as I have often employed in my other writings) but a deliberately free and imaginative redeployment of them for my own "midrashic" purposes. As such, I intentionally emulate traits in rabbinic hermeneutics itself (though admittedly without some of the florid wordplay that is also characteristic of it). My own midrash on the *akedah*, then, whilst clearly both Christian and feminist, enters into conversation with rabbinic interpretation not to supersede but to *attend:* by taking my initial inspiration from elements in that tradition that may seem obscure or tangential, I emulate the simultaneously playful and serious mode of rabbinic exegesis and also its surprising openness to the new. (As Judah Goldin puts it, the story of Abraham and Isaac "rises almost spontaneously in the mind of one generation after another . . . each generation has its own . . . concerns" [Spiegel, *Last Trial*, XVI].) If to standard modern Christian exegetical eyes my method here seems weird or willful (as I am sure it will to some readers), I can only plead that is itself a kind of ascetical experiment in bringing Jewish and Christian traditions of depth and perplexity into the kind of mutual but freeing submission to God that I advocate in this essay as a whole.

9. Already adumbrated in n. 4, above. The massive underlying influence of René Girard in this regard is undeniable, and I was chided at the conference (by Gianni Vattimo and others) for not discussing his work more directly. Whilst it would be a distraction here to advert to a lengthy criticism of Girard's original theory (viz., that sacrifice is an essential and foundational violence against a scapegoat, required for the maintenance of all religion and culture), it should be noted that in his later work Girard makes significant retractions, allowing for the transformative effects of *positive* "mimetic desire," as well as the negative effects of violent competitive desire (and repenting, e.g., of his earlier denigration of the theology of sacrifice in the epistle to the Hebrews). On these points, see the revealing interview with Girard by Rebecca Adams, "Violence, Difference, Sacrifice: A Conversation with René Girard," *Religion and Literature* 25 (1993): 9–33. For a critique of the effects of Girard's influence on postmodern philosophy of religion, especially in its interactions with science,

see my Cambridge inaugural lecture, "Sacrifice Regained: Reconsidering the Rationality of Christian Belief" (Cambridge University Press, forthcoming).

10. London: Routledge, 1990.

11. See Luce Irigaray, "Women on the Market," in *The Logic of the Gift*, ed. Alan D. Schrift (London: Routledge, 1997), 174–89; and Hélène Cixous, "Sorties: Out and Out: Attacks/Ways Out/Forays," in ibid, 148–73.

12. For the development of this theme in Derrida, see Jacques Derrida, *Given Time: Counterfeit Money* (Chicago: University of Chicago Press, 1992), and idem, *The Gift of Death* (Chicago: University of Chicago Press, 1995). For the theme of the *tout autre*, see *Gift of Death*, ch. 4.

13. *Gift of Death*, 96.

14. Ibid. (my emphasis).

15. Ibid., 76: "Would the logic of sacrificial responsibility, within the implacable universality of the law, of its law, be altered, inflected, attenuated, or displaced, if a woman were to intervene in some consequential manner? Does the system of this sacrificial responsibility and of the double "gift of death" imply at its very basis an exclusion or sacrifice of woman? A woman's sacrifice or a sacrifice of woman, according to one sense of the genitive or the other? Let us leave the question in suspense."

16. See, e.g., Derrida, *Given Time*, 4–5, on "Madame de Maintenon," for whom "desire and the desire to give" is the "same thing," thus achieving the "impossible."

17. I comment on this malaise and further analyze the problem of gift and gender as it has now been received in Anglophone theology in "Why Gift? Gift, Gender and Trinitarian Relations in Milbank and Tanner," *Scottish Journal of Theology* 16 (2008): 224–35.

18. Immanuel Kant, "The Philosophy Faculty Versus the Theology Faculty," *The Conflict of the Faculties* (New York: Abaris Books, 1979), 115.

19. Søren Kierkegaard, *Fear and Trembling, The Sickness Unto Death* (New York: Doubleday, 1954), see esp. 64–77 ("Problem 1").

20. See John D. Caputo, *The Prayers and Tears of Jacques Derrida: Religion Without Religion* (Bloomington: Indiana University Press, 1997), 220.

21. See the discussion of *Genesis Rabbah* 58.5 in Sherwood, "Binding-Unbinding," 852. A rather different, and earlier, feminist interpretation of Sarah's role and significance is to be found in Phyllis Trible, "Genesis 22: The Sacrifice of Sarah," in *"Not in Heaven": Coherence and Complexity in Biblical Narrative*, ed. Jason P. Rosenblatt and Joseph C. Sitterson (Bloomington: Indiana University Press, 1991), 170–91.

22. This "incorporative" approach to the Christian doctrine of the Trinity, founded in the Pauline logic of prayer in the Spirit drawing one into the life of Christ (see Rom. 8:9–30) has been a feature of much of my recent theological writing. For a more detailed explication of the exegesis of this passage in the early church and its theological and gendered significance, see my "Why Three? Some Further Reflections on the Origins of the Doctrine of the Trinity," in *The Making and Remaking of Christian Doctrine*, ed. Sarah Coakley and David A. Pailin (Oxford University Press, 1993), 29–56, and "Living into the Mystery of the Holy Trinity: Trinity, Prayer and Sexuality," *Anglican Theological Review* 80 (1998): 223–32. A

more sustained discussion is forthcoming in *God, Sexuality and the Self: An Essay 'On the Trinity'* (Cambridge University Press, 2011).

23. Already in Josephus's account, Isaac joyfully and heroically builds the altar himself (*Ant.*, 1.227); in *Genesis Rabbah* (56.8), he asks Abraham to bind him; in *Sifre Deuteronomy* (32, on Deut. 6. 5), the second-century Rabbi Meir is cited as insisting that Isaac "bound himself" on the altar; and in the *Pesikta de-Rab Kahana*, ed. Bernard Mandelbaum (New York: Jewish Theological Seminary, 1962), 2.451, Isaac is said to have "offered himself upon the altar." See Levenson, *Death and Resurrection*, 192–99, and Kessler, *Bound by the Bible*, 123–25, for these developments in Jewish exegesis.

24. Rembrandt van Rijn, *Abraham and Isaac*, 1634/5, oil on canvas: http://www.artchive .com/artchive/R/rembrandt/abraham.jpg.html.

25. Clearly, my very brief treatment here of some intriguing rabbinical traditions on the *akedah* is selective and—some might say—idiosyncratic. See again n. 8, above, for my defense of this hermeneutical procedure and the use of mutually informing Jewish and Christian traditions on this problematic nexus.

26. *Midrash Tanhuma*, vol. 1: *Genesis*, trans. John T. Townsend (Hoboken, N.J.: Ktav Publishing House, 1989), 143: 5.9 Genesis 25: 1ff., Part III.

27. See Genesis 24:62 for the mention of this place as the one where Isaac was before he went out to woo Rebekah, but the only earlier mention of the same place is Genesis 16:14 in relation to Hagar's flight into the desert after Sarah's outburst of jealousy. From this point of name connection, the author of the *Midrash Tanhuma* concludes that Isaac, after finding a wife for himself, went to bring Hagar back to Abraham to marry. He thus identifies "Keturah" (Gen. 25:1) with Hagar (ibid.).

28. The author of the *Midrash Tanhuma* puts it more laconically: "It is simply that when Isaac took Rebekah, Isaac said: Let us go and bring a wife to my father" (ibid.).

29. *Sifre: A Tannaitic Commentary on the Book of Deuteronomy*, ed. Reuven Hammer (New Haven: Yale University Press, 1986), 32 (see also n. 23 above: Levenson, *Death and Resurrection*, 193, comments that here "child sacrifice has been sublimated into self-sacrifice").

30. *Midrash Rabbah Genesis*, vol. 1, trans. H. Freedman (London: Soncino Press, 1983), 497: "Can one bind a man thirty-seven years old? (another version: twenty-six years old) without his consent?" These ages are worked out from biblical hints of the length of years between Sarah's bearing of Isaac and her death, on the one hand (37), and from the number of years that Abraham spent in Hebron on the other (26).

31. *Mekilta De-Rabbi Ishmael*, trans. Jacob Z. Lauterbach (Philadelphia: Jewish Publication Society of America, 1976), 57.

32. See Gen. 22:11–12; yet from the time of the earliest exegetical reflection, there is perplexity that no mention is made of Isaac after the event on Mt. Moriah, e.g., in vs. 19. On this problem, see Spiegel, *Last Trial*, 3–8, who charts the later traditions that Isaac did die and temporarily went to Paradise before returning to life.

33. See again esp. Spiegel, *Last Trial*, ch. 3, for the medieval slaughters of Jews that intensified these haggadic traditions of death and resurrection. Levenson, *Death and Resur-*

rection, 192–99, insightfully discusses the development of the traditions of Isaac's swooning or actual death, burning to ashes, and resurrection.

34. This convergence and implicit interaction is commented on in Kessler, *Bound to the Bible*, ch. 5, especially in relation to the theme of the treasury of merits (*ʒecut avoth*) accrued by Isaac's ordeal. A particularly telling text here is again the *Pesikta de-Rab Kahana*, 2. 451 (see n. 23): "By the merit of Isaac who offered himself upon the altar, the Holy One (blessed be He) will in the future resurrect the dead, as it is written: '[For he looks down from His holy height; the Lord beholds the earth from heaven] to hear the groans of the prisoner, [to release those condemned to death]' [Ps. 102:20–21]."

35. See R. W. L. Moberly, "The Earliest Commentary on the Akedah," *Vetus Testamentum* 38 (1988): 302–23, which analyzes this interpolation as a first attempt to make Abraham's obedience foundational to Israel and somewhat parallel to Moses's significance. Moberly takes up the issue of the existing feminist "hermeneutic of suspicion" in relation to Genesis 22 in his *The Bible, Theology, and Faith: A Study of Abraham and Jesus* (Cambridge University Press, 2000), ch. 5, and (in my view, rightly) continues to insist that "*thoroughgoing* suspicion lacks adequate criteria for assessing in what way the story might be true" (ibid., 180, my emphasis).

36. This is, of course, according to my earlier definition, a fully "patriarchal" promise about future power and patrilineal descent; whereas the first intervention of the angel (vss. 11–12) is, quite differently, about the test of Abraham's detachment (even from the object of his greatest human love) and thus about his primary and overriding "fear" of God. One might say that this first intervention therefore *breaks* patriarchal attachment rather than fosters it: see below.

37. I refer here to John of the Cross, sketch of Christ on the cross (from the perspective of the Father's gaze), late sixteenth century, reproduced as the frontispiece of John of the Cross, trans. Kieran Kavanaugh and Otilio Rodriguez, *The Complete Works of John of the Cross* (Washington, D.C.: ICS Publications, 1991).

38. Ibid., 745.

39. See Gen. 18:1–5. The icon shown here at the conference was a fourteenth-century representation of *The Hospitality of Abraham* (Benaki Museum, Athens, no. 2973), in which both Abraham and Sarah are depicted serving the three mysterious visitors.

40. The interruption is particularly powerfully portrayed in a fifteenth-century French Bible illustration in which the angel turns Abraham right around 90 degrees from his concentration on Isaac (who is bound on a stone altar slab) and grabs his drawn sword. The angel is seemingly represented as a female figure: see E. Wellisch, *Isaac and Oedipus: A Study in Biblical Psychology of the Sacrifice of Isaac, The Akedah* (New York: Humanities Press, 1954), facing 96.

41. See Moshe J. Bernstein, "Angels at the Aqedah: A Study in the Development of a Midrashic Motif," *Dead Sea Discoveries* 7 (2000): 263–91, for a comprehensive account of differing views of angels that became associated with the *akedah* story over time.

42. In Wellisch, *Isaac and Oedipus*, facing 97. Wellisch comments: "In this crayon-drawing of a boy of fourteen, attending a Child Guidance Clinic, Isaac is shown bowing submissively to Abraham's task."

43. George Segal, *Abraham and Isaac*, twentieth-century sculpture, Princeton University: http://speccoll.library.kent.edu/4may70/exhibit/memorials/segal.html. The sculpture is subtitled "In Memory of May 4, 1970, Kent State University." Here, in contrast to most medieval representations, the figures are directly and shockingly face to face, Isaac kneeling with hands bound, and Abraham's knife drawn in a phallic position as if to stab Isaac directly into his chest. Neither the angel nor the ram are present. Segal has himself acknowledged that he was affected by instances of child abuse and random violence in representing the *akedah* in this way.

44. Relief on the pulpit at Volterra by Bonusamicus, c. 1200. As Wellisch, *Isaac and Oedipus*, facing 81, comments: "In this rendering of the Sacrifice of Isaac the figures of Abraham, Isaac and the Angel, who has womanly characteristics, appear to form a family. The sculptor has movingly conveyed a depth of feeling and pious simplicity in the group."

45. In Wellisch's own words (*Isaac and Oedipus*, 96), stressing the importance of the re-integration of the maternal into the story (reading the angel-as-Sarah): "The Akedah story itself does not give a clear indication of what follows. One can, however, draw the conclusion that it marked the beginning of a new relationship between father and son which initiated a new era in the family relationships of man. Its realization depends on a situation in which selfish aims are abandoned and real personal love and dedication to God's call are possible. From the phenomenological point of view this new relationship can be described as *a covenant between parent and child* which inaugurated a new era of moral code."

46. See Rav Kook, *'Olat Re'iyah*, 82–97, for his commentary on the *akedah*. Unfortunately this is not available in an English translation, but commentary may be found in Zvi Yaron, *The Philosophy of Rabbi Kook*, trans. Avner Tomaschoff (Jerusalem: Eliner Library, 1991), ch. 2, esp. 40–43; and in Jerome I. Gellman's "Poetry of Spirituality," in *Rabbi Abraham Isaac Kook and Jewish Spirituality*, ed. Lawrence J. Kaplan and David Shatz (New York University Press, 1995), ch. 4. The distinctive feature of Rav Kook's rendition of the *akedah* (as beautifully brought out in Gellman's treatment) is that the anti-idolatrous sacrificial urge in Abraham *must* combine both detachment/renunciation and renewed love of earth, family, and relationship. To participate ecstatically in divine love *is* to "return to the servants and donkeys" (see Yaron, *Philosophy of Rabbi Kook*, 43); the upward move of ascent is immediately met with the downward move of divine compassion and mercy for his creation. Here we meet a striking parallel with Christian mystical doctrines of simultaneous ascent and "kenotic" descent.

47. It is surely significant that, in Book II of the *Dark Night of the Soul* (the terrible "Night of Spirit"), John of the Cross describes how God draws so painfully and purgatively close that is it *felt* as an assault that is also (paradoxically) a seeming abandonment. In fact, according to John, it is neither, because what is felt as violent is only seemingly such because the soul is not yet used to this level of intimacy with God; in reality it is the lightest and most tender touch, inviting the soul into union with Christ.

48. I have attempted a sustained argument for the *feminist* worth of such a perspective on submission to God in my *Powers and Submissions: Philosophy, Spirituality and Gender* (Oxford: Blackwell, 2002), esp. the intro. and ch. 1.

49. See my "Pleasure Principles: Towards a Contemporary Theology of Desire," *Harvard Divinity Bulletin* (Autumn 2005): 20–33, for a more detailed enunciation of my thesis

that this ascetic (*not* repressive) perspective should apply equally to heterosexual and homosexual desire. I do want to stress that my thesis here is not to be confused with the conservative agenda to put homosexuals through reparative therapies.

50. Judith Butler, *Undoing Gender* (New York: Routledge, 2004), 15.

51. Again, this argument is made at greater length elsewhere: for the intersection of "twoness" and "threeness" in God and in human sexuality, see my *God, Sexuality and the Self,* esp. ch. 1.

52. I am grateful to those who offered criticisms of the earlier version of this paper as given at the Syracuse conference, in particular: Merold Westphal, Jack Caputo, Jon Levenson, Timothy Dalrymple, Cameron Partridge, and an insightful anonymous reviewer for Indiana University Press. I have attempted to respond to their points in this revised version. I am also deeply indebted to two former doctoral students at Harvard, Mark Nussberger and Shai Held, who provided me not only with research assistance but with many rich textual and bibliographical suggestions.

TWO

The Return of Religion
during the
Reign of Sexuality

Mark D. Jordan

If religion now "returns" to us, how does it come? Like a seasonal wind,
erratic but awaited, that rattles locks and scorches unlucky skin?—or is
religion a plague ever latent in imagined tropics, some venereal fever inevitably imported, to which our citizenry remains vulnerable in its naked
innocence?—or is the religion that returns more particular, more like an
exiled king, an Odysseus, forced to wander, fight other wars, suffer nar-
cotic seductions, before returning home to discover a troop of courtiers
ruining the palace? How do we imagine this religion that returns? And
what does it discover when it comes home?

Religion returns—but the term "religion" is more a disguise than a name,
like the *Oudeis*, the "No one," that Odysseus shouts to the Cyclops. "Religion" is a mystifying abstraction that conceals, that covertly imposes more
familiar figures and histories. The concealed story for many American
audiences is still typically about Christianity and Judaism, though mostly about Christianity. And not any Christianity, but the Christianity of

Christendom, the disciplinary regime of once-dominant churches that could dictate laws and summon the police.

What makes us think that Christianity ever left? Since the Enlightenment, since Revolutions, the disestablishment of certain churches or regnant theologies has been confused with the banishment of religion because "religion" only meant a certain enforcement of Christendom. Disestablishment did not destroy Christianity because Christianity never depended entirely on civil laws and their police. So Christianity continues to occupy languages and bodies, to instruct aspirations and habits, long after its churches are disestablished and its theologies ridiculed.

Our perception of the exile of Christianity depends upon a confusion about disestablishment but also about sex. If anything was supposed to prove our freedom from dead churches and their ridiculous theologies, it was our *orgasmic* enlightenment, our *sexual* revolution. Triumph over Christendom has been a tenet in sexual politics—and, not least, in strategies of American queer activism from the late 1960s on. "The church is the enemy": a slogan equally useful for responding to Anita Bryant, the Catholic hierarchy's rejection of condoms despite AIDS, and today's "faith-based initiatives." Yet we Americans now see—if we ever could ignore—that sexual "liberation" did not silence the discourses of a once-dominant Christianity or quell its political outbreaks.

More than a century after the confessedly premature announcement of God's death by Nietzsche's madman, the cultural place of the Christian God, the throne of the old lawgiver, is still not empty. The death of God has been instead a sort of hide-and-seek. The death of the Christian God, the disappearance of thundering Jehovah, has been only a curious dance with His twin, His other . . . with Sex. (I use "His" for this God quite deliberately.) Instead of confirming Enlightenment and Revolution, the death of God inaugurated another monarchy, the Reign of Sex. The death of God not only made a void into which sex could enter, it fixed the conditions for sex to take power as sexuality—to become King Sex, as Foucault says.[1] And so, when the old God returns—because this God has a habit of rising from the dead—He finds His palace occupied by Sex, His viceroy. The absent God has been replaced by a Sex trained during His long reign and emboldened by His temporary absence. This Reign of Sex is only possible after the Christianity of Christendom.

And yet the interim Reign of Sex—*if* it is only an interregnum—has brought notable changes. Since their return, Christian speeches have embraced the rhetoric of the regime of sexuality—specific categories, but also an ontology of sexual identities. Outside Christian churches, rightly ordered sexuality promises present salvation. Inside many churches, right words about sexuality now determine your eternal salvation. The same churches are havens for outdated juridico-medical theories of sex. The "ex-gay" movement is a living archive of 1950s American Freudianism and other defunct diagnoses of the etiology and prognosis of "homosexuality." There is a new language that even old kings must learn. But then the old king spoke sex too—indeed, practiced his power originally through cunning, curious ways of talking about sex. If evangelical churches have shown themselves adept at mastering the new speech of sexuality, for example, that is because they always had a knack for sex-talk, for words to regulate sex. Christian religion returns during the reign of sex and quickly learns the new words of power. This odyssey too ends with a well-staged and melodramatic homecoming that is sometimes hard to distinguish from a slaughter.

I hope that my little stories have been confusing. I mean to exploit the confusion of our stories about sex and the return of "religion" by describing the relations of Christian speech to modern regimes of sexuality in three moments. In the first, I recall that some famous announcements of the death of God were prescient about the advent of the regime of sexuality. Pronouncing the death of the Christian God meant introducing a better-sexed divinity—but also divinizing better-managed *human* sex. I then show—second moment—some of the relations of Christian discourses to the regime of sexuality under which they survive, toward which they return, before which they already stood. In the final moment, the shortest, the most accelerated, I ask whether some Christian speech might still afford other possibilities for contesting the regime of sexuality. Could the return of this always- and never-familiar religion disrupt the regime rather than copy it and reinforce it? Could the return of another Christianity offer an alternate idiom in which to articulate bodies and pleasures without endorsing the reign of King Sex?

THE DEATH OF GOD AND THE REIGN OF SEX

The premature announcement of the death of God belongs most famously to Nietzsche. The announcement is regularly misunderstood, and many correctives have been offered to prevent further misunderstanding. I step around them to watch again how Nietzsche's representations of the death of God or the demise of European Christendom are followed by his encounter with another divinity, a god notable for sexed beauty and erotic adventures. Let me illustrate this sequence from the obvious example, *Beyond Good and Evil*, the final opera of Nietzsche's Zarathustra-cycle. It presents the monstrous, frightening mask that Zarathustra's teaching must wear in order to "inscribe itself in the heart of mankind with eternal claims."[2] The mask is required by a nihilistic Europe flattened by the shadow of the God it has lately murdered and not yet begun to lament. This means that the book is shouted from beginning to end—or, rather, to just before the end.

Beyond Good and Evil contains a well-known section on "the religious nature (*Wesen*)."[3] Its aphorisms outline a religious "psychology" in Nietzsche's sense. If the outline includes observations on "the religious neurosis" in general (e.g., #47), the religion most evidently under scrutiny is a Christianity of waning European Christendom. The examples in the section are mostly Christian, and Nietzsche presumes an insider's familiarity with churches sufficient to recognize unmarked allusions to Christian scripture, liturgy, and preaching. However much Nietzsche fantasizes a natural-psychological history of all religious neuroses, he can diagnose only the religion that presents itself to him in his patients, in himself. European Christianity has run its course through missionary expansion, imperial enforcement, civil wars of reform, and then sickly abatement. Like any epidemic disease, Christianity risks both outrunning its supply of hosts and provoking them to devise resistance. In earlier times Christianity was virulent enough to consume both a fretting paganism and the "old Asiatic" grandeur of the Hebrew Bible (##49, 52). When raging, its fevers could invert established values, perform vertiginous sacrifices of minds and bodies. But of late it has lost its strength in shrunken or immune populations: it has become the industrialized piety of northerners, who were hardly suitable hosts (## 46, 51, 58). The section on religion in *Beyond Good and Evil* presents fragments from the life cycle of Christendom. The good Europeans about whom Nietzsche writes stand so near the end of that history that they cannot imagine Christianity's epic beginnings—except perhaps by becoming philologists.

The death of the Christian God is learned from diagnostic history. It culminates much later in the book with a prognosis. The most interesting pages on religion in *Beyond Good and Evil* come in the penultimate aphorism (#295). The passage begins with an aria to the "genius of the heart" possessed by a "tempter-God"—"who smooths rough souls and gives them a new desire to taste," "the genius of the heart from whose touch everyone leaves richer . . . broken open, blown on and sounded out by a thaw-wind, [made] less sure perhaps, more fragile, more broken."[4] The tempter-God whose genius grants the experience of desire by his touching and breaks bodies by breathing into them is meant to be Dionysus—though healing touches and thawing breaths belong also to that other god, to Jesus. Nietzsche tells us that he sacrificed his youth to Dionysus and has since spent many hours conversing with him. On what terms? Nietzsche hesitates to tell us *that* much. He is demure: "Perhaps I also must go further in the frankness of my tale than is congenial to the strict habits of your ears? Surely the god in question went further, very much further, in such conversations . . ."[5] The strict habits of Christianized ears: habits required for safeguarding orifices that are always open but also for preserving certain constitutive relations between sex and Christian speech. Nietzsche hesitates to offend against them, to breach them by telling what a god can do when he is not held back by the habit of vulgar shame that is Christendom's afterlife. Dionysus feels no shame while standing naked before Nietzsche, his golden, unbroken skin a rebuke to the loincloth on Jesus' pierced and bloodied body. Dionysus laughs—and so mocks Jesus who never does, whose mournful teaching ends in suffocated silence or else the resentment of unrequited love.

The god Dionysus takes lovers—as against that other god, Jesus, whose aversion to copulation is so great that his mother must be a virgin and his adolescence a chaste void. An erotic life for Jesus is so inconceivable that the canonical gospels never bother to deny one. By contrast, Dionysus's erotic love for human beings is shamelessly avowed. "Under certain circumstances," the god says, "I love what is human," and he gestures to Ariadne, who is present. There are variants in the story of her love for Dionysus, but on Nietzsche's telling she ends by yearning for the god who has abandoned her.[6] Nietzsche has that god disclose that Ariadne is hardly his only human love. "Under certain circumstances": there have been other lovers, there will be other lovers.

The contrast between the old god, Jesus, and the new, Dionysus, could stop here—an ironic reversal of Christianity's triumph over antiquity (because, of course, once Dionysus was the old god and Jesus the new). Jesus, who once rendered the immortal body of Dionysus unseductive, now suffers the same fate in the return of a Greek deity. But Nietzsche does not stop just with the ironic reversal of history. His diagnosis of Christendom leads to a prognosis beyond Christianity. The returning god, he says, loves what is human when the human is his lover. Whatever else it is—and it is many things—the proclamation of the death of the Christian God is an erotic complaint. It is the banishment of the God who refuses His votaries' sex in favor of the god who sometimes wants it.

Wants it how? With whom? Is Dionysus only attracted to Nietzsche for his graceful conversation? Nietzsche hopes not—if we can credit what he writes elsewhere, in a poem called "Ariadne's Lament." Most of the poem appears for the first time in that new gospel, *Zarathustra* Part 4, where it is spoken by the Magician. But Nietzsche later extracted the poem, gave it a new ending, and marked it for inclusion in his *Dionysus Dithyrambs*—a book on his table when he ceased to want to write. "Ariadne's Lament" is a brutal dialogue of desire, abandonment, and surrender. In its final version, it is the midnight voice of Ariadne, "splayed out, shuddering" ("*hingestreckt, schudernd*"), as she hears her lover move near, then retreat.[7] At last Ariadne calls out:

No!
come back!
With all your torments!
All my tears course
their course to you!
and my last heart-flame,
it burns up to you.
Oh come back,
my unknown god! my *pain*!
    my last happiness! . . .

A flash of lightning. Dionysus becomes visible in emerald beauty.

Dionysus:

Be wise, Ariadne! . . .
You have little ears, you have my ears:
stick a wise word inside!—

Must one not first hate oneself, if one is to love oneself?
I am your labyrinth.[8]

The little orifice of the ear, penetrated by divine words. How much Nietzsche wanted some such words spoken to himself! How much he wanted to be Ariadne, "splayed out, shuddering," if only there were a god nearby to lure! But Nietzsche's little ears are also the constricted ears of a Lutheran pastor's son, of a late carrier of the Christian epidemic. He cannot write the emerald-lightning return of Dionysus without quoting that other god, Jesus, the god who is supposed now to be dead, to be only ghost. "Must one not first hate oneself, if one is to love oneself," Dionysus says, but we have heard something like it before, from that other god: "Anyone who finds his life will lose it; anyone who loses his life for my sake will find it" (Matt 10:39). Nietzsche cannot write himself as Ariadne without composing a scene of crucifixion—because a suffering body, "splayed out, shuddering," that calls for the return of an absent God is also, for him as for many of us still, Jesus on the cross calling out for his absent Father. A dying god calls for the return of an absent God: Nietzsche interchanges the roles of Ariadne and Jesus, of Dionysus and Jesus' Father. But Nietzsche also imagines himself the suffering lover of an absent God, imagines himself Jesus calling out for God the deserter, the God who has chosen him only to abandon him.[9]

My remarks are not a reading of Nietzsche. Reading Nietzsche well requires the time for what he calls friendship, a severe devotion over a passionate distance. I have rendered some passages from Nietzsche as a mnemonic device, a reminder that the death of one god is supposed to be accompanied by the return of another; that an erotic complaint against Jehovah or Jesus becomes an erotic invocation of Dionysus. Other mnemonic devices could have been offered. Perhaps they would have been more explicit. Let me gesture toward only two of them—from accomplished readers of Nietzsche.

In Bataille's *Sovereignty*, there is a section entitled "Nietzsche and Jesus."[10] Bataille begins by quoting Gide: Nietzsche was jealous of Jesus to the point of madness. Bataille corrects Gide on many points, but he replies in the first place that there is no madness here. Nietzsche's competition with Jesus is deliberate and prolonged. It is also not solitary. Bataille remarks: "There is always an ensemble of human and divine

forms opposing another ensemble, on one side Nietzsche and Dionysus—
and the Dionysian world—and on the other the believer and the God of
reason—between which Jesus is the mediator" (8:410). Bataille hears in
Gide's use of the word "jealousy" the possibility of *erotic* competition,
then turns it into a paradox: "The object of Nietzsche's jealousy is God"
(407). Again, Bataille recalls that many superficial readers of Nietzsche—
including the young Gide—take the death of God as absolution for their
sexual adventures. But the erotic possibilities opened by the death of God
should be so much more than an excuse for holiday immoralities.

We cannot understand Nietzsche, Bataille writes, because "we belong
to a world . . . where no one can escape from the Christian system without having to adopt at once an equally closed system (or one even more
closed)" (411). Above all, we have lost sight of the sacred, since we inhab-
it a world of objects, and the sacred cannot appear to understanding as an
object. The Dionysian world is precisely not a system of hard objects and
calculable times. It is rupture. We might add to Bataille: it is the world of
Nietzsche's twin and rival, Ariadne, and of her call for violent theophany.
Elsewhere, Bataille will insist upon the way in which the erotic approaches the sacred. But the erotic is of course *not* sex—and certainly not the
"degraded" sex of modern commodification.[11] We cannot understand
Nietzsche—or Nietzsche cannot fully understand himself—because we
live in a sexual world that has excluded the erotic and especially the erotic
encounter with God. The old God must be dead because He wouldn't
have sex with us. So now we have sex with idols, with inanimate effigies,
with a mock-divinity at once insensible and peevish. No one can escape
from the Christian sexual system without having to adopt a system even
more closed.

Which brings me to that other reader of Nietzsche, to Foucault. In an
encomium to Bataille that is also a rewriting of Bataille, Foucault suggests
that discourse on sexuality had been shaped to fit a space left by the death
of God. He writes:

> Sexuality is not decisive for our culture except as spoken and to
> the extent that it is spoken. Our language has been eroticized for
> the last two centuries: our sexuality, since Sade and the death of
> god, has been absorbed by the universe of language, denatured by
> it, placed by it in the void where it established its sovereignty and
> where it, as Law, endlessly poses limits that it transgresses.[12]

For Foucault, who indulges his morose delectation of old churchly moralities, sexuality closes a syntax around sex much more tightly than Christianity ever could. But Foucault also encourages us to read speeches of
sexuality as satisfying longings once elicited and addressed by Christian
theology.

These mnemonic passages from Nietzsche, Bataille, and Foucault
might help us remember that the announcement of the death of God pre-
pares for the advent of sexuality in expected and unexpected ways—by
creating a vacuum to be filled but also by demanding an erotic theod-
icy. The old god must be done away with because He cannot satisfy our
erotic demands. We demand a new god. But instead of Dionysus we get
the regime of managed copulation, of identities, of hygienic genital control. We wanted Dionysus; instead we got Krafft-Ebing—or, worse, the
American Freud. And yet—even the mnemonic devices cannot seem to
remember this—Christian theology did not stop in the nineteenth century. There has been no end to Christian discourses on sex. Indeed,
they have mutated and multiplied, partly in announced opposition to the
regime of sexuality, partly in appropriation or imitation of it. What does
such hardy insistence mean, especially in relation to the new speeches of
sexuality, to the revolutionary theology of the Reign of Sex?

CHRISTIANITY UNDER THE REIGN OF SEX

Christian discourses about sex are now and at once the vanquished
predecessor, the constant alternative, and the chastened collaborator of
discourses about sexuality. There is no way to draw the genealogy of
these relations except as incest. Christian discourses about sex are parent,
sibling, and child to the discourses of sexuality.

This incest of speeches is due in part to the historical precedence of
Christianity—the powerful priority of Christian speeches about sex with
regard to any modern European or American discourse of sexuality. But
the incestuous confusion of speeches we now experience reminds us that
Christian discourses about sex always generated successors or alternatives
to themselves from out of their constitutive tensions. The generational
confusion of speeches, the interruption of clear stages of succession—
these are basic narrative templates for Christianity. The construction of
the Christian Bible out of "Old" and "New" Testaments creates many

tensions, but none so sharp as those around marriage and sex. How can you place Jesus' example of a life beyond sex or his severe suspicion of biological family on top of the Abrahamic promise of divinely protected fertility, the imperative in Genesis to be fruitful, or the notion of an inheritable relation to covenant marked on the foreskin?

As Paul makes plain in Romans, the grafting of gentile Christians onto Israel is an act against nature, beyond nature, that exceeds biological reproduction (Rom 11:24). The memory of that unnatural graft remains in Christian moral theology. Christian discourses about sex have had to struggle from the beginning not only with the severity of their ideals but with their incorporation of contrary speech from a supposedly revered past that must be kept *in the past*. Especially when it comes to sex, Christianity is a discourse that enacts supersession while forbidding return. The patriarchs were commanded to be polygamists. Glory to God's fidelity in His covenant with Israel! But no Christian may be a polygamist. Indeed, it has been a disputed question whether Christians should marry even once.

From the inner tension of supersession, from the prohibition of return to the fertile Israelite body, Christian moralists have learned to edit and translate, to sublimate, contending discourses about sex. They have applied this learning not just to the Hebrew scriptures but to the strange sayings and the more troubling silences of Jesus.[13] If Christian communities were taught early on to tolerate marriage as a concession to lust, they had not only to limit the corruption of erotic pleasure in married sex but to avoid the paradox that all sex between Christians is incest—is sex with someone whom Jesus called brother or sister in a much truer sense than the biological. The exclusivity of vowed monogamy sits uneasily with the universality of Jesus' community of *agápê*. If the approved theological response is to sublate the tension by appeal to celibacy and spiritualized love, the danger is always that a literal *agápê* will return as pure promiscuity.

There is a similar danger with regard to the sexed body of Jesus. It must be simultaneously asserted and controlled, affirmed and evacuated. The complete denial of an erotic life to Jesus is a familiar strategy for avoiding uncomfortable or disruptive inferences from his body. His sex must be reduced to pure virtuality, an official masculinity, an authoritative maleness without any reference to a male member. Once it becomes the habit for all believers to fancy themselves Jesus' ardent lovers, his brides, then his sexed body clearly cannot be allowed to return—except in some indefinite future of abstraction, when he will be an untouchable, androgynous king or else an allegorical lamb. Jesus, who must be the phallus, cannot have a penis—and if he once did, he may not have used it for reproduction or for deliberate pleasure.

The need to manage the return of Jesus' sexed body figures in the Christian ethical register as a silence. In the approved gospels, Jesus can say very little about sex, because to say more would implicate him in knowledge of the details of copulation and of the twists in human desire. So it is that the Christian community must both mark and complete this silence—as Paul does, for example, in 1 Corinthians 7. Paul fills Jesus' silence with the ideal of a life beyond sex that is justified in view of the immanent return of a sexless Jesus, whose coming will disrupt child-bearing and child-making. God takes flesh as a man but puts an end to the cycles of reproduction. It would be better for Christians not to have to talk about sex. It would be better for sexed bodies to heed the call of a life beyond sex.

Paul admits Jesus' silence only to fill it with counsel that is meant to render it unremarkable. We may rather read that silence as both deliberate and remarkable. By refusing to provide detailed sexual legislation (or detailed dietary rules), Jesus kills off a certain type of god, the god whose chief preoccupation is to regulate bodily purity. Paul's speech about sex comes after an event of silence that changes the character of divinity— that banishes one kind of divinity to make room for another. This may account for the curious belatedness of Paul's rhetorical flourishes around sex. He writes most often, not as if he were laying down a new law, but as if all legislation had been accomplished and then superseded. He acknowledges Jesus' silence by reconstruing it as an impatient or disdain-ful reserve—but he does acknowledge it.

These ancient reserves in Christian speech about sex survive as limit-ing negations underneath the enormous elaboration of pastoral discours-es. They qualify or rebuke the endless loquacity about Christians' sexual activity—the loquacity of penitentials, confessors' handbooks, *summae* of moral theology, encyclopedias of casuistry, guides to reformed mar-riage, and summer revival sermons. The reserves are principles of nega-tion that can be invoked unexpectedly to undo the assurance of sexual categories or rules in such texts. When the libraries of Christian speech are rewritten into modern regimes of "secularized" sexuality in a process that Foucault tells and retells—sometimes for the seventeenth-century, most often for the nineteenth—when Christian pastoral discourses pass over into sexuality properly speaking, the ancient reserves, the principles of negation, do *not* pass with them. Much does pass, including a confidence in taxonomies of genital acts, methods for referring acts back to implied species of actors, piety about therapeutic correction, and requirements for unremitting confession. If there are salient differences between medieval Christian theologies of sodomy and nineteenth-century theories of homosexuality, there are also disconcerting family resemblances—as you would expect in any incestuous genealogy. But the most significant difference is not salient because it is a generalized absence—the lack of theological reserve, the erasure of Jesus' marked silence.

The new regime of sexuality does *not* abide by the old reserves underneath Christian speech about sex. The regime's loquacity about sex is not bounded by a supersession that prohibits any return to mere fertility; on the contrary, it serves the purposes of bio-power, the management of fertility. There is no longer a hidden silence at the origin of all detailed legislation, no negative ideal of a life beyond sex and the cycles of reproduction. The new regime understands by natural law, not the slow pedagogy of the Creator's purposes obscured by the cognitive ravages of sin, but a measurable operation of efficient causes. These differences are qualified or conditioned by the similarities, of course. In one sense, modern sexual identities remain intrinsically theological both in their genesis and in their logic. They arise out of Christian pastoral or canonical discourses, and they carry over the rhetorical tropes that make it possible to build a morally decisive role around sexual desire. But in borrowing from moral theology they ignore the limits drawn around Christian theology at its foundations.

A refusal to abide by the old reserves underneath Christian speech changes little on the surface. Perhaps that is why so many Christian communities have thought that they could learn the new language of sexuality in order to contest, correct, or redeploy it. But once they join in ignoring the ancient negations, they are compelled to change the character of their speech. It is not surprising, then, that natural law becomes in some contemporary Catholic documents a fully knowable set of moral propositions. Marriage is no longer a concession to lust: married sexual pleasure has become a Christian right—hence the contemporary genre of the evangelical pillow book. The ideal of the abstemious marriage is replaced by the imperative of fertility, and male-female complementarity becomes not only a universal moral regulation but a cosmic fact and a key to the inner life of the Trinity.

Most strikingly, once churches learn to speak sexuality, they must fit the body of Jesus into the system of well-managed reproduction as its endorsement and guarantee. His is no longer a divine body that refuses to speak sex, that stands apart from marriage and its families. Jesus becomes a presumptive heterosexual—who doubtless would have gotten married if he hadn't been so busy at work; who must have had girlfriends when attending Nazareth High School; who surely fancied certain types of women—say, Miriam, that saucy brunette—and who must have imagined (in a wholesome, healthy way, of course) what it would be like to hold hands with her, to kiss her, to take her to the well-chaperoned prom, to propose to her, to marry her, only then to "make love" to her, with or without the use of artificial means of contraception, depending on his denominational preference.[14] Under the regime of sexuality, everyone should have a sexual identity at the end of a proper sexual development—whether they remain celibate or not. There is no outside, not even for Jesus. If Jesus *could* stand outside, the whole regime would be called into question by his displacement, his refusal to enter the dichotomy between heterosexual and homosexual.

Once Christian speeches capitulate to sexuality in this way, the ancient reserve is indeed undone and Christian chatter about sex no longer deserves to be called Christian *theology*—however it chooses to advertise itself. It is reduced to a pro-natalist ideology, to the marketing of certain marital arrangements, or to a quaint rationale for promoting certain notions of sexual hygiene—not to say, of male privilege. Christian chatter about sex becomes a local *dialect* within the regime of sexuality. It serves as another courtier to King Sex. To say this in Greek: Odysseus comes back to Ithaca and becomes majordomo in his old palace, serving whichever suitor ends up bedding Penelope.

SPEAKING CHRISTIANITY OTHERWISE

Might some Christian theology make another sort of return? Might it still speak otherwise than as sexuality? And how would such speeches recall the old reserve in order to honor its disruptive silence—not least by examining it again?

However familiar the chatter of Christendom seems, especially when it comes to sex, the archive of Christian speeches is barely known and less often read. When it is consulted for its teaching on sex, it is screened through our most pedestrian categories and our simplest assurances about how texts mean and which genres are suited to moral argument. In particular, we look for decontextualized rules about sex when we ought to be looking for ritually or liturgically contextualized characters of desire.

I want to insist that these sacramental characters are not "identities," especially when it comes to sex. Absent a legal code, confronted with gospel narratives and the parables in them, Christian ethics has had to derive its principles from *characters* rather than regulations. The basic element of Christian moral teaching is not a law but a mimetic character. These characters are imitated from proclaimed scriptures and venerated saints. The power to perform the mimesis is a grace mediated through rites or sacraments. Even Christian sin-characters are mimetic in this sense: specific sexual sins are tied to scriptural exemplars, real or imagined. Nowhere is this plainer than with the medieval sodomite, whose sin is conceived as a citation across the time of a scriptural episode. Every sodomite is an exiled citizen of Sodom, still fleeing the pelting fire. The character of a sodomite is performed by an illicit and all-too-bodily return across a space of supersession. However damnable this excess might be, it shares with positive sacramental characters a complex temporality that cannot be captured by any identity. Constituted by scriptural citation in liturgical time, inhabiting a charred past and meriting an emptier eternity of repetition, the sodomite of medieval theology is not a measurable or manageable unit of bio-power—any more than the virgin martyr is.

These sacramental characters of an outmoded Christianity do explain sexual activity by shaping it into selves, but they also deny any final explanation—certainly by human medicine or civil law. The sacramental character of the sodomite, for example, denies that the acts of sodomy can be adjudicated by a set of propositional rules, no matter how numerous. It denies as well that the sodomite can be captured in any life history, any clinical chart, because the sodomite's character is constituted by citation to a scriptural past and by anticipation of a divinely fixed eternity. In these and other ways, even the sin-characters of some traditional Christian theologies acknowledge the ancient reserves underneath Christian speech about sex. This is the other side of supersession: it trains Christian imagination in cross-habitation, in refracted imitation, in non-identical repetition—all under the imperative of the history of salvation. Acknowledging the reserves of silence, one acknowledges as well the limits on embodied performance, and so resists the regime of sexuality at its starting point.

Whatever one thinks about the efficacy of Christian sacraments, one must see them as the indispensable context for many traditional forms of Christian life. The sacraments are, on some theological accounts, means of participation in the ritual power of Jesus. This is a power to perform new selves—a power to transfigure one's person, with all its desires, by inhabiting exemplary characters from past and future. The inhabitation is always incomplete; the performances, refracted and anticipatory. They are closer to camp or drag than to perfect conformity or accomplished identity. But for that very reason they resist the regime of identities proposed by sexuality as its starting point. Some medieval Christian moralities would understand having an identity as damnation—especially in matters of desire.

Jesus' silence about sex is neither a taboo on embodied desire nor an invitation to chatter endlessly about sexual taxonomies. It is a judgment on the adequacy of speech about constitutive desire. After this silence, serious Christian speech about sex might take up dozens of genres—of inquiry, parable, exhortation, invocation, benediction—but each of them would leave the erotic open to refract a past it must revere without repeating and to anticipate a future it must await without picturing. Some Christian theology in the future might yet resist the regime of sexuality by being more accomplished in syncopation and silence, in parody and avowal, than in diagnostic certainties and political programs. Some Christian theology might, but which churchly theology will?

Christianity is a "religion" of return. Christians have long desired the return of a particular body. But Christianity is also a religion that returns somewhat differently each time. The resurrected body of Jesus is not just Jesus' body back again. Despite the testimony of the wounds, it is a different body. It is, for example, a body that can live while being unnaturally opened. The Christianity that has already returned under the regime of sexuality is barely Christian, most especially when it shouts out its fidelity to the categories of sexuality. It may be that some of us await the return of another Christianity—which is likely to come, as stories say the risen Jesus often did, in an unrecognizably divine body.

NOTES

1. Michel Foucault, "Non au sexe roi" (interview with B.-H. Lévy), in his *Dits et écrits, 1954–1988*, ed. Daniel Defert, François Ewald, and Jacques Lagrange (Paris: NRF / Gallimard, 1994), 3:256–69.

2. Friedrich Nietzsche, *Jenseits von Gut und Böse*, Vorrede, as in *Sämtliche Werke: Kritische Studienausgabe*, ed. Giorgio Colli and Mazzino Montinari (2nd ed., Munich and Berlin: DTV / de Gruyter, 1988), vol. 5, p. 12, lines 10–11: "um der Menschheit sich mit ewigen Forderungen in das Herz einzuschreiben."

3. Nietzsche, *JGB*, "Drittes Haupstück: das religiöse Wesen" (Colli–Montinari KSA 5:65.1–2).

4. Nietzsche, *JGB*, #295 (Colli–Montinari KSA 5:237.1–2 / 12–14 / 22–25).

5. Nietzsche, *JGB*, #295 (Colli–Montinari KSA 5:238.22–26).

6. See Claude Calame, *Thésée et l'imaginaire athénien: Légende et culte en Grèce antique* (2nd ed., Lausanne: Payot, 1996), 105–15.

7. Nietzsche, *Dionysos-Dithyramben*, "Klage der Ariadne" (Colli–Montinari KSA 6:398.5).

8. Nietzsche, *Dionysos-Dithyramben*, "Klage der Ariadne" (Colli–Montinari KSA 6:401.9–25). All ellipses are from the original.

9. I here brush against the complicated question of Nietzsche's imagined and performed genders. To pose the question seriously would require me to engage other readers of Nietzsche, including Karl Reinhardt, Luce Irigaray, and Sarah Kofman—or David Farrell Krell, Kelly Oliver, and Claudia Crawford. Here let me only remind these readers that one does not have to be a woman to copulate with a male god—though one is required, in many regimes of speech, to speak this copulation only with the voice of "woman."

10. Georges Bataille, as in his *Œuvres complètes*, vol. 8 (Paris: NRF/Gallimard, 1976), 404–23.

11. For example, Bataille, *L'Érotisme*, part 1, chapters 11 and 12, as in his *Œuvres complètes*, vol. 10 (Paris: NRF/Gallimard, 1987), esp. pp. 128, 136–38.

12. Foucault, "Préface à la transgression," originally published in *Critique* 195–96 (1963): 751–70, reprinted in his *Dits et écrits*, 1:233–50, at p. 248.

13. In these pages, I mean by "Jesus" not a hypothetically reconstructed historical figure but the single protagonist whom faith professes behind the divergences of the four canonical gospels.

14. I wish I could claim to have invented this possibility for parody, but here as in so many other cases parody is prefigured by an aggressive "orthodoxy." For an influential American tale of Jesus as the model for normal adolescence, see Bruce Barton, *A Young Man's Jesus* (Boston, New York, and Chicago: Pilgrim Press, 1914), perhaps especially pp. 78–79.

THREE

Returning God:
The Gift of Feminist Theology

Catherine Keller

DOUBLING BACK

In Christian culture there is something menacing about a *return*, a *second* coming. The Lord should not have had to come twice. He was nice the first time, he tried love, he healed and fed us, and see what happened to him. We threw his gift in his face. The Book of Revelation warns us what a different mood he'll be in when he comes again: he's gonna kick some butt. The storm won't stay in the desert this time, it rains shock and awe upon Babylon, that whore. Her beasts of terror are everywhere; this war must go to the ends of the earth. This *return* has eyes "like a flame"; its protruding tongue is hard, "a sharp two-edged sword."[1] Its very Word is a WMD. It will cut down the enemy empire. It will also penetrate and destroy the traitors within the churches, like that Jezebel, that woman who dares to lead and prophesy. "I am throwing her on a bed . . . ; and I will strike her children dead" [2:22]. Was she teaching too free a love?

"Love" does occur positively in John's Apocalypse: "I reprove and discipline those whom I love" [3:19]. The last letter of the New Testament thus compensates for the excessive love not just of Jezebel but of Jesus. And yet we have to admit that the difference between the love gospel and the apocalyptic rage, the *différance* of a love deferred, has been productive. That tense messianic expectation, charged with threat and hope, has driven, as Ernst Bloch demonstrated, all the revolutionary movements of the West.[2] These include the movements of women such as the St. Simonniennes of the early nineteenth century, with whom Claire Demar founded a journal with other working class women announcing (in her capitals): "The word of the WOMAN REDEEMER WILL BE A SUPREMELY REVOLTING WORD."[3] Indeed, the first religious icon that really got my attention (at age 16) was a bit of feminist apocalypse. It was a poster tacked up in a Massachusetts coffee shop, featuring a magnificent female with long red hair wearing a bearskin over one naked shoulder and holding a staff. The caption (capitalized, of course) read: GOD IS COMING, AND IS SHE PISSED! The full force of the pronoun hit me for the first time and forever; I knew that *She* was pissed because He had usurped her place, He and his armies of butt-kickers. (I was spending time at anti-Vietnam demonstrations.) I did not know that Her Coming presaged the coming of feminist theology, let alone of my going to seminary to assist in Her return. Because the coming would not be ex nihilo; we sensed she'd been around before. She had tried love, she was nurturing, she fed and healed. And see what happened to her, to her incarnation in all women. Oh, the menace of her return was exciting: a second-wave feminist apocalypse, rocking with sex and rage. Of course, this returning she-God soon settled into more sober theological and ecclesial debates. But She never enjoyed unambiguous status, not even as a pronoun, not even within feminist theology.

If feminist theology exists as such, if it is not just the residual oxymoron of an enthusiastic moment, it lives by the tolerance, the need, or the grace of theology. And so—problematically—of its institutionally durable, textually deep, and not altogether inflexible *theos*. The attempt to name ourselves the*a*logians was half-hearted. Its difference doesn't preach any better than, say, the Heideggerian distinction between theology and the*io*logy. And besides, no effort at feminization quite frees itself of patriarchal habit. How could it, after the millennia? Indeed, the specter of a female divinity has also provoked feminist ambivalence about any possible symbolic content, historical antecedent, fabricated image, or self-mirroring icon, let alone archetypal essence of femininity. Femininity projected to infinity—*She* spooked feminists almost as much as patriarchs. Feminist theological ambivalence wields its own double edge. So looking ahead and swinging back, I cannot hope to avoid the slashing tongued s/word of the apocalypse in this meditation. But we might elude its violence. Its double edge might morph into a wider and subtler question, that of an aporetic double genitive: the returning of God.

To Return: Transitive or Intransitive?

So what I am attempting to ask is this: *What is the relation of the "returning God" of feminist theology to the return of religion?* Is our returning God, who comes by way of a few decades of struggle about his/her/its names, a blessing and a renewal of the language of God, of God-talk? Or is it a symptom of the dissolution played out in the willful projection of theological language for political ends? A transformation of God-talk or its well-intending trivialization? What kind of gift is She?

Of course from the start feminist talk of God was confronting the limits of language. And transgressing them. We—and I am pronominally possessed in this paper by the limited collective of "feminist theology," much but not all Christian, which is rather embarrassingly pressing its "we" upon me—have tried altering those pronouns: she rather than he? The hiccup S/he? Alternating she and he? Or "God ain't a he or a she, but a It." Thus, Alice Walker's classic para-scripture: "Whenever you trying to pray, and man plop himself on the other end of it, tell him to git lost, say Shug. Conjure up flowers, wind, water, a big rock."[4] At the same time, we did not want to forfeit the chance, after not centuries but millennia, to recognize our own female faces—not just the face of an other—in the *imago dei*. The experiment in inclusive language allowed us to renegotiate the biblical stories, to retell them with higher voices and more laughter. For the returning God of feminism was never just an apologia for women's leadership. It wasn't just the return of "good old God" in drag. Or, as Nelle Morton put it nearly thirty years ago, "Yahweh in a skirt."[5] We wanted an ancient new metaphor. Maybe God/ess a la Rosemary Ruether? Or a triune "Spirit, Jesus and Mother Sophia" a la Elizabeth Johnson's eminent way of negation and affirmation?[6] Apparently we wanted the impossible. Or more precisely: a metonymics of the possible.

All of this intensity about the naming of God was no less theological than it was liturgical and political. It surely counts as evidence for an unexpected return. Among one subset of progressive thinkers, it has energized, with its argumentative passions, a return not just of a vague religiosity but of theology. It effected a renewal of God-talk just when those thinkers in the West intent on speaking truth to power, or on deconstructing the truth of power, had deemed God good and dead. In this way feminist theology may have pumped a few decades of life force into the God question, into God him/her/itself. This would be a great gift to theology. But the contribution would be *Gift*, German for "poison" indeed, if progress means—as it still inevitably does for most feminists and their sympathizers—transcending God, getting finally beyond religion and its regressive returns.[7]

If, however, the grammar of the *returning of God* turns on itself, in the double genitive, then of course one might doubt that feminist theology is really promoting the coming or coming again of any God. Have we in fact been *giving God back?* Returning God to the shop, like a dress that doesn't fit? Perhaps demanding a refund? Or returning Him to his makers? (As Calvin said, the human heart is a factory of idols.) We feminists in theology have tried our best to feminize, womanize, neuter, or queer God; we have fought with each other and with the lords of patriarchy to open a space for the fullness of women within theology. But, as both sisters and patriarchs sneered knowingly from the start, no matter how much we adjust and supplement and deconstruct and reconstruct God, He will remain pretty much a *he*. Even when there is a liberal willingness to use only inclusive language about the deity in newly written texts, prayers, liturgies—and that is a huge and rare concession—still God brings with him/her/itself the archive: the historical trove of scriptures, prayers, creeds, songs, theologies. And that archive is punctuated percussively, in relentless elegance, with its He's, Lords, and Fathers. In every new class of seminarians someone will say (innocent of Mary Daly) "But the masculine language about God is just metaphoric. We know he isn't a man." I do not break into tears or laughter. I love my students; they know not what they say. And exactly what supersession would I lay on them? What solution? After I communicated with a Viennese friend about the minefields of the U.S. feminist theological discourse, he emailed back in mock exasperation (and precise English): "Holy she/he/it!"[8]

After all, after generations, after so many fresh starts and transgendering subtleties, is the aporia of feminist theology just an oxymoron: God remains a guy no matter how we a/dress him? Doesn't the leadership of church, synagogue, and mosque still overall comprise a boys' club for those made in His image? The impossible dream a low-grade nightmare, the kind one grows accustomed to, full of familiar clichés that no therapy dispels? In this impasse, many of us who are feminists in theology quietly— sometimes so quietly we cannot hear ourselves—say thanks but no thanks. We return the gift. The verb becomes transitive. We may be performing an honorable role, not unlike that of death of God theologians qua *theology;* we are exposing the idol of monotheism within His own household. We do not then return the gift out of ingratitude but out of exhaustion—as though our alchemy had failed to transmute the poison. As though the gift was always after all the "gift of death"—of an Abrahamic sacrifice that, as Derrida noted in passing, implies "at its very basis an exclusion or sacrifice of women."[9] (*That* passing can itself not be given its due, in passing.) The return of the gift that is the gift of death happens, arguably, always too late—except by the grace of an angelic ram. But no substitutionary suffering has long mitigated the organizing violence of the patrilineage.[10]

From this mournful vantage point the religion that is returning across much of the planet appears to be pretty much what it appears to be: the return of patriarchy with a vengeance, whether it is militantly imperial or militantly anti-imperialist. The inviting exceptions at the self-deconstructing fringes of old-line religions would prove only to be— proving the rule.

So it should not be surprising to remember that some of the first voices of feminist theology were carefully keyed into the death of God movement. Naomi Goldenberg, for instance, recognized in 1971 that "we women are going to bring an end to God." Yet she felt that "there was a magnificence attached to the idea of watching him go" and returned with glee to "graduate school to study the end of God."[11] (Indeed, it was to Syracuse that she returned!) And it is in a curt salute to Thomas J. J. Altizer and company that Mary Daly's crucial chapter in *Beyond God the Father* is named "After the Death of God the Father." Is it the death of the deified male, we were asking, or of God Himself? What is the difference?

In the rhetoric of the death of God and its aftermath, ambiguity persists. Is the dying God *any* God that is personlike enough to be called God? Or is the dead One precisely the opposite, the impersonal, immutable, ontotheological abstraction? Or is the dead God a fusion of the changeless God of metaphysics with the particular Other who enshrined Himself as the exclusive Way, the only way to God, the only way God comes? Feminists in religion were quick to recognize, in the classical fusion of a disinterested abstraction (*ontos*) with an invasive nearness (*theos*), the Western hypostasis of a self-interested masculinity. Also we soon recognized the disinterest of death of God theologians, absorbed in the thanatological grandeur of their task, in the terribly particular struggles—institutional, grammatological, sexual, political—of women. But more to the point, we were not interested in declaring the death of just *any* God. We were particular. At least this turned out to be the case for those of us who (unlike Goldenberg and Daly) had variously effected our own return of religion, and more precisely, a return to *theology*.

WAVERING WOMEN

Within Christianity—with at best inexact parallels among the other branches of the Abrahamic patrimony—a spiritual gulf opens between those feminists who made an exodus first from the patriarchal church, then from any church, from theology itself; those who returned the idol and with consequence refused any return on their lost investment; and those of us who (feeling a bit frumpy) remained in some intentional way associated with the church and its symbolic archive. We on this latter side accept from it some gift; we risk from it some death. However ambivalently, however differingly, we conspire more with the theologies of exodus than with the exodus from theology. Feminist theology cannot—except when our anti-essentialism fronts for our whiteness—dissociate itself from the traditions of liberation and Black and gay/lesbian and queer and ecological theologies, of what Cornel West calls "prophetic Christianity" as it is now mobilized against the "new Constantinianism."[12] Under the imperial regime of the first years of this millennium, the call to a prophetic Christianity intensified as it became more apparent among progressives that a secular response is inadequate to swing votes and perhaps even to keep ourselves *progressing*. Even a few writers in *The Nation* began to realize that the religious left may be of some use in countering what George Lakoff called the "strict father" paradigm, that theocratically tinged paternalism that had returned with an anti-Islamic (not to mention Islamic) vengeance.[13] But apart from strategic concessions, our colleagues in other fields retain their transcendent secularism. Under the threat of this two-sided sword—of secular progressivism and of the politico-religious right—feminist theology not surprisingly displays occasional symptoms of apocalyptic hysteria. Repent, for this end of this (phallogoanthropoheterowhite) world is nigh!

Feminist theology is straining to translate logos into flesh, wisdom into work, theory still in process into action still undecidable. Our ecclesial contexts hold our conceptual feet to the fires of an evangelical populism that U.S. progressive thinkers disregard at all our peril. At the same time we struggle at the shifting shorelines of our own finitude, where our still-young traditions fumble and our language falters. Our activist positivism wavers before the evident constructedness of our strategic God-talk. We can no more cash that constructedness into a smug post-Christianity than we can evade the abyssal question channeled through the death-of-God guys.

Will our waver—lacking the decisive either/or of Pascal's wager, let alone Kierkegaard's knight—bring on the death of feminist theology or activate a constructive uncertainty? Deconstruction does not solve the problem; it happily defers the solution. Hints of a feminist apophasis, an "unsaying of God," begin to appear. The ancient apophatic tradition neither erases nor kills God—but returns Him, or any projection of a finite person, to the abyss. And so it fertilizes the abyss. But a mystical solution to feminist problems, given the embeddedness of negative theology in Christian neoplatonic hierarchies, would be premature. So the deconstructive engagement of apophatic theology may protect us from a merely deepened patriarchy.[14] At the edge of this interchange—never an identity—to say "the divine has been ruined by God" is to utter parascripture.[15] If there is a specifically feminist apophasis, it will hover with both positive and negative wings over the face of the abyss. For the abyss, upon closer meditation, is not an empty void awaiting a word of difference—but our always already differential, always already engendering fluidity—what I have called the *tehom*.[16]

The mystical oscillation of those wings over the deep does not escape the world. It does not even escape gender politics. For our language—language itself, or the self-conscious language of feminist theology, or the divine word chasing its male tail—comes upon the evidently fabricated political world of our common embodiment. The *logos* bumps up against its own constructions not just of *theos* but of *kosmos*. Not because there is *no* world, no flesh beyond our language but *because there is so much of it*. Its boundless flowing matter, its *khora* that precedes and exceeds language as surely as any God, floods and short-circuits any given language. It confronts us in our species' *un*common stylizations of gender, and of gender enfleshed in ethnic and racial difference. Thus Ellen Armour pleaded for "whitefeminist theology" to give up on a unifying narrative; instead "to keep woman open as a site of contestation on which and through which theorizing and theologizing differences between women can take place."[17] "Keeping women open" suggests a fluid space, a space churning with the waves of *tehom*, and thus a chance to waver at the boundary between identities, between certainties.

In the opening of women, gender cannot be abstracted from sexuality. So despite decades of fruitful theorizing, we still slip and slide between "gender" and "sex": is sex what I *am* or what I *have* or might not have; or do we *do* sex, like gender, even if we aren't having any? Coming into a similarly principled uncertainty, Judith Butler writes in a retrospective mood: "We try to speak in ordinary ways about these matters, stating our gender, disclosing our sexuality, but we are, quite inadvertently, caught up in ontological thickets and epistemological quandaries. Am I a gender after all? And do I 'have' a sexuality?"[18] These quandaries exceed academic queer theory. They push up against the unspeakable, the apophatic. But Butler does not have the epistemological dilemmas of theology in mind; and even theology would not usually expect to encounter God's ineffability in this fluid opening between sex and gender.

UNDER THE SHEETS

In her satiric novel *White Teeth*, Zadie Smith captures the sexual unspeakable in a conversation between three immigrant women in London, an

AfroCarribean with a Pentecostal background and two Pakistani Muslims. One of the latter, Alsana, is arguing against her niece's feminist insistence upon sexual honesty between partners:

> "All this talk, talk, talk; all this 'I am this' and 'I am really like this' like in the papers, all this revelation . . ." about sex. When really "you do not want to know what is slimy underneath the bed and rattling in the wardrobe."
>
> "Moreover," says Alsana after a pause, folding her dimpled arms underneath her breasts, pleased to be holding forth on a subject close to this formidable bosom, "when you are from families such as ours you should have learned that silence, what is not said, is the very best recipe for family life."
>
> For all three have been brought up in strict, religious families, houses where God appeared at every meal, infiltrated every childhood game, and sat in the lotus position under the bedclothes with a torch to check [that] nothing untoward was occurring.[19]

"What is not said" here signifies no apophatic reserve: this theology keeps sex, not God, unspeakable. Smith's Paki-Allah in lotus position thwarts the orientalism of our tantric icons. For this God under the sheets encrypts instead a common denominator of the Abrahamisms. At the end of the novel, the Jamaican protagonist's mother sits on a folding chair with the other "formidable Witness ladies," holding "a banner between her knees that states, simply, THE TIME IS AT HAND—REV 1:3."[20] Smith published her apocalyptic novel (with a comically counter-apocalyptic conclusion) in 2000. It was there to contest the millennial return of a multiply monotheistic patriarchy.

When it is the sexually censorious God who returns, the one who sniffs out our sex acts and sends us to war, the breaking of silence about sex and the breaking into theological speech by the second sex become a single double-edged project. What discourse can unseat that God of the bedroom flashlight? What discourse will break that sexual silence? Straight talk of God's nonexistence?

Too straight, replies feminist theology. We want a discourse that gets under the sheets of theology. That bends the prohibitive logos against itself rather than mounting an opposing prohibition. That seduces rather than silences theology itself. Rather than a heroic atheology, would feminist theology not, even or precisely as a theos-logos, be returning that disembodied, disembodying deity to the *nihil* of His own creation?

Would we then be returning one God for another? Negotiating—under the cover of the sheets—a kind of trade? Thus the theologian Marcella Althaus-Reid, as satiric in her genre as Smith in hers, declares a Queer God, with a Trinitarian orgy of love instead of omnipotence, "the omnisexuality of God." Her satire is revelatory. Behind it, but coming up close, very close, lies the multigenerational tradition, passing through a great diversity of gender and sexual voice, of an embodied divinity—of a "return [of] the lost presence of the polyamorous body to its theological discourse."[21]

Well, sure, the incarnation. That so-called *skandalon* was made decent almost from the start. The passion of its excessive love was effectively funneled into apocalypse: God became flesh and paid the price. Isn't that why he is returning to kick butt? The Jews wouldn't admit he was God, the pagans never got it, the liberal oversexed Christians lost it, and they are all gonna get it. Gift indeed.

No doubt.

And yet there may be another return, another way of picking up where that lone incarnation left off. It is possible to receive that single, overused, endlessly re-gifted corporeality as still a gift—indeed, a gift that strange to say has barely been opened. For it got wrapped hardly a century after the swaddling clothes in the doctrine of an absolute metaphysical exception, that of the one-and-only, once-for-all clothing of human carnality in divinity. The exception proved the rule: the rule of the discarnate deity, on the throne and in the lotus, over all the naughty bodies. What if we make the temporarily orthodox move to read that one body as a primary disclosure of something unspeakable about God—what Paul found scandalous for his own monotheism and foolish for the Greeks, what for a moment was tantalizingly new. But his church-body, with its multigifted, interlimbed body, already began to define itself by its exclusions of sexually improper bodies. If he and the Fathers soon sacrificed that provocative newness on the altar of an absolute singularity, they only wanted to protect the novelty of the Christ-event. To guard it from all coming, competing novelties, they swathed its unspeakable flesh in Christological exceptionalism. The Christ could henceforth be passed down in an orderly fashion through the hierarchy of re-gifters. At least this was the hope. Otherwise the love that shines or flows on the just and the unjust alike will grow wild, wanton, out of bounds. Unspeakable effects were showing up early right in the churches, clearly symbolized by John of Patmos's warning to "Jezebel's" congregation and Paul's to the Corinthian women prophets.[22]

CARNAL APOPHASIS

Yet what would the divine love, the love that *is* the divine, *be*—if not love infinitely out of bounds? Its infinity would not unfold in indifference to all the different bodies but in intimacy with them, through them, *as* them. Job's ostrich and leviathan, Jesus' sparrow and lily, hint at the amorous return of a divinity that hadn't ever left. Where would she/he/it go? Out of the bounds of monotheism, perhaps. Out of the triangulated Trinity. Out of our mind. But Christendom in its dominant thrust "reproves and disciplines" the amatory imaginary. By opposing the exceptional incarnation to our routine carnality, the body (*soma*) to all flesh (*sarx*), one might say that the re-gifted Christology in effect puts a stop to further incarnation: *incarnatus interruptus*.

So one might in response call upon a marginal but tenacious sub-tradition from which feminist theology sometimes unknowingly draws, according to which the incarnation that was Jesus reveals a boundless process of divine embodiment. It has antecedents in every mystical pan-entheism, from Irenaeus and Dionysius through Nicholas of Cusa and Angelus Silesius; or in John Wesley's designation as "practical Atheism" any denial that God is the soul of the universe, the *anima mundi*.[23] It has taken the form since Charles Hartshorne, mobilized for ecofeminist theology by Sallie McFague, of the God whose body is the universe. Incarnation is no longer the exception but the rule. An unruly rule, however: the doctrine of the incarnation can no longer be abstracted from its *carnality*. This divinity embodied in all the flesh of the world surely materializes under the sheets: taking pleasure in our pleasure and suffering in our sorrows. Might it unseat the One with the flashlight more effectively than a straight non-God?

The omniamorous deity suggests a pancarnality, a species not of pantheism but of panentheism, which allows room for interplay. If the God-trope is still inviting, it will no more reduce to the *totality of bodies* than to a *single body*. The divine would not be exhaustively incarnate in all or in anything, yet nothing would materialize outside of the divine. For the margin of the unknowable, which reserves alterity in the midst of intimacy, or, to put it crudely, transcendence in the midst of immanence, remains irreducible. The logos thus poetically written into the flesh of the universe is not contained by any revealed word. It may lure language from the darkness that enfolds every body; in that darkness, in its invisibility, lurk waves of possibilities. The possibilities (like future chances for feminist theology) offer themselves for embodiment. Not, as Jean-Luc Marion suggests, possibilities already realized in Christ the eternal logos for us to receive as pure and unilateral gift. Perhaps more like *posse ipsum* (possibility itself) of Cusa, Alfred North Whitehead's "primordial nature of God," or Richard Kearney's *God that May Be*. Its attractive power would gently and precisely take the place of omnipotence. But precisely in its margin of alterity, it opens a way, as the Black church says, where there is no way, a possibility in the face of the impossible.

The trope of God will in this sense invariably signify some personal relationship to the possible, a relationship that collapses the impersonal infinity, like the probability wave, into a particular actualization. But isn't this relationality just what insults the projection-busting intelligence? God, however we translate him/her/it/they or you, seems to remain *personal*. The personhood that presumably protects the alterity, the otherness of God and thus our ability to relate to God, is not nearly *other* enough. He gets frozen in his high but still literally He-ness, his personal pronominality, and his metaphysical nominality. Neither truly and apophatically transcendent (unquestionable verbal utterances confused with faith) nor amorously and boundlessly immanent (no flesh besides Jesus). But at this edge of projective personhood, feminist theology also, and rightly, falters. Is our divine gal-pal any freer from the person-problem than the guy in the sky? Indeed, would any widened range of metaphors, picking up where the interrupted incarnation left off, overcome the intimacy of what is called "a personal relationship with God"? They may get loose from the reified *person*, praying with Meister Eckhart (and Caputo next to him) for "God . . . [to] make me free of 'God.'"[24] But then if the feminist unsaying of the divine patriarch were finally to yield a bottomless uncertainty as to any theologically or politically or even queerly correct names, whether new or ancient, would we fall silent again? Will feminist theology turn out to have been a women's auxiliary of the death of God brotherhood after all? Not in theological effect so different from its mirror opposite, the churchier tradition inaugurated by Paul's "women should be silent in the churches"?[25]

INTERCARNAL GIFT

To return to the opening question: what gift does feminist theology offer in our returning God? This, at least: in our inside struggle with the *theos-logos*, possibilities keep opening where they weren't. In an indeterminate space between sex and gender, between theism and atheism, between language and silence, between too much and too little. In this space nothing we say of God, including the presumption of His/her/its existence, can be believed to be *true*. But God might remain a gifted metaphor for the space itself, in which truth might be told. "In spirit and truth" [John 4:23]. As Vattimo says, in the same Johannine spirit: "The truth that shall set us free is true only because it frees us. If it does not free us, we ought to throw it away."[26] Indeed, feminist theology does a lot of tossing; we seem to be returning God to His makers over and over and over. To her makers too. Over a couple of generations we have never rested with any single naming strategy. We return our own images ever again, restlessly, nervously, creatively, lest they turn to idols. Still some of us find "God" returning. Even through the porthole of that aporetic, gendering *o* of *theos*.

Will the returning deity perhaps swing both ways—received as gift, returned as idol—always? A waver without end? Maybe the gift can only be received if we can claim the double return—beyond its embarrassed impossibility—as a possible strength.

The strength of this possibility seems to appear only as we face its improbability. Up close, like Cusa's "cloud of the impossible," the aporia itself evinces a certain *porosity*. Reading Derrida with a little help from Caputo, this might be the point where "the borders of the kingdom become porous."[27] Caputo's exegesis of the *basileia tou theou* echoes the passionate priorities of prophetic Christianity. And yet every pore threatens to close again: how can we linger long with the term "kingdom"? And who wants a "queendom," but for a term or two? The translation of the kingdom of God into "the commonwealth of God" requires yet another detour.[28]

The linguistic hesitation both exasperates and illustrates. Nonetheless, as Caputo was saying: at the point of hospitable porosity, the borders waver "in a kind of 'holy undecidability' between theism and atheism, among Christian, Jew, and Muslim, between theology and a-theology . . . religion and religion without religion, and this precisely in the name of the God who loves the stranger."[29] It is the Hebrew tradition of the love of the stranger that seems to have served as Jesus' hermeneutical key, opening into even stranger loves of the immoral and the enemy, loves not performing self-martyring masochisms but amatory excess. The deconstructive undecidable is not indecision. It marks the pause, the uncertainty as to our own certainties, by which we give some alien, or some alien voice in ourselves, a chance. If as feminist theologians (for instance) we accept the undecidability in our work as precisely our receptiveness to the excess, the unexpected, the gift, then it need not paralyze action. It may *free* us to make our uncertain decisions. To sin boldly. Even to go ahead and do theology.

The gift, then, is neither the undecidability itself nor the impossible as such. The gift would be the particular possibility that offers itself, that lures us to receive it, to *realize* it. To embody it. But we do not escape the aporia of a return of that which had never quite come: the aporia of an interrupted giving that is a refused reception. The incarnation, like "the gift," has been so neatly packaged in its substantive singularity, its bounded nominality—this one gift, boxed, and no other. If the coming, the other who comes, is not the *same* returning with a vengeance, then in the difference of this coming the pores of possibility open amorously.

The gift of the possible may, however, also resist a certain deconstructive gesture of purification: the purely impossible, the pure alterity, pure death, pure promise, messianicity purged of any embodied messiah, signifiers cleansed of the marks of matter, ground, earth, flesh. Or a utopic democracy pure of our paltry experiments so far, the absolute "to come" of a pure gift, a gift without—*return*. Is it the imagined *purity* of the gift that renders it the impossible, that threatens to reify the impossible as the ideal, to dream the impossible dream? *The impossible surely does confront us, but it is the possible that lures us.* That offers its gift. Left in a hyperbolic dream of purity, the gift becomes the impossible itself; for the gift supposedly brooks no return, not even that of gratitude. So "return," in the currently unavoidable gift discourse, denotes *reciprocity,* as in giving a gift *in* return. It is not the Derridean sense of the unconditionality but of the purity of the gift that feminist theology may have to return, as in *not accept*. Here is the one point where I may agree with John Milbank against Derrida and Jean-Luc Marion (at one point where they agree). Against the opposition of reciprocity to the gift, Milbank insists on an "asymmetrical reciprocity," though he unwittingly sacrifices reciprocity itself to the impassibility, which for him characterizes "the absolute creative power of the Father."[30] And unilateral power bodes far worse for feminists than unilateral gift!

We all might concur, however, that a gift is not a gift if it is withheld because reciprocation is uncertain. Love takes the risk of *initiating*. It makes the first improbable offering. Readers of the Gospels are asked to emulate that omniamorous gesture—without presuming any return. At the same time, they are asked to receive that gift, the seed, the treasure—and indeed, to bear fruit. To actualize the possible. In one problematic parable the steward is fired for not investing and making a *return* on the money. Impure gifts indeed. And clumsy parable. But it captures something disturbingly unsentimental: the gift may be unconditionally *given*—but any future relation depends on its *active reception*. Not because an absolute Boss fires us, but because to take a gift is to take a self-constitutive action. So how would a gift-giver, even an anonymous one, be indifferent to the reception? That would be no gift but a mere give-away.

The care for the difference of the receiver and the difference made by the gift make the gift a gift. But the difference made, in enjoyment or transformation, *is* the return—not to the giver as such (though expressions of gratitude may intensify joy) but to the world the giver loves. This love that shines or rains on just and unjust alike would not signify indifference to whether the unjust remain unjust. It continues to shine, no matter how dense the clouds of impossibility. This counter-apocalyptic *agape*, beyond judgment, always returns. What it can offer may, however, be sorely diminished.

Actualizing this radiance, we too radiate; we risk ourselves—not returning something to its giver, not giving *back* but giving *forth*. In *eros* we rightly desire the reciprocity, but in *agape* we may not *count* on it. The privileging of *eros* against any unilateral *agape*, against any sacrifical economy, had made possible the emergence of feminist theology in the first place.[31] Unilateral grace is just the other side of the blade of unilateral power. If I give with no interest in receiving your response, I am devoid of vulnerability, I am pure act. A unilateral *eros*, however, does not on the longer run effectively counterbalance a unilateral *agape*. That *eros* realizes itself, not in a passionate demand and not in a pious self-sacrifice, but in the agapic embodiment of passion, the com/passion that makes passion possible again—after loss.

I am just suggesting that feminist theology will not refuse and return the very concept of gift along with the supreme giver in an act of suicidal theocide. But what we offer is not a unilateral but a relational gift. If we want to deconstruct omnipotence, a desire that most feminist and all process theologians share with Caputo, we might need to accept an *impure* gift *as* a gift. Outside of ancient ritual contexts of purification, the "pure" itself will always echo the unmixed, the One, the Same— and perilously imply a cultured transcendence of those primitive tribal potlatches re-narrated by Marcel Mauss, at the origin of the twentieth-century gift-debate.[32]

Might we for a change imagine icons of an *infinite impurity,* incarnate in the dust and the dirt of us all? Mingled in the multiplicity of selves, sexes, species, stars, its divinity would find itself infinitely enmeshed in reciprocity with the creation. Down on the ground, at any rate, on a planet endangered by an imperial denial of our interdependence, the web of creation might not mend without a counter-apocalyptic conversion to grateful interrelation. Ingratitude is devouring the life of the planet. It reeks, as ecofeminism demonstrates, of millennia of matricidal disdain of the dirty work of the earth, and of all the mothers—and of all the others of class, race, and species who render material and thankless service. Whose ever-returning gifts we take for granted.

The grant may be running out. To waver in indecision about, for example, global warming is not to deepen but to damage the animate space of deconstructive undecidability.[33] This collective paralysis, compounded by systemic ingratitude, merely renders the apocalyptic scale of destruction all the more certain. Not surprisingly, many gifted younger folk find hope for the future impossible. What matters in the face of unpromising odds is *not the impossibility of the gift but the gift of the possible.* The possibility, for example, that we earthlings will better actualize the promise of our genesis collective. Life is the ferment of possibility: actively receiving the gift of our shared life, whether or not the metaphor of a divine giver becomes explicit, releases the effervescence of gratitude. We actualize our possibilities only in enmeshed networks of asymmetrical reciprocity; our bodies are networks of networks within larger networking fields. This boundless multiplicity of interdependent socialities offers a theological supplement to the singular event of incarnation.

We may call this supplement—the alternative to the history of the *incarnatus interruptus*—the "intercarnation." It might be narrated as the becoming body of God—but only if the God-metaphor does not defeat the multiplicity.[34] This khoric intercarnality will not sustain what Laurel Schneider is calling "logic of the One."[35] It supports cooperation by way of mutual differentiation. Forgive me if I preach, but I am suggesting that for the difficult relationality that forms the matrix of feminist theology in its specifically Christian heritage, the porosity of the borders of the *basileia,* both now and coming, amplifies the porosity of the shared body—returned and returning—of the Christian messiah. The aporia of "his" impossible representation, an inclusion by exclusivism, is still enshrined in the arguments for the non-ordination of women, let alone the monopoly on salvation of the returning religious right. An aporia is answered only by *poria,* porosity. And that body, only nameable as Christ if the word opens rather than closes its own boundaries, itself signifies and amplifies the porosity of our every body. And so the body of the intercarnation infinitely exceeds that particular, if infinitely signifying, body. The "flesh of the world," in Merleau-Ponty's promising invocation, exceeds the sum of its bodies. Indeed, bodies subjugated by Christian conquest still exhibit the porous, intercarnal relationality in ways lost to the conquerors. The intercarnate body resembles, for example, Sylvia Marcos's account of the Mesoamerican body as "a vortex generated by the dynamic confluence of multiple entities, both material and immaterial and often contradictory." Those entities, or elements, marked according to a non-Western gender binarism, combine and recombine in endless and vulnerable interplay.[36]

UNCERTAIN RETURNS

The love that brings this network of reciprocity to fruition may itself be barely tolerable. Ask Hadewijch, the thirteenth-century Beguine and poet of *Minne,* the troubadour's name for love and the poet's name, a grammatically feminine noun, for God. "Where is now the consolation and the peace of Love with which she provided me so splendidly at first?" Hadewijch yearns for her return. There is no triumphalism in this eschatology:

> At great favors before the time,
> And at great promises before the gift,
> No one can rejoice overmuch.
> Both have largely failed us:
>> False joys
>> That implied the possession of Love's being
> Have swept me far from myself.[37]

What an achingly evolved self, that she can write her disappointment and yet return with undiminished ardor to that self from which she had been swept, and so to the love of Love. Medieval mystics did not need to worry about the "great promises" of global capitalism and the "false joys" of its favors; we do. Yet this erotic mysticism that tilts toward apophasis communicates the struggle of a woman to find voice, a struggle with the cruelty of men and the queerness of Love. It opens a truth-space beyond the possession of truth, God, or being, beyond the possessable *being* of Love. (Thus perhaps Marion's apothegm, "Gxd loves without being.")[38] "I let Love be all that she is; I cannot understand her fierce wonders," writes Hadewijch.[39] Incomprehension, however, does not silence the poetry. "Because I wish to live free," she persists, practicing a trying discipline of double-return: "I cannot do without this gift,/I have nothing else: I must live on Love."[40]

If feminist theology is to receive the very gift it gives, it perches close to this amorous apophasis. It cannot flee its epistemological double edge of affirmation and negation. I suspect that we are learning to be humbled rather than humiliated by the quandaries and thickets of our discourse of sex, gender, and love—divine or human. When the *eros* of variously affirmed sexualities bubbles into the struggle of love for a sustaining justice, then we construct a pluralism of embodied difference rather than a relativism of indifference. And in the theological register of this relational pluralism reverberates the endless multiplicity of divine names—for the nameless.

In Cusa the epistemological double return becomes the cosmological double fold, the rhythm of the infinite unfolding into finite bodies, and all bodies folding back in the *complicatio*. For any divinity I can unfold is unfurling, unfinished, unfolding in our own unpredictable becomings, which fold or crumple back as her multiplicative body. Under the sheets, perhaps, of the old luminous darkness. Or of some new dark energy. Perhaps the double gesture of folding will prove more effectual than the double-edged sword. The unfolding of the infinite as the manifold makes manifest an irreducible plurisingularity only hinted at in the Trinity.[41] It may help us shift now from the feminist logos of the *cutting* edge to something more promising than "postfeminism." Transfeminism?

Amidst the bottomless waters of becoming, *genesis,* we need our edges, our shorelines—like Caputo's God-name, harbors of an unknowable event. When the harbor-keepers seek to enclose the waters, the returning deep swells like a tidal wave. The unknown God appears apocalyptically shrouded as the dead or as the deadly One. All the love in the universe cannot evaporate for us the uncertainty of what is coming. Or who. Or not. The gift of feminist theology will not have been a maternal security to replace that of an expiring father. Feminist theology, by whatever name, has always been beginning again, and never from nothing. "In the beginning there can only be dying, the abyss, the first laugh" (Hélène Cixous).[42] In beginning again, the possibility arises, weeping with laughter, of a just and ecological intercarnality.

We cast God on the waters, and she returns—manifold.

NOTES

1. Revelation 1:14, 16. Biblical citations will be taken from the New Revised Standard Version.

2. I explore Bloch and other apocalyptic posthistories in *Apocalypse Now and Then: A Feminist Guide to the End of the World* (Boston: Beacon, 1996).

3. Claire Demar, *"Ma Loi d'avenir,"* cited by Leslie Wahl Rabine, "Essentialism and Its Contexts: Saint Simonian and Poststructuralist Feminists," in *The Essential Difference*, ed. Naomi Schor and Elizabeth Weed (Bloomington: Indiana University Press, 1994), 133.

4. Alice Walker, *The Color Purple* (San Diego: Harcourt Brace Jovanovich, 1982), 168.

5. Nelle Morton, *The Journey Is Home* (Boston: Beacon Press, 1985).

6. Elizabeth Johnson, *She Who Is: The Mystery of God in Feminist Theological Discourse* (New York: Crossroad, 1992).

7. The theme of "the gift" has played a key role in the margins between poststructuralism and theology, for example as unwrapped in a companion volume to the present one, *God, the Gift and Postmodernism*, ed. John D. Caputo and Michael J. Scanlon (Bloomington: Indiana University Press, 1999).

8. I thank Roland Faber, who now teaches in Claremont, for permission to quote him. Most of his writing is more serious! See, for example, his *God as Poet of the World: Exploring Process Theologies*, trans. Douglas W. Stott. (Louisville and London: Westminster John Knox Press, 2008).

9. Jacques Derrida, *The Gift of Death*, trans. David Willis (Chicago: University of Chicago Press, 1995), 76.

10. Sarah Coakley's essay in this volume, in which Isaac appears as a feminist hero, will counterbalance any facile feminist dismissal of the Abrahamic sacrificial symbolism.

11. Naomi R. Goldenberg, *Changing of the Gods: Feminism and the End of Traditional Religions* (Boston: Beacon Press, 1980), 3.

12. See Cornel West, *Democracy Matters: Winning the Fight Against Imperialism* (New York: Penguin Press, 2004).

13. George Lakoff, *Don't Think of an Elephant: Know Your Values and Frame the Debate* (White River Junction, Vt.: Chelsea Green Publishing, 2004).

14. Building in feminist directions on the subtle tensions between the Christian apophatic discourse and poststructuralism, see the excellent essays by Sigridur Gutmarsdottir, "Feminist Apophasis: Beverly J. Lanzetta and Trinh T. Minh-ha in Dialog," *Feminist Theology: The Journal of the Britain & Ireland School of Feminist Theology* (January 2008); Mary Jane Rubinstein, "Unknow Thyself: Apophaticism, Deconstruction and Theology after Ontotheology," *Modern Theology* 19:3 (July 2003).

15. See Kevin Hart's reflection on this bit of Derrida in *Trespass of the Sign: Deconstruction, Theology and Philosophy* (New York: Fordham University Press, 2000), 47; "My position," writes Hart indispensably, "is not that deconstruction is a form of negative theology but that negative theology is a form of deconstruction," 186.

16. See Keller, "The Cloud of the Impossible: Embodiment and Apophasis," in *Apophatic Bodies*, ed. Chris Boesel and Catherine Keller (New York: Fordham, 2010). See also Keller, *Face of the Deep: A Theology of Becoming* (London and New York: Routledge, 2003).

17. Ellen T. Armour, *Deconstruction, Feminist Theology, and the Problem of Difference: Subverting the Race/Gender Divide* (Chicago: University of Chicago Press, 1999), 183.

18. Judith Butler, *Undoing Gender* (London and New York: Routledge, 2004), 16.

19. Zadie Smith, *White Teeth* (New York: Vintage, Random House, 2000), 65.

20. Ibid., 438f. Her capitalization.

21. Marcella Althaus-Reid, *The Queer God* (London and New York: Routledge, 2003), 53. See especially ch. 3—"Queering God in Relationships: Trinitarians and God the Orgy."

22. See Bernadette J. Brooten, *Love Between Women: Early Christian Responses to Female Homoeroticism* (Chicago: University of Chicago Press), 1996. See also Antoinette Wire,

Corinthian Women Prophets: A Reconstruction Through Paul's Rhetoric (Minneapolis: Augsburg Fortress Press), 1995.

23. John Wesley, "Upon Our Lord's Sermon on the Mount, III," discussed in John B. Cobb Jr., *Grace and Responsibility: A Wesleyan Theology for Today* (Nashville: Abingdon Press, 1995), 50.

24. Meister Eckhart, "Sermon 52: Beati paupers spiritu, quoniam ipsorum est regnum caelorum," in Meister Eckhart, *The Essential Sermons, Commentaries, Treatises, and Defense,* ed. Edmund Colledge and Bernard McGinn (New York: Paulist Press, 1981), 202, 200; John D. Caputo, *The Weakness of God: A Theology of the Event* (Bloomington: Indiana University Press, 2006), 33, 271–3, 277.

25. 1 Cor. 14:34

26. Gianni Vattimo, "Toward a Nonreligious Christianity," in John D. Caputo and Gianni Vatimo, ed. Jeffrey W. Robbins, *After the Death of God* (New York: Columbia University Press, 2007), 45.

27. Caputo, *Weakness of God*, 269.

28. John B. Cobb Jr., "Commonwealth and Empire," in *The American Empire and the Commonwealth of God: A Political, Economic, Religious Statement,* ed. David Ray Griffin, John B. Cobb Jr., Richard A. Falk, and Catherine Keller (Louisville: Westminster John Knox Press, 2006).

29. Caputo, *Weakness of God*, 269.

30. John Milbank, *Being Reconciled: Ontology and Pardon* (London: Routledge, 2003), 160; see my "Is That All? Gift and Reciprocity in Milbank's *Being Reconciled*," in *Interpreting the Postmodern: Responses to 'Radical Orthodoxy,'* ed. Rosemary Radford Ruether and Marion Grau (New York & London: T&T Clark, 2006).

31. Rita Nakashima Brock, *Journeys by Heart: A Christology of Erotic Power* (New York: Crossroad, 1988); Rita Nakashima Brock and Rebecca Parker, *Proverbs of Ashes: Violence, Redemptive Suffering, and the Search for What Saves Us* (Boston: Beacon Press, 2001).

32. Vis-à-vis Mauss, the "primitive" gift, deconstruction, and radical orthodoxy, see Marion Grau's illumining "'We Must Give Ourselves to Voyaging': Regifting the Theological Present," in *Interpreting the Postmodern.*

33. For a multilayered analysis of the relations between deconstruction and ecology within theology and philosophy, see *Ecospirit: Religions and Philosophies for the Earth,* ed. Laurel Kearns and Catherine Keller (New York: Fordham University Press, 2007).

34. Catherine Keller, "The Flesh of God: A Metaphor in the Wild," in *Theology That Matters: Ecology, Economy, and God,* ed. Darby Kathleen Ray (Minneapolis: Fortress Press, 2006).

35. Laurel Schneider, *Beyond Monotheism: A Theology of Multiplicity* (London and New York: Routledge, 2007).

36. Sylvia Marcos, *Take from the Lips: Gender and Eros in Mesoamerican Religions* (Boston: Brill, 2006), 64.

37. Hadewijch, "Defense of Love," in *Hadewijch: The Complete Works,* trans. Columba Hart (New York: Paulist Press, 1980), 176.

38. Jean-Luc Marion, *God Without Being*, trans. Thomas A. Carlson (Chicago: University of Chicago Press, 1991), 138.

39. Hadewijch, "The Noble Valiant Heart," *Hadewijch*, 184.

40. Hadewijch, "Subjugation to Love," *Hadewijch*, 194.

41. In *Face of the Deep* I translate the Elohim of Genesis, which is grammatically plural yet takes the singular verb, as "Manyone," and as a co-creative plurisingularity.

42. Hélène Cixous, *"Coming to Writing" and Other Essays*, ed. Deborah Jenson, trans. Sarah Cornell, Ann Liddle, and Susan Sellers (Cambridge: Harvard University Press, 1991), 41.

FOUR

Religion, Feminism, and Empire: The New Ambassadors of Islamophobia

Saba Mahmood

The complicated role European feminism played in legitimating and extending colonial rule in vast regions of Asia, Africa, and the Middle East has been extensively documented and well argued for some time now.[1] For many of us raised in this critical tradition, it is therefore surprising to witness the older colonialist discourse on women being reenacted in new genres of feminist literature today, with the explicit aim of justifying the U.S. "war on terror" in the Muslim world. It seems at times a thankless task to unravel yet again the spurious logic through which Western imperial power seeks to justify its geopolitical domination by posing as the "liberator" of indigenous women from native patriarchal cultures. It would seem that this ideologically necessary but intellectually tedious task requires little imagination beyond repositioning the truths of the earlier scholarship on Algeria, Egypt,

Indonesia, and India that has copiously and rigorously laid bare the implicated histories of feminism and empire.

Yet it is important for feminists to address the relationship between contemporary feminist discourse and Euro-American imperial domination of the Middle East. While ordinary Americans and Europeans seem to have lost their enthusiasm for the Bush-Blair strategy of unilateralist militarism (whether in Iraq, Afghanistan, or Iran), they continue to trust the judgment offered by their politicians and media pundits that Muslim societies are besotted with an ideology of fundamentalism whose worst victims are its female inhabitants. This judgment further entails the prescriptive vision that the solution lies in promoting "democracy" in the Muslim world and Western values of "freedom and liberty" through religious and cultural reform so that Muslims might be taught to discard their fundamentalist propensities and adopt more enlightened versions of Islam. What concerns me most in this essay is the role that freedom, democracy, and gender inequality have come to play in this story, and the ease with which Islam's mistreatment of women is used as a diagnosis as well as a strategic point of intervention for restructuring large swaths of the Muslim population, if not the religion itself. How have the tropes of freedom, democracy, and gender equality—constitutive of a variety of traditions of feminist thought—facilitated the current Euro-American ambition to remake Muslims and Islam? What do these tropes obfuscate, and what forms of violence do they condone? Lest I be misunderstood, let me be clear about my use of the term "liberal feminism": I use this term to designate those currents within feminism in which the connections between a certain analysis of gender inequality and the politics of empire are most dense and pervasive. I am fully aware that there are other traditions of feminist thought that are critical of this imbrication.[2]

NATIVE TESTIMONIALS

The empirical terrain from which I want to think through these issues is the plethora of recently published nonfiction bestsellers written by Muslim women about their personal suffering at the hands of Islam's supposedly incomparable misogynist practices. Since the events of 9/11, this vastly popular autobiographical genre has played a pivotal role in securing the judgment that Islam's mistreatment of women is a symptom of a much larger pathology that haunts Islam—namely, its propensity to violence. Calls for the reformation of Islam, now issued from progressive, liberal, and conservative podiums alike, are ineluctably tied to its oppression of women. The argument is simple: women are the most abject victims of the ideology of Islamic fundamentalism. The solution lies in bringing "democracy" to the Muslim world, a project that will not only benefit women but will also make them its main protagonists. In our age of imperial certitude, it seems that the fate of Muslim women and the fate of democracy have become indelibly intertwined.

Many of the authors of these accounts have been handsomely rewarded by conservative political parties and think tanks internationally, and some have been catapulted into positions of political power, having few qualifications other than their shrill polemic against Islam. Given their public prominence, the authors of this genre perform a quasi-official function in various American and European cabinets today: lending a voice of legitimacy to, and at times leading, the civilizational confrontation between "Islam and the West."

As will become clear, however, the popularity of these authors extends beyond their conservative supporters to liberal and progressive publics who dismiss the poor writing and gross exaggerations characteristic of this genre as incidental to its real merits: the truth of Islamic misogyny. The ideological force of this literature lies to a great extent in the ability of the Muslim woman author to embody the double figure of insider and victim, a key subject within Orientalist understandings of women in Muslim societies. These autobiographical works are, however, also distinct from earlier colonial accounts in which it fell to Europeans to reveal the suffering of indigenous women.

The fact that this genre of Muslim women's biographies speaks to a range of feminists, many of whom oppose an imperialist agenda toward Islam, is particularly disturbing. A number of well-known feminist critics have endorsed these books, and several of the bestsellers are either taught or widely read within women's study circles.[3] While the authentic "Muslim woman's voice" partially explains the popularity these books command, it is the emancipatory model of politics underwriting these accounts that provokes such pathos and admiration among its feminist readership. It is this emancipatory model with its attendant topography of secular politics and desire for liberal freedoms that I wish to examine in this essay.

In what follows, I will make three related but distinct arguments. In the first section of the essay, I will examine the symbiotic relationship between the authors of this genre of Muslim women's literature and conservative political parties and think tanks in America and Europe, a relationship that should serve to mute the enthusiastic reception these books have received in many feminist circles. The second section of this essay analyzes the particular kinds of elisions and inaccuracies, so characteristic of these autobiographical accounts, that have helped construct an essential opposition between Western civilization and Muslim barbarism (or fundamentalism). Finally, the third section examines current arguments for bringing democracy to the Muslim world and the role the figure of the oppressed Muslim woman plays in these arguments. I draw attention to the singular and reductive conception of religiosity underwriting current calls for democracy in the Muslim world, one that enjoys wide currency among a range of feminists (Pollit 2002) but that needs to be criticized for the forms of violence it entails and the narrow vision of gender enfranchisement it prescribes. In this section I also discuss how the liberal discourse on freedom, endemic to various traditions of feminist thought, blinds us to the power that nonliberal forms of religiosity command in many women's lives. If indeed feminists are interested in distancing themselves from the imperial politics of our times, it is crucial that these forms of religiosity be understood, engaged, and respected, instead of scorned and rejected as expressions of a false consciousness.

One of the most successful examples within this genre of Muslim women's literature is Azar Nafisi's *Reading Lolita in Tehran*. Since its publication in 2003, this book was on the *New York Times* bestseller list for more than 117 weeks, has been translated into more than 32 languages, and has won a number of prominent literary awards. Although Nafisi's writing exhibits aesthetic and literary qualities that make it unique among the works I discuss here, it shares with these other writings a systematic exclusion of information that might complicate the story of women's oppression within Muslim societies.

A second book published to wide acclaim—though it does not have the literary pretensions of the former—is Canadian journalist Irshad Manji's *The Trouble with Islam: A Muslim's Call for Reform in Her Faith*. This book has been translated into more than 20 languages, republished in over 23 countries, and was on the Canadian bestseller list for 20 weeks during the first year of its publication. Manji's shrill diatribe against Muslims has won her a prominent public profile: she regularly appears on a variety of television networks (including BBC, CNN, and FoxNews); her op-eds are published in prominent international dailies (such as the *New York Times*, the *Times of London*, the *International Herald Tribune*, the *Sydney Morning Herald*); and she is invited to give lectures at elite academic institutions despite the fact that her writings and speeches are full of historical errors and willful inaccuracies about Islam.

A third sample of this genre, Carmen bin Laden's *Inside the Kingdom: My Life in Saudi Arabia*, is an account of her marriage to one of Osama bin Laden's 25 brothers and the years of claustrophobic (albeit plush) boredom she spent in Saudi Arabia. Translated into at least 16 languages, with translation rights sold in more than 27 countries, the book was on the bestseller list in France for months after its initial publication as well as on the *New York Times* bestseller list during the first year of its publication.

In France a number of such books reached high acclaim at the time of the passage of the controversial law banning the display of the veil (and other "conspicuous" religious symbols) in public schools. Leading these publications was Fadela Amara's *Ni putes ni soumises*, which received two prominent literary awards (Le Prix du livre politique and Le Prix des Députés in 2004), sold over 50,000 copies, and has been translated into multiple languages. A sequel to the book, *Ni putes ni soumises, le combat continue*, has sold out prior to its publication. An equally popular first-person account attesting to Islam's barbaric customs is *Bas les voiles!* written by Iranian dissident Chahdortt Djavann (2003), whose quote on the dust jacket exemplifies the enunciative position that constitutes this literary genre: "I wore the veil for ten years. It was the veil or death. I know what I am talking about."

Both Amara and Djavann provided personal testimonies against the veil to the Stasi Commission (a government-appointed investigative body that recommended the ban), which reportedly moved the presiding officials to tears. These women's highly dramatized statements, marshaled as "evidence" of the oppressive character of the veil in the Stasi Commission's report, played a key role in securing French public opinion against the veil and creating a communitas of shared aversion to Islam's religious symbols and the misogyny to which they give expression.

Other European countries, including Holland, Spain, Sweden, and Germany, also lay claim to their own ambassadors of Islam's patriarchally oppressed. These authors authenticate and legitimize the Islamophobia sweeping Europe today, lending a voice of credibility to some of the worst kinds of prejudices and stereotypes Europe has seen since the rise of anti-Semitism in the 1930s. These authentic Muslim voices have played a crucial role in shoring up support for the passage of a number of anti-immigration laws in Europe targeting the poorest and most vulnerable sections of the population. It is no small task that these female "critics of Islam" perform, and indeed their service is recognized by the conservative political forces of contemporary Europe and America who have bestowed considerable honors on this group.

Neoconservatism and Women's Suffering

Consider, for example, the mercurial rise of Ayaan Hirsi Ali in Dutch politics. A woman of Somali descent, Hirsi Ali had no public profile until she decided to capitalize on the anti-Muslim sentiment that swept Europe following the events of 9/11. Excoriating Muslims for their unparalleled barbarity and misogyny, she scored points with the right wing when she attacked the Dutch government's welfare and multicultural policies for fostering and supporting the culture of domestic violence supposedly endemic to Islam and Muslims. In highly staged public statements, Hirsi Ali has characterized the prophet Muhammad as a pervert and a tyrant, claiming that Muslims lag "in enlightened thinking, tolerance and knowledge of other cultures" and that their history cannot cite a single person who "made a discovery in science or technology, or changed the world through artistic achievement" (Hirsi Ali 2006:152–53, Kuper 2004). Soon thereafter the right-wing People's Party for Freedom and Democracy offered her a ticket to run for member of parliament, a seat she won by popular vote in January 2003 despite the fact that she had little qualification for such a position.

Dutch immigration services discovered that Hirsi Ali had lied to gain entry into the Netherlands, fabricating the story of her flight from a forced marriage and a vengeful natal family. Threatened with the repeal of her Dutch citizenship, Hirsi Ali resigned from the Dutch parliament and was immediately granted a position at the American Enterprise Institute, a

RELIGION, FEMINISM, AND EMPIRE · 83

prestigious right-wing think tank in Washington, D.C. Predictably, Hirsi Ali also published a memoir, *The Caged Virgin: An Emancipation Proclamation for Women and Islam* (2006), a title highly reminiscent of the nineteenth-century literary genre centered on Orientalist fantasies of the harem (cf. Alam 2006). Despite the fact that Hirsi Ali's personal story of suffering under Islamic customs has been discredited and that her book is full of absurd statements (e.g., "[Muslim] children learn from their mothers that it pays to lie. Mistrust is everywhere and lies rule," 2007, 25–26), it has done quite well. *The Caged Virgin* (2006) has sold translation rights in 15 countries, and she is considered the contemporary doyen of "conservative left criticism." Such excess and hyperbole has been handsomely rewarded: not only do left critics like Christopher Hitchens (2006) hail her publications, but Hirsi Ali received the Simone de Beauvoir Freedom Prize in February 2008.

The arguments of these authors read like a blueprint for the neoconservative agenda for regime change in the Middle East. Irshad Manji is a case in point. Her book *The Trouble with Islam* (2004) is breathtaking in its amplification of neoconservative policies and arguments—all told in the voice of a purportedly self-critical and reformist Muslim woman who wants to bring her lost brethren to the correct path. While inflammatory hyperbole is characteristic of this genre, Manji uses language aimed at injuring and offending Muslim sensibilities. Her text is littered with sentences that describe Muslims as "brain-dead," "narrow-minded," "incapable of thinking," "hypocritical," "desperately tribal," and "prone to victimology" (2004, 22, 30, 31). She brands Islam as more literalist, rigid, intolerant, totalitarian, anti-Semitic, and hateful of women and homosexuals than any other religion, and describes its rituals as more prone to inculcating "mindless and habitual submission" to authority. Manji's denunciations of Islam and Muslims are matched by the unstinting praise she reserves for the "West," "Christianity," "Judaism," and "Israel." She finds the Western record unparalleled in human history for its tolerance, its "love of discovery," "openness to new ideas," and so on (2006, 18, 20, 204–18).

Like Hirsi Ali, Manji supported the U.S. invasion of Afghanistan and Iraq and subsequently the Israeli destruction of Lebanon in the summer of 2006—all in the name of cleansing the Muslim world of "Islamic fanatics and terrorists" (2006a). In her book, Manji, in Manichaean fashion, upholds Israelis as paragons of virtue, capable of self-criticism and tolerance, while Palestinians are condemned for inhabiting a culture of blame and victimhood. She goes so far as to say that Israel's discrimination against its Arab citizens is a form of "affirmative action" (2004, 112). Manji has been promoted by the pro-Israel information lobby, the Middle East Media Research Institute (MEMRI), and the infamous Daniel Pipes, who reviewed her book in glowing terms and with whom she has appeared at Israeli fundraising events.

Despite the cozy relations Manji enjoys with neoconservative luminaries, it would be a mistake to underestimate the broad public presence she commands. Not only do her polemical op-eds appear in prominent international dailies, but she is routinely invited to lecture at a wide range of liberal arts colleges and universities and asked to comment on political events of international import on major television and radio talk shows. Her reviewers often benignly overlook the factual errors and polemical oversimplifications that characterize her work. In an early review published in the *New York Times Book Review*, Andrew Sullivan (2004) writes:

> *The Trouble with Islam* is a memorable entrance. It isn't the most learned or scholarly treatise on the history or theology of Islam; its dabbling in geopolitics is haphazard and a little naïve; its rhetorical hyperbole can sometimes seem a mite attention-seeking. . . . But its spirit is undeniable and long, long overdue. *Reading it feels like a revelation.* Manji, a Canadian journalist and television personality, does what so many of us have longed to see done: assail fundamentalist Islam itself for tolerating such evil in its midst. *And from within.* (10, emphasis added).

The last caveat is telling: Manji's identity as a Muslim lends particular force to her Orientalist and racist views, reaching audiences that ideologues such as Bernard Lewis and Daniel Pipes cannot. Apart from her vitriolic attacks on Islam, what makes Manji so valuable for someone like Sullivan is her "distinct tone of liberalism"—"a liberalism that," he writes, "seeks not to abolish faith but to establish a new relationship with it. If we survive this current war without unthinkable casualties, it will be because this kind of liberalism didn't lose its nerve. Think of Manji as a nerve ending for the West—shocking, raw, but mercifully, joyously, still alive." Note the providential role this imaginary is expected to play in the Muslim world. Not only is it a harbinger of joy and mercy for Iraqis whose country has been destroyed by the U.S. military occupation, but it promises to reorchestrate every Muslim's relationship to his/her faith.

SELECTIVE OMISSIONS

In this section I focus on how elisions and inaccuracies in these accounts have helped secure a monochromatic picture of Islam. Using Azar Nafisi's celebrated *Reading Lolita in Tehran* (2003) to make this point, I focus on how the description Nafisi provides of women's lives in post-Revolutionary Iran can be complicated by a short recounting of recent developments in Iranian politics to yield a very different picture.[4] Instead of her simplistic view of "gender apartheid," we get a more nuanced understanding of post-Revolutionary Iranian politics, one that should lead secular feminists to rethink many of their assumptions about Islam, gender inequality, and political enfranchisement.

Nafisi's *Reading Lolita in Tehran*, with its literary pretensions and invocations of great "Western Classics," stands in contrast to Manji and Hirsi Ali's books. Indeed, much of its appeal stems from the fact that it plays on Nabokov's subtle masterpiece *Lolita* in a manner that makes Nafisi's narrative palatable to sensibilities critical of the strident opportunism of the other texts. *Reading Lolita in Tehran* is a first-person account told from the point of view of an Iranian professor of English (Nafisi herself), who, after resigning from her post at an Iranian university out of frustration over clerical control of the curriculum, gathers several of her female students to teach them classics from Western literature in the privacy of her home. Nafisi uses these sessions as a means not only to denounce clerical political rule but also to express her visceral distaste for Iranian cultural life—both contemporary and historical. She paints a stultifying picture of life in post-Revolutionary Iran—a life devoid of any beauty, color, inspiration, poetry, debate, discussion, and public argumentation. In this suffocating environment, it is only the Western literary canon that offers any hope of redemption in its irrepressible power to foment rebellion and critique and its intrinsic capacity to incite critical self-reflection.

Despite the difference in tone between Nafisi and authors like Hirsi Ali and Manji, the fundamental message her memoir communicates is not that different: Islamic societies are incapable of thought, reflection, and creativity; and their propensity to violence is most evident in their treatment of women. At one point in the memoir, Nafisi sweepingly declares that Iranian university students are only capable of obsequious sycophantic behavior toward their instructors because "from the first day they had set foot in the elementary school, they had been told to memorize. They had been told that their opinions counted for nothing" (220). Such declarations are coupled with gratuitous statements such as: "It is a truth universally acknowledged that a Muslim man, regardless of his fortune, must be in want of a nine-year-old virgin wife" (257). The contempt that Nafisi reserves for Iranians and Muslims stands in sharp contrast to the utter adulation she reserves for the West, from its cultural accomplishments to its food, its language, its literature, its chocolates, and its films. As must be clear by now, this dual theme of abhorrence of everything Muslim and sheer exaltation of all things Western is a structural feature of this genre of writing.

This image of Iranian life is ruthless in its omissions. During this period, not only has Iranian clerical rule faced some of the toughest challenges from a broad-based reform movement in which women played a crucial role, but Iranian universities have been at the center of this political transformation. This is in keeping with Iran's long history of student involvement in almost all protest movements of any significance in the modern period, including the overthrow of the shah. One of the most interesting accomplishments of the last three decades is the establishment of a feminist press and a critical scriptural hermeneutics that is quite unique in the Muslim world (Najmabadi 1998). During the same period about which Nafisi writes so disparagingly, Iran has produced an internationally acclaimed cinema, which is just as fiercely critical of various aspects of contemporary Iranian society as it is reflectively ponderous about the existential meaning of modern life itself. None of this has been easy or without cost for those who have struggled against the absolutist impetus internal to the clerical establishment in charge of the Iranian state apparatus. But it is important to note that dissent has come not only from secular leftists and liberals but from the clerics themselves, many of whom had supported the Revolution at its inception but who became the most trenchant critics of the establishment's corruption and totalitarian control.[5] Social and political critique, in other words, has become a deeply integral aspect of post-Revolutionary Iranian life.

Reading Lolita in Tehran fits the Orientalist paradigm: it reproduces and confirms the impressions of its Western audience, offering no surprises or challenges to what they think they already know about Iran and its rich cultural and political history. Like Delacroix's famous painting *Women of Algiers*, Nafisi's memoir only embellishes the tapestry of anecdotal prejudicial impressions that the spectator brings to her reading of the object at hand. One cannot help but wonder how Nafisi's book would have fared had it surprised its readers with social facts that do not neatly fit her readers' structure of expectations, such as the fact that the literacy rate for women shot up dramatically under Islamic rule from 35.5 percent in 1976 to 74.2 percent in 1996, or that more than 60 percent of Iranian students in higher education are women, or that post-Revolutionary Iran has had more women representatives elected to the parliament than the U.S. Congress (Bahramitash 2006, 235). In addition, the population growth rate in Iran declined from 3.2 percent in 1980 to 1.2 in 2001 as a result of one of the most effective family planning and public health initiatives launched in recent history. If indeed Iranian women have been able to achieve this kind of political and material enfranchisement under conditions of Islamic clerical rule, then how does this complicate the rather simple diagnosis that Islamic rule is and always will be oppressive of women?

Nafisi's book fitted neatly into the geopolitics of the Bush White House that declared Iran to be part of the "axis of evil," and neoconservative plans to attack Iran were made public (Hersch 2006). It is hard not to read Nafisi as providing the cultural rationale for such plans, particularly those extended to her by the neoconservative establishment. Bernard Lewis, the Orientalist ideologue of the current U.S. imperial adventure in the Middle East, calls the memoir "a masterpiece," and Nafisi was given a prestigious position at the Johns Hopkins School of Advanced International Studies, where her friend Fouad Ajami, another prominent conservative ideologue, directs the Middle East program. The fact that Nafisi was awarded such a position, even though she had no substantial publishing record or a comparable position at a similar institution, attests to the considerable service she performed for the scions of the U.S. empire.

Political patronage aside, Nafisi has also been promoted as a cultural icon by corporations eager to showcase their socially responsible side. The manufacturer of the luxury car Audi, for example, promoted Azar Nafisi (along with media figures like David Bowie and the actor William H. Macy) as part of "Audi of America's 'Never Follow' Campaign" to sell the brand to affluent and educated potential buyers. Nafisi has appeared in Audi advertisements for magazines as diverse as *Vanity Fair, Wired, Golf Digest, The New Yorker,* and *Vogue* (see Salamon 2004). Inasmuch as automobile advertisements do not simply sell cars but also forms of social identity, Audi's promotion of Nafisi shows the extent to which a genuine concern for Muslim women's welfare has been evacuated of critical content and whittled down to a commodified token of elite chic. The project of "Saving Muslim Women" is reminiscent these days of the "Save the Whale" campaign: while the latter might have contributed to the well-being of the species the campaign sought to protect, the former, I fear, might well obliterate the very object it champions.

Indeed, this is a conclusion that echoes Hamid Dabashi's assessment in his devastating review of *Reading Lolita in Tehran.* Apart from the political service the text renders, Dabashi (2006) criticizes the book cover for the "iconic burglary" it performs. The cover of the book shows two young veiled women eagerly poring over a text that the reader infers to be *Lolita* "in Tehran." Dabashi shows that this is a cropped version of an original photograph that portrayed two young students reading a leading oppositional newspaper reporting on the election of the reformist candidate Khatami, whose success was widely attributed to votes cast by Iranian women and youth. In censoring the photograph and denuding it of its historical context, Dabashi argues, the book strips these young women "of their moral intelligence and their participation in the democratic aspirations of their homeland, reducing them into a colonial harem." For Dabashi, insomuch as the book cover places the veiled teenage women within the context of Nabokov's celebrated novel about pedophilia, it reenacts an old Orientalist fantasy about the incestuous character of the East, simultaneously repulsive and tantalizing in its essence. It is hard to escape the conclusion that the women whose suffering Nafisi sets out to capture must be obliterated in their particularity, both narratively and iconically, so that they can be re-enshrined as the "caged virgins" of Islam's violence. The fact that Nafisi's book has drawn accolades from feminist writers such as Susan Sontag and Margaret Atwood is disquieting in that even vocal critics of the conservatism now sweeping Europe and America remain blind to the dangerous omissions that texts such as Nafisi's embody and to the larger political projects they facilitate.[6] It is crucial that feminist writers and cultural critics learn to read such texts more critically, a reading that must ground itself in a familiarity with the complexities and ambiguities that attend even the much-spurned Iranian clerical regime and the politics of dissent it has spawned.

But What about Islam's Abuse of Women?

The reader might object at this point that even though accounts of Muslim women's suffering have been opportunistically used to serve a political agenda, is it not the case that Islamic societies exhibit a forbidding record of misogynist practices? How can anyone concerned about women's well-being not criticize and condemn such unspeakable atrocities? By way of an answer, let me begin by stating categorically that I fully acknowledge that women in Muslim societies suffer from inequitable treatment and are disproportionately subjected to discriminatory acts of violence. Any feminist concerned with improving Muslim women's lot, however, must begin not simply with the scorecard of Islam's abuses but with the terms through which an act of violence is registered as worthy of protest, for whom, under what conditions, and toward what end.

Let me flesh out these points by considering the much-publicized issue of "honor killing," a widely condemned practice that received international media attention even prior to the events of 9/11 but has since surfaced more dramatically in the genre of literature I discuss here. "Honor killing" is generally understood to be an "Islamic practice" in which women suspected of engaging in illicit sexual behavior are murdered by male family members. This practice might be compared to acts of man-on-woman homicide common to many Western societies. Consider, for example, the following comparable statistics: various reports show that in a country of 140 million people, almost 1,000 women are killed per year in Pakistan (which, along with Jordan, has one of the highest recorded instances of "honor killings").[7] The Family Violence Prevention Project, on the other hand, reports that approximately 1,500 women are killed every year by their spouses or boyfriends in what are called "crimes of passion" in the United States, which has a population of 280 million (slightly more than three women are murdered by their boyfriends or husbands every day in the United States).[8] Despite these parallel statistics, discussions of "honor killings" are seldom analyzed within a comparative context. Instead, most discussions construct "honor killing" as symptomatic of "Islamic culture" (note the elision between religion and culture in this formulation), while acts of man-on-woman homicide in the United States are presented as acts of either individualized pathology or excessive passion. In this logic, American men are represented as acting out of jealousy (a "natural" emotion) against their sexual rivals (albeit swept away by its force), while Muslim men are understood to be compelled by "their culture," irrationally and blindly acting out its misogynist customs and traditions. An individualized account of domestic violence in the West is secured, in other words, against a tautological account of "Islamic culture." Once this premise is conceded, it follows that an appropriate strategy for combating this form of violence in the West is to transform individual behavior, whereas in Muslim societies one would need to reform, if not eradicate, "Islamic culture." Such a polemical account, in its drive to quantify sexism (West equals less; Islam equals more), fails to realize that both forms of violence are equally cultural as they are gendered, each depending upon distinct valuations of women's subordination, sexuality, kinship relations, and various forms of male violence. Any opposition to these different (if comparable) acts of male violence requires a precise and grounded understanding of the social relations and cultural grammar that give meaning and substance to such acts.

The point I am making here is rather simple and straightforward: no discursive object occupies a simple relation to the reality it purportedly denotes. Rather, representations of facts, objects, and events are profoundly mediated by the fields of power in which they circulate and through which they acquire their precise shape and form. Consequently, contemporary concern for Muslim women is paradoxically linked with, and deeply informed by, the civilizational discourse through which the encounter between Euro-America and Islam is being framed right now. Feminist contributions to the vilification of Islam do no service either to Muslim women or to the cause of gender justice. Instead they re-inscribe the cultural and civilizational divide that has become the bedrock not only of neoconservative politics but also of liberal politics in this tragic moment in history.

WOMEN, DEMOCRACY, AND FREEDOM

In these last two sections, I want to examine the work that the rhetoric of democracy and freedom has come to perform in the "war on terror," paying particular attention to the secularity of this rhetoric and its constitutive assumptions. As is evident from even the most cursory reading of the media, progressive and conservative strategists agree these days that one of the most compelling strategies for eliminating Islamic fundamentalism consists of empowering Muslim women by educating them and giving them access to economic resources and political representation. The logic underlying this project is rather simple. In the words of *New York Times* reporter Barbara Crossette (2001): "When women's influence increases . . . it strengthens the moderate center, bolstering economic stability and democratic order." The conventional wisdom seems to be that insomuch as feminism is "the opposite of fundamentalism" (Pollit 2002, xiv), and fundamentalists are supposed to hate democracy, it follows that empowering women will further the cause of feminism, which in turn will help eliminate Islamic fundamentalism.

Apart from the more complicated fact that a number of Islamist movements—those pejoratively referred to as fundamentalist in the literature I cite here—seek to broaden the scope of political debate in the Muslim world rather than narrow it, I want to question the facile equation made between democracy and women's socioeconomic status: the idea that promoting the latter will automatically lead to the former. This equation is easily put to the test if we look at the conditions under which women lived in Iraq prior to the first U.S. war on Iraq in 1990. Despite the fact that Iraq was not a democracy under Saddam Hussein, Iraqi women enjoyed one of the highest rates of literacy in the third world and were widely represented in various professions, including the army and public office. At the height of Iraq's economic boom, Saddam Hussein implemented a series of policies to attract women to the workforce by providing them incentives such as generous maternity leaves, equal pay and benefits, and free higher education (Chew 2005; Bahdi 2002). In this important sense, Iraq was no different than a number of socialist countries (such as Cuba, the former Soviet Union, and Eastern Europe), where the lack of liberal democracy did not translate into the marginalization of women from the socioeconomic and political life of these countries.

Iraqi women's condition declined after the Iran-Iraq war (1980–1988), but suffered the most serious setback after the first Gulf War (1990–1991) and the subsequent economic sanctions imposed by the United States in cooperation with the United Nations and its European allies. Female literacy dropped sharply after the Gulf War, and Iraqi women's access to education, transportation, and employment became increasingly difficult. The current U.S. occupation of Iraq is the most recent chapter in twelve years of debilitating sanctions that directly contributed to the most dramatic decline in Iraqi women's living conditions. Needless to say, in the current situation of violence, chaos, and economic stasis, women (along with children, the elderly, and the disabled) are the most vulnerable victims of this disorder, and they are not likely to experience even a modicum of social order in the foreseeable future. Not only has Iraqi women's dramatic loss of "life and liberty" failed to arouse the same furor among most Euro-Americans as have individualized accounts of women's suffering under Islam's tutelage, but a number of political pundits now suggest that perhaps the promotion of electoral democracy in the Middle East is not a good idea after all, since it might bring Islamist political parties to power (as indeed was the case in the 2005 elections held in Palestine and Egypt) (Feldman 2006; Friedman 2006). Apart from the fact that these commentators find Islamist ascendance to political power inimical to American strategic interests, the fate of women under Islamic regimes is often marshaled as the ultimate reason for thwarting Islamist success at the polls. Note here once again the neat equivalence drawn between Euro-American strategic interests and women's well-being, between democracy (narrowly defined in electoral terms) and women's status.

One heart-rending appeal for instituting democracy by legislating women's freedom was made by Barbara Ehrenreich in an op-ed piece written for the *New York Times* in the lead-up to the 2004 American elections. In this piece, Ehrenreich upheld Carmen bin Laden's memoir *Inside the Kingdom* as the manifesto that all Democrats should embrace in their policy toward the Muslim world. As I mentioned earlier, *Inside the Kingdom* is Carmen's account of her luxurious life both in Switzerland, where she was raised and currently resides, and in Saudi Arabia, where she lived as the sole wife of one of the rich scions of the bin Laden family for several years. Much of the book lists the claustrophobic character of her life in Saudi Arabia, one punctuated by extended luxurious vacations in Europe, palatial houses with an army of servants, and lavish parties. Carmen, much like the authors I mentioned earlier, brims with her adulation for the West, its lifestyle, and its "opportunities." Carmen's zeal for a Western lifestyle is only matched by her sneering and derogatory portrayal of Saudi women. For Carmen, they are doomed to a herd mentality by the straitjacket of their cultural traditions: "You never develop as an individual in the Middle East. People may manage to escape their tradition for a short while, but those rules catch up to them" (16).

It is this account that inspired Barbara Ehrenreich's plea to the Democratic presidential candidate John Kerry to make gender parity a corner stone of his foreign policy in the Middle East, for the real enemy, she opined, is not terrorism but an "extremist Islamic insurgency whose appeal lies in its claim to represent the Muslim masses against a bullying superpower." Ehrenreich erroneously but predictably reduces the heterogeneity of Islamic movements to the likes of Osama bin Laden and, in due course, treats the practice of veiling (now so common in large parts of the Muslim world) as nothing but the entrapment of Muslim women in this patriarchal ideology. As a number of scholars have shown in the last fifteen years, *pace* Ehrenreich, not only is the Islamic movement quite diverse, but a number of its constitutive strands have strong support among women, who are the backbone of the welfare work undertaken by this movement (Abdo 2004; Deeb 2006; Mahmood 2005). Far from curtailing women's freedoms, Islamic movements have often been the vehicles for women's participation in the sociopolitical life of their societies. One of the grave costs of Ehrenreich's argument is that it fails to account for the complicated social shifts, challenges, and political transformations Islamic movements have produced that do not fit the simplistic logic of patriarchal subordination and authoritarian politics.

The fact that Carmen bin Laden's model of white elite bourgeois femininity is the symbol of this vision of "democracy" should alert us to its imperialist underpinnings. Callous and unrelenting in the modes of sociability and subjectivities it seeks to remake, this vision ridicules and scorns women whose desires and goals do not fit the telos of a liberal lifestyle. It is precisely because Ehrenreich is so sure that this insurgency is not in the best interests of women that she is led to conclude that it is up to the United States (better led by the Democrats than Republicans) to free these enslaved souls. This missionary zeal to remake "cultures and civilizations" has strong resonances with colonial projects of the nineteenth and early twentieth century, when European powers, also outraged by what they took to be Islam's degradation of women, undertook cultural and educational reform to civilize the local population. British regulation and policing of practices of widow sacrifice (*sati*) in India and feminine genital cutting in Sudan, symbolic of the colonized cultures' barbaric treatment of its women, seldom benefited those whom they were supposed to save. As Mani has noted, indigenous women were neither the objects nor the subjects of these reforms; rather, they were the ground on which European and national battles were fought for competing visions of empire and modernity (Boddy 2007; Mahmood 2005, esp. chap. 1 and epilogue).

SECULARISM AND EMPIRE

Calls for secularizing and liberalizing Islam so that Muslims may be taught to live a more enlightened existence are issued from a variety of quarters these days, left and right alike. These calls strike a chord with secular feminists (from a variety of political perspectives) who have long been convinced that religion is a source of women's oppression. While critical of neoconservative militaristic belligerence, many liberal feminists support a broad-based strategy of slow *progressive* transformation, one in which, as Katha Pollit (2002) puts it, "organized religion [is made to] wither away or at any rate modulate away from dogma and authority and reaction toward a kind of vague, kindly, nondenominational spiritual uplift whose politics if it had any, would be liberal" (ix). This seemingly benign vision encodes a secular conception of religiosity in which religion is treated as a private system of beliefs in a set of propositional statements to which an individual gives assent. Secularism, often reduced to its doctrinal principal (the separation of religion and state), operates here as a sociocultural project, authorizing a privatized form of religious subjectivity that owes its allegiance to the sovereign state (rather than to traditional religious authority). Importantly, the autonomous individual is the protagonist animating this secular liberal model of religiosity, a self-choosing subject who might appreciate the spiritual truths religious traditions symbolize but is enlightened enough to understand that these truths command no epistemological or political force in this world. These aspects of secular culture, now often noted under the rubric of secularity, are propagated not only through the agency of the state but through a variety of social actors and organizations that might well be critical of various policies and prerogatives of the state.[9]

Embedded in this secular conception of religiosity (echoed in Katha Pollit's quote above) are a number of presuppositions about autonomy and freedom that resonate with liberal feminist thought. The most obvious is the powerful trope of the autonomous individual—capable of enacting her own desires free from the force of transcendental will, tradition, or custom—that continues to animate many strains of feminism despite trenchant philosophical and anthropological critiques of such a limited conception of the subject (see Butler 1993; Mahmood 2005, chap. 1). A second assumption central to this secularized conception of religiosity is the understanding that a religion's phenomenal forms—its liturgies, rituals, and scriptures—are inessential to the universal truth it symbolizes. The precise form that scripture and ritualized practices take, in other words, is regarded as inconsequential to the spirituality (immaterial and transcendental) that they are made to substitute.

This secularized conception of ritual behavior makes it difficult for most secular feminists to entertain the claim made by many Muslim women that the veil is a doctrinal command. Women who contend that the veil is part of a religious duty, a divine edict, or a form of ethical practice are usually judged to be victims of false consciousness, mired in a traditionalism that leads them to mistakenly internalize the opinions of misogynist jurists whose pronouncements they should resist.[10] The veil— reduced either to its symbolic significance (a symbol of Muslim identity or women's oppression) or its functional utility (the veil protects women from sexual harassment)—is seldom entertained as an expression of and a means to a Muslim woman's submission to God's will, despite repeated evidence that for many veiled women this understanding is central (Mahmood 2005; Fernando 2006; Scott 2007). To take such a claim seriously would require stepping out of the simple opposition liberalism constructs between freedom and submission, instead exploring the forms of submission internal to a particular construction of freedom and the system of gender inequality in which such a construction resides. Sadly, this is not the direction in which the Euro-American public debate is headed (as evident in the French ban on the veil and the attempts in other countries to follow suit). Instead, contemporary calls for reforming Islam are built upon a narrow vision of a secularized conception of religiosity that mobilizes many of the liberal assumptions about what it means to be human in this world.

The problem of this prescriptive vision of secularized religiosity lies in its singularity and certitude that brooks no argument and makes no adjustments for different ways of living, both religiously and politically. It is the telos of a liberal-democratic Protestant society—whose ethos is condensed in the cosmopolitan sensibilities and pleasures of its enlightened citizenry—that is posited as the Mecca toward which all Muslims should conscientiously head. Apart from the infeasibility and singularity of this vision, what strikes me as imperialistic is the chain of equivalences upon which such a vision rests. It is not simply Islamic militants who are the object of this unrelenting prescription, but all those Muslims who follow what are considered to be nonliberal, orthodox, and conservative interpretations of Islam, key among them the wearing of the veil, the strict adherence to rituals of Islamic observance, the avoidance of the free mixing of the sexes, and the adjudication of public and political issues through religious argumentation. Insomuch as the appellation of fundamentalism has now come to enfold within itself not simply Islamic militants but also those who embrace this range of practices, calls for the liberalization of Islam are aimed at the transformation of these Muslims, making their lifestyles provisional if not extinct through a process of gradual but incessant reform.

As I have shown elsewhere (Mahmood 2006), the prescriptive force of this liberal project is not simply rhetorical. It enjoys the support of the U.S. State Department, which recently allocated over $1.3 billion under an initiative titled "Muslim World Outreach" to transform the hearts and minds of Muslims through a range of theological, cultural, and pedagogical programs. Part of a broader strategy of the White House National Security Council, this initiative is engaged in training Islamic preachers, establishing Islamic schools that propagate liberal interpretations of Islam, reforming public school curricula, and media production (which includes establishing radio and satellite television stations, producing and distributing Islamic talk shows, and generally shaping the content of public religious debate within the existing media in Muslim countries). What is notable about this broad-based multipronged strategy is that it is not the militants but the ordinary "traditional" Muslims who are the targets of this reform, in that they are seen as woefully lacking in the kind of secular sensibility required of modern subjects.[11] This project bears obvious similarities to the U.S. State Department's Cold War strategy with one exception: the current campaign has an overt theological agenda that abrogates the same secular liberal principal—the right to religion and freedom of conscience—that the United States is supposed to be fostering among Muslims through this campaign. There are many ironies in this attempt of the U.S. government to orchestrate Islamic reform in the Muslim world, but one that merits some reflection is how this policy of promoting liberal religiosity in the Middle East sits in tension with the Bush White House's active promotion of a particular form of evangelical Christianity at home. As I have argued elsewhere, these seemingly opposite tendencies need to be analyzed as part of what constitutes secularism today—particularly the understanding that secularism is not simply an evacuation of religion from politics but its re-orchestration.

Furthermore, it is not clear to me that inculcating a liberal religious sensibility among Muslims is necessarily going to decrease militant attacks on the United States or other Western European powers. This is not because all Muslims are violent but because the grievances they hold against the West have more to do with geopolitical inequalities of power and privilege. Even Osama bin Laden was clear in his message at the time of the World Trade Center attacks: he wanted American troops out of Saudi Arabia, a just solution to the Palestinian-Israeli conflict, and an end to Euro-American domination of Muslim resources and lands. His ends, if not his means, speak to a wide range of Arabs and Muslims who are currently witnessing one of the most unabashedly imperial projects undertaken in modern history, a project that, as a number of observers have pointed out, has done more to fuel the militant cause than to eliminate it.

The Muslim World Outreach program seeks to build alliances and networks with what it calls "moderate" Muslim scholars who promote a liberal interpretation of Islam and who largely echo the programmatic vision championed by the U.S. State Department through this initiative. The fact that calls for liberalizing Islam are now increasingly made by a range of prominent Muslim intellectuals—such as Khaled Abul Fadl, Nasr Hamid Abu Zayd, Abdolkarim Soroush, Hasan Hanafi—is testimony to the hegemony that liberalism commands as a political ideal for many contemporary Muslims, a hegemony that reflects, I would submit, the enormous disparity in power between Euro-American and Muslim countries today. In their reflections, it is Islam that bears the burden of proving its compatibility with liberal ideals, and the line of question is almost never reversed. They do not ask, for example, what it would mean to take seriously the orthodox practices of Islam embraced by many in the Muslim world right now and rethink some of the secular liberal values that are so readily upheld today, such as freedom of choice, autonomy, and indifference to religious forms of belonging. What would such a dialogue look like? How would such a conversation change our world-making projects?

As a number of critics of liberalism have pointed out, it is a characteristic of liberal thought—which, we must remind ourselves, cuts across conservative and radical projects—to assimilate unfamiliar forms of life within its own projection of the future, a future that is defined by the unfolding of the liberal vision itself. All life forms that do not accord with this futurity are to be subsumed within a teleological process of improvement and are destined to become either extinct or provisional. This attitude toward difference seems not only to animate calls for Islamic reformation but also to be operative in contemporary strands of feminism—particularly in its certainty that women's sensibilities and attachments, those that seem so paradoxically inimical to what are taken to be women's own interests, *must* be refashioned for their own well-being. It is this arrogant certitude that I want to question here. Does the confidence of our political vision as feminists ever run up against the responsibility that we incur for the destruction of life forms so that "unenlightened" women may be taught to live more freely? Do we fully comprehend the forms of life that we want so passionately to remake so that Muslim women and men may live a more enlightened existence? Can we entertain the possibility that practices like the veil might perform something in the world other than the oppression and/or freedom of women? Have we lost the capacity to be able to hear the voices of Muslim women that do not come packaged in the form of Ayaan Hirsi Ali, Azar Nafisi, and Irshad Manji? Would an intimate knowledge of lifeworlds that are distinct, and perhaps even opposed to our cosmopolitan lifestyles, ever lead us to question the certainty with which we prescribe what is good for all of humanity? At a time when feminist and democratic politics run the danger of being reduced to a rhetorical display of the placard of Islam's abuses, these questions offer the slim hope that perhaps a dialogue across political and religious differences—even incommensurable ones—can yield a vision of coexistence that does not require making certain lifeworlds extinct or provisional. It requires of us to entertain the possibility, perhaps too much to ask in the current imperial climate, that one does not always know *what* one opposes and that a political vision at times has to admit its own finitude in order to even comprehend what it has sought to oppose.

NOTES

This essay would have been impossible without the research assistance of Noah Salomon, Michael Allan, Stacey May, and Mark McGrath. I am thankful not only for their help in locating the materials but also for keeping me abreast of the enormous popularity this genre of literature enjoys in various public forums. My thanks to Jane Collier, Charles Hirschkind, and Joan Scott for their critical comments, and to Mayanthi Fernando for introducing me to the French examples in this genre. I presented this essay at the Center for Middle East Studies at UC Berkeley and to the faculty resident group at the University of California Humanities Research Institute in Spring 2006. I am grateful to the audiences at both these forums for their suggestions and comments. A longer version of this essay appears in *Women Studies on the Edge*, ed. Joan Scott (Durham, N.C.: Duke University Press, 2007). I would like to thank Duke University Press for permitting the republication of this piece in its current version.

1. A small sample of this vast scholarship includes Ahmed 1992; Alloula 1986; Lazreg 1994; Mani 1998; and Spivak 1988.

2. For a more developed critique of liberal feminism in relation to Islam, see my *Politics of Piety* (2005), esp. chap. 1.

3. On Azar Nafisi, see, for example, Atwood 2003; on Carmen bin Laden, see Ehrenreich 2004.

4. For the most comprehensive treatment of Nafisi's text as part of the growing genre of what many call the "new Orientalist literature," see Keshavarz 2007.

5. Some of these people include clerical luminaries such as Shariat-Madari, Mahmoud, Taleqani, Abdollah Nouri, and Hossein Ali Montazeri. For an account of the dissent from within, see Abdo and Lyons 2004.

6. Susan Sontag, for example, offers the following praise for Nafisi: "I was enthralled and moved by Azar Nafisi's account of how she defied, and helped others to defy, radical Islam's war against women. Her memoir contains important and properly complex reflections about the ravages of theocracy, about thoughtfulness, and about the ordeals of freedom—as well as a stirring account of the pleasures and deepening of consciousness that result from an encounter with great literature and with an inspired teacher." See the Random House website: www.randomhouse.com/acmart/catalog/display.pperl?isbn=9780812971064 (accessed September 4, 2006).

7. See www/hrcp-web.org/women.cfm# (accessed March 9, 2007); and the Amnesty International Report issued in September 1999 at www.amnesty.org/library/Index/eng ASA330181999 (accessed March 9, 2007).

8. See the Family Violence Prevention Project website at www.endabuse.org/resources/facts.

9. For recent scholarly work on the understanding of secularism not so much as an abandonment of religion but as its reformulation along certain lines, see Asad 2003; Mahmood 2006.

10. Nawal al-Saadawi (2004), a prominent secular Egyptian feminist, expressed this view on observing a sign displayed by French Muslim women protesting the recent ban on the veil that said: "The veil is a doctrine, not a symbol." Saadawi found this slogan to be an expression of the false consciousness of the protesting Muslim women, a sign of their naïve complicity with the capitalist plot to keep the Muslim world from coming to a "true political consciousness." Once again, any concern with religious doctrine cannot but be a ruse for material power in this kind of an argument.

11. For an extensive elaboration of the threats traditional Muslims pose to U.S. strategic interests and the "Western lifestyle," see Benard 2003.

References

Abdo, Genieve. 2004. *No God but God: Egypt and the Triumph of Islam.* New York: Oxford University Press.

Abdo, Genieve, and Jonathan Lyons. 2004. *Answering Only to God: Faith and Freedom in Twenty-First Century Iran.* New York: Henry Holt.

Ahmed, Leila. 1992. *Women and Gender in Islam: Historical Roots of a Modern Debate.* New Haven: Yale University Press.

Alam, Fareena. 2006. "Enemy of Faith." *New Statesman,* 24 July 2006, 54–55.

Alloula, Malek. 1986. *The Colonial Harem.* Minneapolis: University of Minnesota Press.

Amara, Fadela. 2004. *Ni putes ni soumises.* Paris: La Découverte.

Amara, Fadela, and Mohammed Abdi. 2006. *Ni putes ni soumises, le combat continue.* Paris: Seuil.

Asad, Talal. 2003. *Formations of the Secular: Christianity, Islam, Modernity.* Stanford: Stanford University Press.

Atwood, Margaret. 2003. "A Book Lover's Tale: A Literary Life Raft on Iran's Fundamentalist Sea." *Amnesty International Magazine* (Fall 2003). www.amnestyusa.org/magazine/fall_2003/book_lover/ (accessed 7 March 2007).

Bahdi, Reem. 2002. "Iraq, Sanctions, and Security: A Critique." *Duke Journal of Gender, Law, and Policy* 9 (1): 237–52.

Bahramitash, Roksana. 2006. "The War on Terror, Feminist Orientalism, and Oriental Feminism: Case Studies of Two North American Bestsellers." *Critique: Critical Middle Eastern Studies* 14 (2): 223–37.

Benard, Cheryl. 2003. *Civil Democratic Islam: Partners, Resources, Strategies.* Pittsburgh: Rand Corporation.

Bin Laden, Carmen. 2004. *Inside the Kingdom: My Life in Saudi Arabia*. New York: Warner.

Boddy, Janice. 2007. *Civilizing Women: British Crusades in Colonial Sudan*. Princeton: Princeton University Press.

Butler, Judith. 1993. *Bodies That Matter: On The Discursive Limits of "Sex."* New York: Routledge.

Chew, Huibin Amee. 2005. "Occupation Is Not (Women's) Liberation." *Znet*, 24 March, 26 August 2006. www.zmag.org/content/showarticle.cfm?ItemID=7518.

Crossette, Barbara. 2001. "Living in a World without Women." *New York Times*, 4 November 2001, 4.1.

Dabashi, Hamid. 2006. "Native Informers and the Making of the American Empire. "*Al-Ahram Weekly*, June 1–7. www.mltoday.com/Pages/Commentary/Dabashi-Native Informers.html (accessed 24 August 2006).

Deeb, Lara. 2006. *The Pious Modern*. Princeton: Princeton University Press.

Djavann, Chahdortt. 2003. *Bas les voiles!* Paris: Nouvelle Revue française.

Ehrenreich, Barbara. 2004. "The New Macho Feminism." *New York Times*, 29 July 2004, 19.

Feldman, Noah. 2006. "The Way We Live Now: The Only Exit Strategy Left." *New York Times*, 30 July 2006, 9.

Fernando, Mayanthi. 2006. "French Citizens of Muslim Faith: Islam, Secularism, and the Politics of Difference in Contemporary France." Ph.D. diss., University of Chicago.

Friedman, Thomas. 2006. "The Kidnapping of Democracy." *New York Times*, 14 July 2006, 19.

Hersch, Seymour. 2006. "Annals of National Security: The Iran Plans." *The New Yorker*, 17 April 2006, 30–37.

Hirsi Ali, Ayaan. 2006. *The Caged Virgin: An Emancipation Proclamation for Women and Islam*. New York: Free Press.

———. 2007. *Infidel*. New York: Free Press.

Hitchens, Christopher. 2006. "Dutch Courage: Holland's Latest Insult to Ayaan Hirsi Ali. *Slate* 22 May 2006. www.slate.com/id/2142147 (accessed 28 August 2006).

Keshavarz, Fatemeh. 2007. *Jasmine and Stars: Reading More than Lolita in Tehran*. Chapel Hill: University of North Carolina Press.

Kuper, Simon. 2004. Of All Things European: Guru of the Week—Big Thoughts in Brief—Ayaan Hirsi Ali. *Financial Times Weekend Magazine*, 27 March 2004. http://search.ft.com/ftArticle?queryText=kuper+hirsi+ali&aje=true&id=040327001305 (accessed 8 March 2007).

Lazreg, Marnia. 1994. *The Eloquence of Silence: Algerian Women in Question*. New York: Routledge.

Mahmood, Saba. 2005. *Politics of Piety: The Islamic Revival and the Feminist Subject*. Princeton: Princeton University Press.

———. 2006. "Secularism, Hermeneutics, and Empire: The Politics of Islamic Reformation." *Public Culture* 18 (2): 323–47.

Mani, Lata. 1998. *Contentious Traditions: The Debate on Sati in Colonial India*. Berkeley: University of California Press.

Manji, Irshad. 2004. *The Trouble with Islam: A Muslim's Call for Reform in Her Faith*. New York: St. Martin's.

————. 2006a. "Don't Be Fooled by the Fanatics." *Times Online*, 5 August 2006. www.muslim-refusenik.com/news/the-times-2006-08-05.html (accessed 30 August 2006).

————. 2006b. "How I Learned to Love the Wall." *New York Times*, 18 March 2006, A15.

Nafisi, Azar. 2003. *Reading Lolita in Tehran*. New York: Random House.

Najmabadi, Afsaneh. 1998. "Feminism in an Islamic Republic." In *Islam, Gender, and Social Change*, ed. John Esposito and Yvonne Haddad, 59–84. New York: Oxford University Press.

Pollit, Katha. 2002. Introduction. In *Nothing Sacred: Women Respond to Fundamentalism and Terror*, ed. Betsy Reed, ix–xviii. New York: Nation Books.

Reed, Betsy, ed. 2002, *Nothing Sacred: Women Respond to Fundamentalism and Terror*. New York: Nation Books.

Saadawi, Nawal al-. 2004. "An Unholy Alliance." *Al-Ahram Weekly*, 22–24 January 2004, 15 February 2007. http://weekly.ahram.org.eg/2004/674/op2.htm (accessed 9 March 2007).

Salamon, Julie. 2004. "Author Finds That with Fame Comes Image Management." *New York Times*, 8 June 2004, E1.

Scott, Joan Wallach. 2007. *Politics of the Veil*. Princeton: Princeton University Press.

Spivak, Gayatri Chakravorty. 1988. *In Other Worlds: Essays in Cultural Politics*. New York: Routledge.

Sullivan, Andrew. 2004. "Decent Exposure." *New York Times Book Review*, 25 January 2004, 10.

FIVE

It's All About the Blues:
The Black Female Body
and Womanist God-Talk

Kelly Brown Douglas

"How can you, a black woman, possibly be a Christian?" This was the question posed by one of my students that inspired my most recent book, *What's Faith Got to Do With It: Black Bodies/Christian Souls.*[1] What my student, Gabrielle, recognized was the pervasive role that Christianity has played in the oppression of black women. She did not understand how one who identified as a womanist theologian, one therefore committed to the "life and wholeness of entire people," especially black women, could affirm a religious tradition that so often militated against black female well-being. Gabrielle's question implied that there was something about the Christian religion itself that was incompatible with black women's quest for life and wholeness.

Of course, in many respects Gabrielle's concern was not new. This was the question raised in the 1960s by Malcolm X as he deemed Christianity "the white man's religion" and thus a religion completely unsuitable for black people. How, he wondered, could black people be a part of a religion that had been used to justify the enslavement of their bodies? It was also the concern of post-Christian philosopher Mary Daly as she recognized Christianity's long history of complicity in the oppression of women. She posited that if Christianity had been used that way (i.e., to oppress women) and had a long history of being used that way, then perhaps there was something wrong with Christianity itself, hence making it a undesirable religion for women.[2] Unlike the questions of Malcolm X and Mary Daly, Gabrielle's brought to the forefront of religious/theological inquiry black women's reality (for black *male* experience was the focus of Malcolm X's analysis and *white* women's experience was the focus of Daly's). Gabrielle's focus was on the role Christianity had played in the exploitation of the black female body. Implicit, perhaps, was the recognition that Christianity's complex role in human oppression is exemplified by its role in the oppression of black women.

Indeed, as black women's experience reflects the intersecting/interactive realities of race, gender, and sexual oppression, any appreciation of the complicated relationship between religion, sexuality, and gender must take into account the role of religion, in this instance Christianity, in the exploitative manipulation of the black female body/sexuality. "Writ large" on black women's bodies are the religious contradictions involved in gender/sexual oppression. It is only in understanding, therefore, how the black female body/sexuality has been "put-upon" by the insidious interaction of social-cultural and religious narratives that we can begin to move toward theological and religious paradigms that affirm the intrinsic relationship between religion and sexuality, and hence between God and sexuality—a relationship that, in fact, does not confound the well-being of any body/sexuality. Thus, it is through an examination of black women's exploited bodies that I will concern myself with the topic at hand, "Feminism/Womanism, Sexuality, and the Return of Religion."

Before proceeding, however, I must clarify an underlying presupposition concerning the nature of sexuality. For as suggested in my earlier statement, I believe that when properly understood sexuality is inextricably linked to religion in that the positive valuation of sexuality is essential to one's relationship with the transcendent, with God. Drawing upon Christian ethicist James Nelson's definition, sexuality involves our self-understanding and our way of relating in the world as embodied, gendered beings. Nelson puts it best when he says:

> Sexuality is a sign, a symbol, and a means of our call to commu-
> nication and communion. This is the most apparent in regard to
> other human beings, and other body-selves. The mystery of our
> sexuality is the mystery of our need to reach out to embrace oth-
> ers both physically and spiritually. . . . [Sexuality] is who we *are*
> as body-selves who experience the emotional, cognitive, physical
> and spiritual need for intimate communion-human and divine.[3]

And so it is that I affirm that sexuality, in all of its mystery, is about who
we are as relational beings. It is that aspect of ourselves that compels us
toward relationship. It is also an essential mechanism by which we enter
into relationship. In this regard, as suggested by Nelson, sexuality is not
the whole of who humans are, but it is basic to all that humans are. And
most particularly, as it relates to this discussion, sexuality is basic to our
relationship with God. A person's ability to enter into right relationship
with God corresponds to one's ability to affirm who she/he is as a sexual
being, in short, to affirm her/his sexuality. Sexuality and religious discourse, sexuality and God-talk are thus naturally linked.

Yet social/cultural and religious narratives tend to essentialize sexuality. Within these narratives sexuality typically becomes a matter of
sex; it becomes virtually synonymous with intimate/genital activity.
Again, while sexuality certainly involves sexual intimacy, this is not
the whole of what it is. Nevertheless, sexualized essentialization of sexuality contributes to its "demonization," that is, to its being considered
evil/sinful, and hence to the notion that sexuality is an anathema to God.
Such a notion portends trouble for certain human bodies. Again, it is
through the exploration of the exploited black female body/sexual that
religion's troubling influence on sexuality becomes clear. Let us now turn to
this exploration.

There is, I contend, no tradition that helps us to better understand the
complexity of black women's oppression, and religion's role therein, than
that of the blues, specifically that of blues-singing women. This tradition
also provides important insight for moving toward a reclaiming of right
relationship between religion and sexuality. Let us see how this is the case
by first examining the meaning of black women's "put-upon" body. Ann
Petry's novel, *The Street* provides the framework for this examination and
entrance into the blues tradition.[4]

Before I begin, it should be noted that my use of Petry's novel in framing the discussion reflects my particular womanist methodology. I have adopted a methodology that foregrounds black women's literature because I embrace what many black female literary critics have long pointed out: literature has historically provided a "safe space" for black women to explore and give voice to their experiences. Furthermore, my use of this particular novel by Petry is compelled by the womanist mandate proclaimed in the title of Alice Walker's womanist prose *In Search of our Mother's* Garden.[5] Implied in this title is the need for black women to search the often-overlooked resources and wisdom that our black mothers have left to us. I am highlighting Ann Petry's *The Street* because it has often been ignored as the American classic that it is. As a classic, it provides one of the most penetrating looks into the complex social-historical experience of black women, and hence the reality of their "put-upon" bodies.

BLACK WOMEN: A SEXUALIZED BODY

"You Know How They Are." Through the turbulent quest of her protagonist, Lutie Johnson, to provide a good life for her son—one that will allow him to avoid a future existence on the streets that are "meant to keep Negroes in their place," Petry exposes how black women have been sexualized by the racially coded patriarchal world in which they are a part.[6] Essentially, through the fictionalized Lutie, *The Street* tells the story of black women as they have struggled to "make do and do better" for themselves and their families in a world in which their bodies have been victimized by sexual abuse and racially sexualized commodification. In so doing, the novel subtly exposes Christianity's complicity in the unrelenting torment of the black female body/sexual. It is through the comments of a mother to a daughter—Mrs. Chandler, for whom Lutie Johnson is a live-in domestic—that we gain insight into the sexualized oppression of black women. Mrs. Chandler's mother cautions her about Lutie, "Now, I wonder if you are being wise, dear. That girl is unusually attractive and men are weak. Besides, she's colored and you know how they are" (45). How is it that Mrs. Chandler's mother is suggesting "colored" women are? Upon overhearing the comment, Lutie knows exactly what is meant. Despite the fact that Lutie is a "highly respectable, married, mother of a

small boy," she realizes that because of her blackness white people assume "she had to be a prostitute. If not that—at least sleeping with her would be a simple matter, for all one had to do was make the request. In fact, white men wouldn't even have to do the asking because the [black] girl would ask them on sight" (45).

These assumptions, which Lutie knows all too well, reflect the way white culture has characterized black women and men. Briefly stated, white culture depicts black women and men as over-sexualized, inexorably licentious beings. A sexualized white supremacist ideology has undergirded and sustained white tyranny against the black body since the slavocracy. This ideology caricatures black women and men as hyper-sexualized beasts controlled by lust (i.e., the unrelenting urges of their genitalia). Black women and men are thereby seen as immoral animals driven by abnormal sexual proclivities. Specifically, black men are characterized as rapacious predatory bucks, and black women as promiscuous seductresses. Black men are thus considered mandingos, and black women are considered Jezebels. Such derisive portrayals have provided, throughout history, ideological justification for violent attacks on black bodies such as the lynching of black men and the rape of black women. White lynchers often deceitfully posited black men's predatory behavior in relation to white women as a "reason" for lynching them (which oftentimes included castration). At the same time, white men were regularly considered hapless victims of black women's seductive wiles and thus permitted to rape black women with impunity. The notion of a black women being raped by a white man was virtually absurd, given the sexualized assumptions of white culture.

White cultural sexualization of black persons is typical of discourses of hegemonic power. As the late French philosopher Michel Foucault has argued, power naturally attaches itself to the sexuality of those it subjugates, all in an effort to control them. Foucault argues that sexual discourse is one of the most effective mediums through which oppressing power is exercised.[7] In short, to question or impugn the sexuality of another bolsters one's own claims to superiority because it suggests another group's inferiority. If one can establish that a people's sexual behavior is deviant, then one can also suggest that they are abnormal and likely inferior. As established earlier, sexuality is integral to one's very humanity. It involves a person's self-image, relationships with others, and relationship to God.

Therefore, to malign a people's sexuality is to call into question their very humanity and to taint their web of relationships—"human and divine." Thus, Mrs. Chandler's mother warns her daughter of Lutie, "You know how they are." Mrs. Chandler's mother is essentially speaking the "truth" that she knows—the truth of white culture that blackness is a marker of cunning hyper-sexuality, hence irrepressible immorality. Thus, in the mother's mind, Lutie Johnson is a source of temptation. She is an evil that has entered into the Chandler home.

Unfortunately, it is not just Mrs. Chandler's mother who has internalized the racially sexualized message of white culture—so too has Lutie. This reveals perhaps the most insidious aspect of white culture, that is, the way it penetrates the black psyche. Reading the novel, we find that not only did Lutie know the assumptions to which Mrs. Chandler's mother was referring, but she had incorporated them into her very self. We see this in her self-regard, in her regard for others—especially black men—and in her circumscribed life reality.

One of the first things Lutie seems to note about the people she encounters is the degree of their blackness. Upon seeing Mrs. Hedges (a woman who runs a brothel and looks out the window all day), Lutie immediately observes that "the woman was very black" (5). As if to confirm the sinister nature signaled by this blackness, Lutie goes on to describe Mrs. Hedges as having "eyes of a snake" (6). Likewise, in her initial contact with Supe (the superintendent of her apartment building) Lutie notices that his hands are blacker than the flashlight he is carrying. In Lutie's mind, Supe's blackness corresponds to his menacing nature (to which I will return below).

As if to separate herself from the reality of blackness (which she tries to escape by trying to break loose from the street), Lutie never ascribes blackness to herself. She says of her hands, "they were brown and strong" (71). Even then, Lutie attempts to escape the darkness of her hands by gloving them in white. Interestingly enough, not even those who encounter Lutie describe her as being black, as if she is better than what blackness represents. Supe, when thinking about Lutie, pictures her "bare *brown* legs," and her "soft *brown* skin" (98, emphasis added). After she escapes from his rapacious advances, Supe comes to resent her brownness because it signals to him that she thinks herself too good to be with a black man. He imagines that "she didn't like *black* men, had no use for them" (282, emphasis added). Boots, a black man who offers Lutie a job as a singer, is equally taken by her "long legs, straight back, [and] smooth *brown* skin" (263). To him, her brown skin means that if he is to "have her" he would have to marry her. In short, the color-coded narrative of white culture seems to have penetrated not just Lutie's psychology but also that of the other black men and women on the street. In this way Petry points to its impact on actual black lives, a point to which we will return later.

For now it is important to note that just as Lutie assimilated white cultural notions of blackness, she also assimilated the concomitant racially sexualized narrative. This can be seen most especially in Lutie's responses to black men. In Lutie's mind, black men always had lustful intentions. Consequently, in all of her encounters with them she presumed they were angling for a sexual relationship with her, and thus she treated them accordingly. And so, in her first encounter with Supe, she immediately assumed that his gaze on her as she walked up the stairs in front of him was libidinous (even though she wondered later if she had not really mistook him on that first encounter). Nevertheless, she did everything she could after that to avoid his company. Likewise, in her first encounter with Boots she immediately began to contrive ways to avoid what she believed to be his lecherous intentions. Unfortunately, both of these men would prove Lutie correct as both eventually try to rape her (perhaps signaling how their views of black women have been similarly warped by white culture). Nonetheless, Lutie's self-image is definitely refracted by the sexualized notions of white culture. It is this refracted self-image that she subsequently projects onto black men, thus automatically viewing them as lustful predators—again affirming white culture's sexualized image of the black male, thereby distorting her relationships with them.

As aware as Lutie is of her sexualized image, she tries to avoid living into it. This is seen most in her efforts to gain what she considers "respectable" employment, employment that did not exploit her body by preying upon her sexuality. Yet in a society governed by white cultural ideology, the jobs most available to black people are those which exploit their bodies as a source of body labor: domestic work, manual labor, earthy labor, or entertainment. Reflective of this reality, the "respectable" jobs that were available to Lutie were as a domestic worker (which became untenable because it required that she live away from home), or as a hand presser at a steam laundry (which did not pay well). The jobs that would pay her more and were there for the taking, as an entertainer or a prostitute, Lutie considered unrespectable. She believed that each of the jobs, in their own way, supported the sexualized stereotype of black women thereby rendering them as sexual objects since they made money off of their sexualized bodies. It is interesting to note that the only time Lutie identifies with her own blackness is when her efforts to develop her singing talents are frustrated by a white man's licentious desires. She thinks to herself, "If you were born black and not too ugly, this is what you get, this is what you find" (321). Essentially, in spite of her diligent efforts to escape the sexualized reality of her blackness, Lutie discovers that there is actually no escape.

Before moving on it is important to recognize that Lutie's sensitivity, if not hyper-sensitivity, to the hyper-sexualization of the black body, reflects a dominant response within the black community. In an effort to offset white cultural sexualization of them, black people have, in various ways, projected a standard of "acceptable" decorum governed by a norm of *hyper-proper sexuality*. This hyper-proper sexuality is characterized by a strident determination to sever the link between blackness and "abnormal" sexuality. Thus historically, there have been consistent efforts within the black community to shape black behaviors and morals in such a way that it complies with what is deemed by narratives of power—white patriarchal heterosexual narratives—to be a "proper" sexuality. A discussion of the many implications of this hyper-proper sexuality goes beyond the scope of this paper.[8] For now, it is sufficient to note the palpable reality of this standard within the black community as this community has tried to navigate their racialized sexualization by white culture. It was such a standard that surely guided Lutie's decisions concerning employment as well as her own comportment.

Eventually, however, her disgust for the street and the influence it is beginning to have on her eight-year-old son leads Lutie to accept the least objectionable of the unacceptable jobs: that as an entertainer. She accepts Boots's offer to sing for his band at the local nightclub. Though Petry does not explicitly identify Lutie as a blues-singing woman, there is little doubt that she is. This is evident through the way she is able to connect to her audience when she sings—in a way that makes them stop whatever they are doing and listen. The call and response, "the shared communal feeling" between the singer and the audience, was a signature of the blues performance.[9] It was the recognition that the story the blues singer sang was their own story. The personal became communal. Lutie's singing was described in this way:

> Her voice had a thin thread of sadness running through it that made the song important, that made it tell a story that wasn't in the words—a story of despair, of loneliness, of frustration. It was a story that all of them knew by heart and had always known because they had learned it soon after they were born and would go on adding to it until the day they died. (148)

The story that Lutie's singing conveyed was the "blues," the facts of black life, "its aches and pains, grievances, pleasures and brief moments of glory."[10] Through the fictionalized Lutie, Ann Petry captures the reality of what the classic blues-singing women represented in regard to black women's complex life of struggle. This tradition becomes of particular importance in our consideration of religion/God-talk and sexuality.

The "classic blues tradition" was that which brought the blues to the urban centers of the North during the periods of the Great Migrations. With the 1920 release of Mamie Smith's *Crazy Blues*, the 1920s and 1930s recording industry's "race market" began. This was a market that was defined by the classic blues. The classic blues tended to be performance oriented, accompanied by instrumentation, and more commercialized than the folk blues of the South, typically sung by a "wandering lone male." Yet the classic blues, while perhaps more sophisticated in terms of performance and instrumentation, still maintained the fundamental integrity of the blues as a music that was born out of black peoples' trials and triumphs, articulated the pains and joys of black living, and thus spoke to the deepest feelings of black women and men. The classic blues moved the blues tradition up North, making it available to a variety of audiences; yet its primary audience remained "blues people," that is, the black community. In many respects the classic blues "bridged the gap between folk blues and the world of entertainment."[11] Again, the classic blues tradition broadened the blues audience as it made the blues a part of the commercial recording industry.

The classic blues tradition was dominated by women like the fictionalized Lutie. They were women such as Ma Rainey, Bessie Smith, Ida Cox, Sippie Wallace, Victoria Spivey, and many others. Although these women did not write many of the songs that they sang and recorded, the blues they sang and interpreted reflected the realities of black women's lives. This brings us to the meaning of the blues.

As suggested by the description of Lutie's singing, the blues is about more than a music form: a twelve-bar, three-line structure. The blues is about a people. It is part of an expressive culture that emerged from "the circumscribed world of a segregated minority."[12] The blues is black people's music and hence black people's story. As Leroi Jones aptly stated, "Blues could not exist if the African captives had not become American captives."[13] Thus, reflecting the facts of black living, the blues is the "unvarnished, or unpainted back-alley actualities of everyday flesh-and-blood experience."[14] Essentially, the blues tells "the story of humble, obscure, unassuming [black] men and women."[15] So to reiterate, the classic blues tradition, one represented by Lutie, tells the story of black women as they navigate the difficult and often treacherous terrain of being black and female in a society that devalues both their blackness and their womanhood. In telling the story of black womanhood, classic blues-singing women would sing unabashedly about the loves, the troubles, the trials and tribulations, and the triumphs of black women's lives. Sometimes the stories they told in song were theirs, sometimes they were not. But to be sure, they were the stories of the women for whom and to whom they sang—poor, obscure black women trying to make it in a hostile world. And so the blues women sang:

> Hey, people, listen while I spread my news
> Hey, people, listen while I spread my news
> I want to tell you people all about my bad luck blues
>
> Did you ever wake up, just at the break of day
> Did you ever break up, just at the wake of day
> With you arms around the pillow where your daddy used
> to lay?[16]

As Ma Rainey, Bessie Smith, and others sang black women's story, they did not do so unreflectively. They sang with an awareness of the racially sexualized narrative that attempted to seize control of their bodies and circumscribe their lives. They sang, for instance, of the sexualized meaning of blackness. Bessie Smith sang "Young Women's Blues," which says, "I'm as good as any woman in your town / I ain't no high yella, I'm a deep killer brown / I ain't going to marry, ain't gon' settle down / I'm gon drink good moonshine and run these browns down."[17]

Clearly one of the most pervasive aspects of the classic blues tradition is the explicit sexual themes. The blues women sang unapologetically about their intimate sexuality. They sang about their sexual needs, wants, and preferences. For instance, Ma Rainey sang "One Hour Mama":

> I'm a one-hour mama, so no one-minute papa
> Ain't the kind of man for me
> Set you alarm clock papa, one hour that's proper.
> I may want love for one hour.
> Then decide to make it two.
> Takes an hour fore I get started,
> Maybe three 'fore I'm through.
> I'm a one-hour mama, so no one-minute papa
> Ain't the kind of man for me.[18]

Or Bessie Smith sang, "I Need a Little Sugar in My Bowl":

> Seem like the whole world's wrong since my man's been gone
> I need a little sugar in my bowl
> I need a little hot dog on my roll.[19]

These women would also sing matter-of-factly about homoerotic love. Ma Rainey sang, for instance, "Prove It to Me Blues:

> They said I do it, ain't nobody caught me
> Sure got to prove it on me
> Went out last night with a crowd of my friends
> They must've been women, 'cause I don't like no men.[20]

The sensual sexuality so predominating within the classic blues can be interpreted as affirming the sexualized stereotype of black women, a stereotype that many black women, like Lutie, so desperately tried to escape. However, to see the blues women as fulfilling and affirming the stereotypes of their blackness would be to miss the subtlety of what they are doing, and indeed the significance of the blues as it relates to religious discourse. For instead of reinforcing the stereotypes, in boldly singing of the intimate sexuality they were actually subverting it. That they sang so fervently and so often about sexual/sensual relationships can be seen as a form of "signifying protest" against the sexualized stereotype of blackness. According to Henry Lewis Gates, signifying is "repeating with a difference"; the blues women are repeating in song a sexual stereotype not only with a difference but to make a difference.[21] In so doing, that is, by singing so brazenly about sexuality, they are taking control of their own sexuality. They are portraying black women as agents of their own sexual bodies. As blues interpreter Maria Johnson says, blues women are "affirming and reclaiming black female sexuality."[22] They refuse to be confounded by the sexualized stereotypes of them or restrained by the black community's hyper-proper response to that stereotype. If Lutie represents those women who confronted the stereotype by promoting a hyper-proper sexual norm, the classic blues women dealt with it by ignoring it. In essence, by signifying upon it, they signaled that it had no power over them and their bodies.

Moreover, by foregrounding intimate sexuality they were not only protesting against white cultural hyper-sexualization of them but also against the very systems/structures that would seek to deny their freedom. For power always encumbers the sexuality of those it subjugates. Such has been the case for black people since slavery. The lack of freedom meant the lack of sexual agency, that is, the inability to choose one's partners, to marry, to engage in romance. Thus, to claim sexual agency is indeed to claim one's freedom. Angela Davis explains it this way:

> Sexuality . . . was one of the most tangible domains in which emancipation was acted upon and through which its meanings were expressed. Sovereignty in sexual matters marked an important divide between life during slavery and life after emancipation.[23]

As the classic blues women sang about black female sensual relationships, they were offering a social protest as well as telling a personal story. Yet even though the blues aptly reflected the story and protest of black bodies, they were rejected by a significant segment of the black community. Black church people typically considered the blues "devil's music." Worse still, they considered those who sang them as having "made a pact with the devil."[24] Neither the blues nor the women who sang it were readily accommodated by the black church—the religious context of most black people.

While some have suggested that the blues was labeled devil's music because it often referred to the devil, particularly that sung by men, it is clearly the explicit, if not (to some) illicit, sexual themes that have earned the blues this moniker. What is behind such a rejection of sexuality that a church community would reject its own sung story and castigate those who would bravely sing that story? Understanding this brings us even closer to understanding this complex relationship between religion and sexuality as well as to a way to "right" that relationship. Again, it is through Ann Petry's Lutie Johnson that we gain insight into this problem.

PLATONIZED CHRISTIANITY

"Ain't No Restin Place for a Sinner Like Me." Throughout the novel Lutie is haunted by the voice of her dead "Granny." Granny's voice consistently emerges to impart "wisdom" to Lutie as she navigates her black female reality. When seeking training for her singing voice, Lutie hears Granny's caution about white men's lusty ways, words similar to Mrs. Chandler's mother's caution to her daughter about black women's supposed seductive nature.[25] While Mrs. Chandler's mother represents the "lies" of white culture, one can say that Granny represents its truth. In this sense, for Lutie Granny is the voice of wisdom concerning the entanglements of a world controlled by whiteness. But Granny's voice is significantly more than that. It also warns Lutie of the temptations of sin, which means the temptations of the flesh. Granny's voice consistently projects a standard of piety that considers sinful anything that gives in to the passions of the body, meaning, of course, lustful sex and that which may lead to it—"secular" singing and entertaining. Thus, as Lutie contemplates the reality of life on the street, she hears her Granny's voice singing, "Ain't No Restin Place for a Sinner Like Me." Lutie sees herself as the sinner of Granny's song not simply because of her blackness but because of who she is as an entertainer, and herein lies the significance of Granny's voice.

Granny's voice resonates with an influential strand within Christianity that demonizes the body and virtually renders sexuality an anathema to God. It is thus this tradition that compels the black church to reject blues-singing women. Let us look briefly at this tradition, which I have spoken of in many places before as a Platonized Christian tradition.[26]

Platonized Christianity emerged as early Christian thinkers and apologists integrated into their Christian theologies the most prominent philosophies of their day, most significantly Platonic and Stoic thought. Specifically, the Platonic belief in the world of forms as being different and superior to the world of sense coalesced in Christian thought with the Stoic regard for reason and disregard for passion. In assimilating this philosophical thinking into their Christian thought, a significant strand of Christian theology adopted a paradigm for interpreting the world that esteemed the immaterial (i.e., things of the mind, reason, soul) and devalued the immaterial (i.e., things of the flesh, passion, body). This dualistic worldview eventuated into a body-devaluing theological tradition, namely, Platonized Christianity. It is important to note that even as I label this Christian tradition Platonized, I am aware that more than Platonic thought contributed to it. Moreover, there are those interpreters of Platonic thinking that suggest that the dualistic rigidity often attributed to Platonic thought is not accurate in its representation. To be sure, it is Neoplatonic thought that would create such a rigid divide. Moreover, recognition of the "Platonic split" does not preclude that about Platonism which might have contributed in a positive manner to Christianity. Nevertheless, with all of this said, it has been the Platonic split that has given way to the pervasive dualism found in Western thinking and worldviews. If nothing else, Western thought has built upon the Platonic split in such a way that this thought is characterized by a privileging of that which is rational, the mind/reason, and a devaluation of that which is not, the body/passion.

The point is that the Platonic split found its way into Christianity (again intermingled with Stoicism), thereby producing a tradition that invariably places the body in an antagonistic relationship with the soul. The soul is divinized, and the body is demonized. The soul is revered as a key to salvation while the body is seen as a salvific impediment. The body is considered a source and cauldron of sin. The locus of this bodily sin is passion, that is, sexual pleasure. This "sacred" disdain for the body/sexual pervades the Christian theological tradition, particularly as it has given way to a definite sexual ethic. The writings of the Apostle Paul, especially as they have been interpreted through an Augustinian reading, are perhaps most responsible for the predominance of this body-denouncing, theo-ethical tradition.

Specifically, Platonized Christianity promotes a dualistic sexual ethic. It suggests that there are only two ways in which to engage in sexual activity: one is tolerably good, and the other is intolerably sinful. Procreative sex is that which is good; non-procreative/pleasurable sex is sinful. A Platonized sexual ethic does not allow for a third sexual option. It does not, for instance, recognize the possibility of intimate sexual activity as an expression of a loving relationship—whether it is procreative or not. In sum, a Platonized Christianity is a body-less Christianity in that it is grounded in the notion of the body as potentially bad. Thus, all that issues forth from the body, that is, sexuality, is seen as sinful (which is, needless to say, ironic for a religion with an incarnate revelation at its core). It is Platonized thinking that makes sexuality an anathema to that which is sacred. Because it affirms a split between the body and the soul, it fosters a profound opposition between sexuality and God (especially as sexuality has been characteristically essentialized within this tradition to be mean sexual intimacy).

Platonized Christianity became an influential part of the black religious tradition during the Christian revivals of the eighteenth century. During these revivals a significant number of black women and men were converted to evangelical Protestant thought, the principal conduit of Platonized thinking of Christianity in the United States. Black church people most affected by this evangelical—that is, Platonized—tradition tend to stridently assert the dictums of the Apostle Paul to the Corinthians that one should "make no provision for the flesh," but if one must engage in sexual activity, "it is better to marry than to burn with passion."[27] Given the presence of this Platonized thinking within the black church community, it is easy to see why the blues and the women who sing blues are not welcome in the church. Both are virtually demonized. The black church essentially won't tolerate matters of the flesh. Indeed, it is the case that the black church's Platonized sexual ethic basically provides a sacred canopy for the black community's sense of hyper-proper sexuality, thus making violation of this norm not simply a social violation but also a sin. As Angela Davis notes, the church practically "valorized" the very ideology that deemed black people inferior.[28]

It should also be recognized that white cultural sexualization of black people is also that which no doubt significantly contributes to the black church's fervent adoption of a Platonized religious narrative in the first place. Inasmuch as black church people can diligently cling to a Platonized ethic, they can sever the connection between their blackness and hyper-sexuality—and thus perhaps not simply effect their salvation but attest to their very humanity. So it is no wonder that this Platonized Christianity has such a prominent place in the black church community.

But of course even as it may allow for a certain affirmation of black humanity, Platonized Christianity also compels the marginalization of certain persons within the black church community itself. This fact is made clear in Ann Petry's novel in a subtle but decisive manner. The black church as an institution is virtually absent from the novel. While one gets a strong sense of Lutie's spirituality, she never speaks of the church or a relationship to the church. It is as if she realizes that given her life of the flesh, as an entertainer, the church does not provide a space for "a sinner like [her]." In fact, the one instance in which the church is mentioned, its Platonized character is enunciated as it is juxtaposed to the nightclub in which Lutie performs. This is seen when at the close of one chapter the church is implicated through the experiences of Supe:

> He had only contempt for the people who slobbered about their sins and spent Sundays pleading for forgiveness, he had never been able to rid himself of a haunting fear of retribution . . . the retribution which . . . awaited men who lusted after women—men like himself.[29]

At the beginning of the next chapter, following the description of Supe's regard for the church, the nightclub is described as a place where "all of them—the idle ones and ones tired from their day's labor—found sur-cease and refreshment."[30]

Essentially, the church is regarded as a place of judgment for blues people, while the nightclub is seen as a place of shelter. Not only does the nightclub accept what the church rejects, but it provides a sanctuary for those that the church vilifies. This juxtaposition is the reified manifestation of a Platonized religious ethic. And so again, the blues, which have a home in the "juke joints," is barred from the church just as are blues-singing women. Angela Davis makes it plain: "Blues singers were (and to some extent still are) associated with the Devil because they celebrated those dimensions of human existence considered evil and immoral according to the tenets of Christianity. . . . [B]lues singers are unmitigated sinners and the creativity they demonstrate and the worldview they advocate are in flagrant defiance of the . . . prevailing religious beliefs."[31]

As censorious as the Platonized black religious tradition has been of blues women, it must also be noted that this tradition has had positive value in black women's lives. Petry points to this through the one Christian symbol that is predominant in her novel: the cross. In brief, Min (the woman who lives with Supe) brings the cross into the apartment she shares with Supe and prominently displays it above their bed. This cross for Min is a source of protection, for it prevents Supe from kicking her out, and most importantly from violently abusing her body. In one intense interaction between Min and Supe, Supe literally refrains from striking Min because he envisions her body framed by a cross. For Supe, therefore, the cross is a symbol of judgment that places restraints upon his behavior.[32] Without going into detail, what Petry is alluding to through her demonstrative use of the cross is the way in which a Platonized tradition has provided black women with agency over their bodies. Protecting their bodies became for many black women a matter of "protecting sacred space."[33] With a Platonized ethic they were spiritually empowered to claim control over their bodies.[34] At the same time, through Supe, Petry also reveals how the judgment of a Platonized tradition might also have positive value. For it has prevented black men and women from engaging in behaviors or activities that are detrimental to their well-being and the well-being of the community.[35] With that said, however, this tradition is problematic since it still demanded the rejection of the blues women.

Yet like Lutie, even though the church rejected them, the blues women were not without a strong spirituality, that is, a connection to God. This could be seen in their very songs as they often referenced or called upon "the Lord." For instance, in "The Blues the World Forgot," Ma Rainey sang:

Everybody cryin mercy, tell me what mercy means.
Everybody cryin mercy, tell me what mercy means.
If it means feeling good, Lord, have mercy on me.[36]

And in "Countin the Blues" Rainey sang:

Lord, I got the blues this morning
I want everybody to go down in prayer, Lord, Lord.[37]

Furthermore, despite their rejection by the church, the blues-singing women were church women. Many of them grew up in the church and first sang publicly in the church. Some of them ended their blues-singing careers in order to return to the church, while others returned after their careers ended. Most of all, the blues women were more than aware that singing the blues placed them outside of the church. Ida Goodson knew this at an early age, since her parents constantly warned her that singing the blues was the "Devil's work." Consequently, Goodson hid her playing of the blues on her piano from her parents. It is indeed recognition by the blues women that they were an affront to the church that brings us to the importance of the blues to restoring a right relation between sexuality and religion, sexuality and God.

"It's All about the Blues"

Just as the blues signifies upon the sexualized stereotypes of white culture, so too it signifies on the black church's Platonized sexual ethic. It does this as it "repeats" that which is an affront to the black church, but with a difference—without shame. The blues rescues sexuality from its sinful space. That about which the black church rarely speaks, blues women boldly proclaim. In their proclamation they are doing more than simply "thumbing their noses" at black church piety. Rather, they are pointing to the integrity of the black religious tradition itself. For as black religion emerged within the enslaved community, it was shaped, not by a Platonized theology (defined by body/soul splits), but by an African heritage in which there were no sacred/secular splits. This was a religious heritage in which all life was considered sacred—including the body, the flesh, sexuality. This is the religious heritage that undoubtedly allowed the enslaved crafters of black faith to appreciate the meaning of an incarnate God. For to be sure, inasmuch as Platonized thinking diminishes the body, then a Platonized Christianity obscures its very core, the incarnate revelation of God. Black religion, however, as it was shaped in slavery, was able to recognize that God's embodiment was crucial to any understanding of God's meaning in human history. Black religion, again as created by the enslaved, also attested that it is only via the body/flesh that human beings can reach out to God and most significantly that God can reach out to them.

The point being made is this: as the blues women signified upon the church in their celebration of sexuality, they were also calling the black church back to its own religious tradition—sans Platonized thought—a tradition that affirms the sanctity of the body/sexual. Indeed, this is the tradition that pulsates through the spirituals as they consistently maintain a connection between soul salvation and bodily freedom. They also testify to an incarnate God that is Jesus, who reaches out to black people and cares for their very bodies. In this regard, what the blues women also remind the black church community is again that which the enslaved understood: it is from the vantage point of a blues people (those that are more oppressed, a "bodied" people in a world that depreciates the body) that an embodied, incarnate God can best be understood. For it is the case that the incarnate God entered history in a blues context (a manger), and moreover Jesus' ministry consistently showed his compassionate solidarity with the blues people of his own day—even to the point of crucifixion.

This compassionate solidarity is witnessed to in *The Street* by way of Min's profound identification with the cross. That Jesus was crucified reveals the measures to which God will go to show compassionate solidarity with the most oppressed of society, in the case of Jesus, with the crucified class of people.[38] It is no wonder, therefore, that the cross/crucifixion is so central to black faith, as again seen in spirituals such as "Were You There When They Crucified My Lord." Therefore, it must be reiterated that the blues, that which is deemed devil's music, actually resonates with the spirituals, that which is considered sacred music. Like the spirituals, the blues refuses to diminish the sacred worth of the sexual body.

One of the ways in which the blues differs from the spirituals, however, is that the blues explores the sexual implications of the acceptance of the body. Specifically, blues reveals that the refusal to devalue the body, and hence to demonize sexuality, allows for an acceptance of sexuality not as simply an object of lust or procreation but as an expression of loving relationship (opening the way for homoerotic intimacy). Also, sexuality is viewed as a vehicle through which loving relationship can be experienced (opening the way for an appreciation of who Jesus was as a sexual being).

Let me conclude with this: When my student, Gabrielle, asked me how a black woman could be a Christian, my response came easily, for inasmuch as the Christian religion is an incarnate/bodied religion (and it is), then it is the religion of blues women.

NOTES

1. Kelly Brown Douglas, *What's Faith Got to Do With It? Black Bodies/White Souls* (Maryknoll, N.Y.: Orbis Books, 2006).

2. See Mary Daly, *Beyond God the Father: Toward a Philosophy of Women's Liberation* (Boston: Beacon Press, 1973), 72.

3. James Nelson, *Embodiment: An Approach to Sexuality and Christian Theology* (Minneapolis: Augsburg Publishing House, 1978), 17–18.

4. Ann Petry, *The Street* (New York: Mariner Books, Houghton Mifflin Company, 1946).

5. Alice Walker, *In Search of Our Mothers' Garden* (New York: Harcourt, Brace Jovanovich, 1983).

6. Petry, *The Street*, 323. Hereafter page references will be in the text.

7. See Michel Foucault, *The History of Sexuality: An Introduction*, vol. 1, trans. Robert Hurley (New York: Vintage Books).

8. A historically significant example of the institutionalization of hyper-proper sexuality, especially as regards black women, was the Negro Women's Club movement, later to become the National Association of Colored Women (NACW). Negro club women such as Mary Church Terrell, Anna Julia Cooper, Fannie Barrier Williams, and Ida Wells Barnett, believing that black women were to be the paragons of sexual purity for the black community, adopted Victorian notions of sexual purity.

9. Daphne Duval Harrison, *Black Pearls: Blues Queens of the 1920s* (New Brunswick, N.J.: Rutgers University Press, 1988), 57.

10. Harrison, *Black Pearls*, 6.

11. Paul Oliver, *Blues Fell This Morning: Meaning in the Blues* (New York: Cambridge University Press, 1960), 6.

12. Paul Oliver, *The Story of the Blues* (Boston: Northeastern University Press, 1969, 1997), 1.

13. Leroi Jones, *Blues People: The Negro Experience in White America and the Music That Developed from It.* (New York: Morrow Quill Paperbacks, 1963), 17.

14. Albert Murray, *Stompin the Blues* (Cambridge, Mass.: Da Capo Press, 1976), 50.

15. Oliver, *Story of the Blues*, 3.

16. Lyrics cited in Angela Y. Davis, *Blues Legacies and Black Feminism: Gertrude "Ma" Rainey, Bessie Smith, and Billie Holiday* (New York: Pantheon Books, 1998), 200.

17. Ibid., 356–57.

18. Lyrics cited in Hazel Carby, *Cultures in Babylon: Black Britain and African America* (London/New York: Verso, 1999), 19.

19. Lyrics cited in Davis, *Blues Legacies*, 238.

20. Ibid.

21. See Henry Lewis Gates Jr., *The Signifying Monkey: A Theory of African American Literary Criticism* (New York: Oxford University Press, 1988).

22. Maria V. Johnson, "Jelly, Jelly, Jelly Roll: Lesbian Sexuality and Identity in Women's Blues." From *Woman and Music*, reprinted at HighBeam Research, Inc., 2006 at www.highbeam.com, 1.

23. Davis, *Blues Legacies*, 4.

24. Ibid., 123.

25. See for instance, Petry, *The Street*, 45.

26. My most developed discussion of Platonized Christianity is found in *What's Faith Got to Do With It? Black Bodies/White Souls* (Orbis, 2006). The discussion below is taken from this book.

27. See the First Epistle to the Corinthians, chap. 7.

28. Davis, *Blues Legacies*, 131.

29. Petry, *The Street*, 140.

30. Ibid., 143.

31. Davis, *Blues Legacies*, 124.

32. See Petry, *The Street*, 138–140; 358-59.

33. Marla Frederick, *Between Sundays: Black Women and Everyday Struggles of Faith* (Berkeley and Los Angeles: University of California Press, 2003), 190.

34. See my discussion of this in *What's Faith Got to Do With It?* 176.

35. See James Baldwin's discussion of the value of this kind of Platonized ethic in "Down at the Cross: Letter from a Region in My Mind," in *Fire Next Time* (1963; reprint, New York: First Vintage International Books, 1993), 20. Baldwin explains that without the strict flesh-denying ethic of the black church, he may have ended up on the streets or dead like those of his peers who were not in the church.

36. Lyrics cited in Davis, *Blues Legacies*, 207

37. Ibid., 210.

38. See a fuller discussion of this in my *What's Faith Got to Do With It?* 100–103.

SIX

Nihilism, Sexuality, Postmodern Christianity

Gianni Vattimo

Allow me to start with a (not so) paradoxical thesis: the central importance of sexuality in human life is a belief that is more and more vanishing, its believers being increasingly reduced to psychoanalysts and priests (and not only Catholic priests). This paradox holds literally in the measure in which these two "categories" of "sex believers" are in fact the representatives of social authority and of the leading "norm" of an order that is still largely based on the oedipal rule that dominates the reproduction of social life and the self-preservation of society. The strength of this social normality depends on the lack of an alternative model of family, education, theory, and practice of authority. Conservatives claim that such a lack proves that the "oedipal" order is the sole natural one. As an Italian, I am every day confronted with the "naturalism" of the Catholic Church—but I imagine that in the United States, not to speak of the Islamic world, the situation is not very different. The current campaign of the Italian church against the proposed law that would legitimate the so-called *unioni di fatto*, non-married couples, hetero- or homosexual, is precisely based upon the claim that family is "naturally" heterosexual. The state should not recognize any

right to unions different from this natural model; otherwise it would promote the dissolution of the basis of all social order, which is assured only
by the monogamic, heterosexual, reproductive, and (possibly) indissoluble
union that is the traditional (in the Christian West) family.

There is at least one very important point in the obstinacy with which
the Church continues to condemn, among all perversions, homosexuality; and that's not only a matter of inner discipline, as one might suspect,
given all the scandals of pedophilia recently discovered in many Catholic
milieus and the obvious problems existing in all-male institutions like the
seminars. The point is that the Church is clearly aware that the defense of
the exclusively reproductive legitimacy of sexuality is an essential element
of its claim to represent the "natural" order established by God the Creator himself, which has been perturbed by the original sin but which Jesus
would have restored, entrusting the administration of the salvation—in
terms of sacraments and of teaching the truth—to the same Church.
Within the struggle against the homosexual "marriages," the Church
includes many different intentions: basically, and often legitimately, the
defense of the "nature" of human being, which it sees threatened by bio-
technologies, genetic manipulation, and so forth.

On this path, the Church has encountered recently a very unexpected
ally, namely, Jürgen Habermas, who has started to talk of "human nature,"
which is rather surprising for a philosopher who has always defended a
historistic, Hegelian-Marxian view of the human being. The worries of
Habermas are only in part similar to those of the Pope: to defend human
nature means for Habermas to limit the reduction of human life, body,
embryos, genetic code, to a merchandise that can be eventually patent-
ed, sold, and bought on the market. For the Pope, the question is that
of remaining faithful to the essence of human being such as it has been
established by God the Creator. In this latter case, the Church is always
again the authority that prevented biologists from making autopsies in
the Middle Ages and generally opposed in all times the effort of scientists
to know more about nature and to manipulate it technically for the best
interest of humans. That is the reason why the Church is so strongly
interested in sexuality. As one can see in one of the last documents of
the Italian bishops, sexuality is for them something "which cannot be
changed," a sort of natural limit that has to be respected also, or exactly,
because it cannot be changed. One can see here the usual naturalistic fal-

lacy on which so much of the Catholic ethics is based, a clear violation of the so-called law of Hume (deriving a norm from a fact). Now that it becomes more and more possible to change also this aspect of nature, and the "natural fact" is no longer a fact, where are we going to look for the will of God?

All these observations on sexuality, nature, the will of God, have a strong connection with the theme of nihilism and postmodernity. The view I have developed already in some of my writings is that nihilism is the postmodern interpretation, or version, of Christianity—in my opinion the sole one that can save it from the dissolution or from a violent end in a universal religious war. Put into different terms: the death of God announced by Nietzsche is not simply the death of Jesus on the Cross. Death of God means, in Nietzsche, the final dissolution of the supreme values and of the metaphysical belief in an objective eternal order of being, that is, nihilism. I am not going to repeat here all the development that the notion of nihilism has undergone in Heidegger's theory of the end of metaphysics; I'll only remind you that Heidegger's struggle against metaphysics was not a theoretical one, since it was ethically motivated by the refusal to accept the totalitarian political and social order (the *totale Verwaltung* of the Frankfurt School), which was being created on the basis of the culminating phase of metaphysics (positivism, scientism, etc.).

Nihilism is Christianity insofar as Jesus did not come into world to show the "natural" order, but to disrupt it in the name of charity. Loving my enemy is not exactly what nature commands, and above all, is not what "naturally" happens. Now, when the Church defends the natural order of monogamic reproductive family against any charity toward (naturally!) gay people, or prohibits the priesthood to women (again, in the name of a pretended natural vocation of the woman) it shows a preference for the God of the natural order against the message of Jesus. It is not surprising that a church oriented in this sense is also "naturally" reactionary, always on the side of the existing (dis)order, except in the case that this order violates some specific rights of the clergy (see the Italian history of the late nineteenth century and of the Lateranian Treaty between the Church and the Italian state in 1929). As Joachim of Flore taught prophetically in the Middle Ages, the History of Salvation has moments and phases. Using Joachim's terminology freely, we may say that we are living in the age of the Spirit; namely, we live in an epoch that through science and technology can do without metaphysics and the metaphysical God, in a nihilistic epoch where our religiosity can develop finally in the form of a charity that no longer depends on truth. There is no longer any reason to say that *"amicus Plato sed magis amica veritas"*—the principle on the basis of which the church(es) in the past killed heretics of every kind. There is (should be) nothing but charity, hospitality, toward the other.

Let's not miss the point. In the age of Spirit, that is, in the age of the end of metaphysics, why should the Christian believers still worry about the "natural order"? Natural order, from a no longer metaphysical (objectivistic, authoritarian, reactionary) point of view is (not), but the way things usually go—remember that even a still metaphysical thinker like Kant based the need for a life after death on the refusal of the ethical disorder of this nature.

But: what about God the Creator? One of the main points of controversy between Christian thought and (modern, or even premodern) science has always been the question of creation. Is it still so? Shall we really believe that Jesus was persuaded of being THE son of God the Creator in this sense? We now agree more or less completely that even the qualification of God as the Father can be demythologized without putting at risk our Christian faith. Could it not be the same in the case of the origin of the material world? There is some truth in the positivistic thesis following which the development of the natural sciences reduces progressively the field of theology. The enquiry on the origin of the material world is a matter of science, like the laws of astronomy and the option between Ptolemaic and Copernican model. The Bible is not a handbook of natural sciences; even the Church takes this for granted now, having decided that Galilei had not to be condemned. Just imagine how different Christian faith would be if it were not committed to defend a specific "description" of the way the world has been formed. The necessary atheistic impact of the modern cosmological consciousness (the long history of the physical world, the possible multiplicity of universes, extraterrestrial life, etc.) could be radically eliminated. Christian revelation is exclusively concerned with the possible salvation of our souls; this too is no longer thought of in terms of physical survival, but rather as an experience of plenitude in the current life, in the light of a hope for the resurrection, the parousia. How many Christians today still believe literally in a post-death life imagined as a continuation of the present one, with the addition of eternal beatitude or punishment? *Regnum dei intra vos est* might very well mean that eternal life in the Grace is something which is experienced here and now. . . . I have usually fought against the atheistic impact of modern cosmology by refusing the claims of natural experimental science to be objective and therefore true. It works on the basis of paradigms that cannot be considered as a view from nowhere; the language game of science has nothing to do with that of religion—no one can claim the absolute ultimacy. I still hold this opinion. But nevertheless, I admit that my attitude toward the "objectivity" of natural sciences can be much more friendly if I realize that I don't have to fear scientific cosmology as a threat to my faith.

In many senses, what the (Catholic) Church does today in relation to sexuality and, more generally, in its defense of "nature" (family, genetic manipulation, biblical anthropology) is the same thing it did against Galilei and the Copernican cosmology. The Pope wants to impose a view of natural world that is continually belied by the sciences. Take the example of creationism against Darwinism. It is very possible that even Darwinism is belied, but surely not on the basis of the literal "truth" of the Old Testament text.

May we really do without the biblical, Old and New Testamentary mythology? I don't think so. I would not wish a church without saints and Christmas and Easter rituals and so forth. But I don't want to be obliged to accept such an elaborated doctrine like that of transubstantiation in order to go to the Mass. To take Christian mythology as if it were a description of reality alternative to that of sciences is an authoritarian abuse that the Church should abandon in order not to scandalize the faithful.

Let me just (try to) come back to the central theme of sexuality. Like the forms of family in history, sexuality itself has undergone profound changes in terms of cultural practices and the freedom of individuals. Why should a Christian not accept that one is free to change his or her sex, for instance? As to the abuses Habermas fears as strongly as any "papist," let's try to be clear. Habermas thinks that it is a violation of nature, the "natural" freedom of the newborn, a genetic manipulation which would predispose her or him to be especially oriented toward an activity (to become a musician and not, e.g., a pilot). But on such a basis one should also prevent the parents from any intervention directed to prevent the newborn from getting cancer or another illness, or some grave deformity. Examples like these show that it is impossible, and inhuman, to decide bioethical questions on the basis of the "respect for nature." Although this criteria can help, it is more and more visible that also the worries of Habermas can be coped with only by a positive legislative effort, based on the consensus first of all of the persons directly concerned. I am aware that this seems a too-simplistic and limited criterion. But a more specific discussion of the matter can show that it is possible to establish good norms in the bioethical field without referring to such vague criteria as "nature."

SEVEN

Promised Belief

Hélène Cixous

A very long time ago, in 1965, in a prehistory, in a twilight of the soul torn by nagging little apocalypses, I used to write "things," literary larvae, that came together one night under the roof of a book called *Le Prénom de Dieu*, or *The First Name of God*, which I entrusted to Jacques Derrida to read. And everything had already begun in the name of *The First Name of God*.

FIRST EPIGRAPH

The First Name of God describes God the unnamable through Anagrams, spells it out "in back of the open book" without managing "to decipher the first word of the book." It says without saying, in an undertone, murmurs, *writes* rather this absent cause, this name of names that makes the whole language quake. "Therefore, Pseudo-Denis would say, to this Cause of everything that transcends everything, it is both the proper anonymity and all names of all beings, so as to ensure its universal royalty." But the cruelty of these tales perturbs a climate, a certain serene tranquility, in negative theology. In attempting to strip clean a hollow place of language where God's name can resound, in discovering—in a fabulous, dream-like experience—this place, empty, but familiar to us in our experience of being open to the coming of God, *The First Name of God* speaks before God. It disperses the name of God, shatters it, breaks it into anagrammatic fragments. "Your name is spelled out in every direction, Lord, and NOW, and MORD, and WON and DROL, you are *Dieu*, you are *God*, you are DEAD." From this moment forth the name of God, name of names, is no longer the center. It is nothing more than the play of his fingerprints on the skin of our language and our body's speech. What *The First Name of God* no longer lets into its writing, what it establishes the disappearance of, is the certitude of the name of God as the "original" of all names and "fixed point" of all languages. An objection Pseudo-Denis foresaw. The deity, he said, is participated in; "like the central point of a circle, it participates in all the radii that make the circle, as the multiple prints of a single seal participate in the original, that is wholly and identically immanent in each of its prints, without in any way fragmenting itself. . . . One might however object: the seal is not whole and identical in all its prints. I say this is not the fault of the seal." But *The First Name of God* hasn't the form of this objection. It is both the affirmation and the objection, its accomplice, at once. It is written in the form of a question: what if there were no seal before the print? If the whole- and identical-ness of the name of God were only the dream of a reading trying to "decipher the first word of the book," giving form to that which it desires, indestructibly: the seal, the past present of the print, the writing of a name not fragmented, unscratched, by the anagram. The name of God is one possibility in the syntax and in the game of first names. The game of our first-naming experiences is before God, ahead of God, in anticipation of God, both younger and older than he is. To give the marks in our flesh, of a first nickname of God to be read, newly the before in the before-God, to manage to write the here-before God, such is the attempt of this book which brings together the sparse tales, fragmentary marks of an "ultimate revelation," the one that "was given, sparingly, in a dream."

What I have just read to you, handed over, is a key, the heretofore unpublished remains of a secret: the first text Jacques Derrida ever wrote, looking at Hélène Cixous's text. That was in 1965. As you see, already, first of all, always, *at the beginning* of writing, *at the place of entering in* (to literature, to thought, to life and its death), the question is "God." Of

Dieu and *d'yeux* (of God and of eyes): the two of us, each worrying at the other, we've never ceased *asking for news. Dreaming* God? Who, what?

Before *The First Name of God* came all of literature that is the Promised Land without which, without whose extra-real phantasmatico-realistic existence I wouldn't have survived the deserts of my short but already cruel history. Literature, another Latin word, Jacques Derrida would say, like *religion.* Like Promise. *Literature* like *Religion.* My sole religion. My foreign Religion, my foreign re-legion, Greco-Roman for sure but not only, my alter Land, slaked by many a flood, bathed in more than one language, raised up, washed across borders, breathed on by more than one culture, a place promised to the meteoric upheavals of totally unexpected planets, a landing strip each time improvised to receive the marvelous event of a Letter freshly invented, never yet seen, never yet read, *ULO,* as Jacques Derrida was to say of *The First Name of God, jungfraudsmessongebook* as James Joyce would say of his *Finnegans Wake.*

In my foreign Religion, Literature, I live and work, I would tell myself, in the lost land in which French, the French language, speaks. In this idiom, attributed to me at birth, God's name is *Dieu.* In French *Dieu* (*d'yeux*) is an incalculable sum of eyes. At the same moment, the very moment, I was wondering what to do about God, what to think about God, literally and the word, what to think about the first initial of the name, the *D,* what there was to think, was there something to think? about God, bequeathed to me by Greco-Roman history, while in the next room Omi, my German grandmother, was praying in German to *Lieber Gott,* in whom she didn't believe, but to whom she nevertheless confided her disbelief, at the moment, the very same, I was reading *Portrait of the Artist as a Young Man,* and lo and behold there's *Dieu* calling himself *God* in English. Speaking to Stephen Dedalus c/o James Joyce, he took care to introduce himself in his language, the language of James Joyce, English in other words. Well, we've all at some point or other of our childhood had this brainwave of a Genius which Stephen Dedalus sums up:

"But though there were different names for god in all the different languages in the world . . . still god remained always the same god and god's real name was god."

God is in fact the one and only case of a given name independent of its language: a given name is not translated no matter what countries are traversed or intentions made manifest. Daedalus is Daedalus in Dublin or Paris. But Dieu calls himself *God* in English, he translates his name for his interlocutor; the unit of his name doesn't belong to any language in particular. God is not a concept, he is both singular and universal. Therefore a name exists which is not a word but a being and a being who answers to a multitude of names without being in any way altered by this.

And so I had written, without knowing (him), my first "book" before any book, in the name of the First Name of God. Later, this God, or the word *God*, left its mark and title on a fair number of my texts, returning, without my being able to do a thing about it, signing this or that page or scene in the course of its revolution's parabola. For years I failed to notice this. The way you overlook the light of day and the evidence staring you in the face. Then I saw. It might have been when the God so-called made an appearance under the name of Beethoven. (*Beethoven for ever or the existence of God*). I don't know exactly when I noticed the reiteration, the insistence, the ghostly returns. (Yet—this is a parenthesis—at the age of ten following the brutal death of my father I had dethroned God, a conscious, revolutionary dethroning, a decapitation of prayer: never again did I say to God, I'm not speaking to you. Never again to begin by God, never again ask for grace. I put my father in his place. I was young, I didn't know the tricks of substitution. Did I see I was deifying my father? I defied God. Later, when I wasn't looking, God stole back, surreptitious, underground, a textual sovereign, not that I gave him back his crown, but to stop God? How can you get along without a word that has no limits, when you throw your whole life into the creation of a world, the other one, the other world, the world raised to the nth power, in a gesture of virtual omnipotence, but still . . .)

It's no coincidence if God each time the same and other is invited or invites himself, as witness, into all the places where a person wakes up a poet, that is, a literary prophet. You find this God, so-called, in the place and in lieu of God in all possible positions, playing all the parts, active, discreet, central, sitting in a corner of the book buffing his nails, wearing a judge's robe, or invisible or unemployed, in his own name or not, in Flaubert, Dostoievski, as the figure of eternity in Proust, today as tomorrow and in biblical days, synonymically in Genesis of which literature is another figure.

SECOND EPIGRAPH

TO JACQUES RIVIERE
102 boulevard Haussman
[Friday 6th February 1914]

Sir,

Finally I have a reader who *divines* that my book is a work with a dogma and structure! . . .

I found it more honest and more refined as an artist not to let it be seen, not to proclaim that I was in fact on a quest for Truth, nor to say in what for me this consists . . .

Only at the end of the book, when life's lessons have been assimilated, will my thought show itself. That which I express at the end of the first volume, in the parenthesis on the Bois de Boulogne I set there just as a screen to bring to a close a book, which for material reasons could not go beyond five hundred pages, is *the opposite* of my conclusion. It is a stage, apparently subjective and dilettantish, on the way to the most objective and believing of conclusions.

No, had I no intellectual beliefs, were I trying merely to remember and layer my memories with my life, I would not bother, ill as I am, to write. This evolution of a way of thinking: I didn't wish to analyze it in the abstract, but rather recreate it, bring it to life. Thus I am forced to paint the errors, without believing in the necessity of stating that I consider them errors; too bad for me if the reader thinks I take them for truth. The second volume will accentuate this misunderstanding. The last, I trust, will dispel it. . . .

Marcel Proust.

Let me keep the word *belief* here. I myself believe in literature. My belief is a sort of religion in which I might be the only believer, and which I call the All Might Other.

All these interrogations which *make* and *find* [*font*] God, which found [*fondent*] God (careful, I am speaking to you of God in French), which perform and perfuse God (the word the being, the thing that makes my sentence shudder when, uttering the name, invariably brief as a thunderclap, *Thor!* Zeus! as a last breath, as a first cry, I receive its shock, its echo—I don't believe one ever utters this name, this word, this cry, believer or not, without a secret shudder), Jacques Derrida evokes their myriad secret powers, such as he translated them into his language— derridean—in his tremendously powerful meditation on the Island of Capri entitled *Foi et Savoir (Faith and Knowledge)*, first published in 1996. I quote from its 7th moment:

> 7. . . . . Here we shall be besieged by all the questions of the name, and of what "is done in the name of": questions of the name or the noun "religion," of the names of God, of whether the proper name or noun belongs to the system of the language or not, hence of its untranslatability, but also of its iterability (that is of what makes it a site of repeatability, of idealization and thus, already, of tekhné, of technoscience, of tele-technoscience in long-distance calling, in calling from a distance), of its link to the performativity of calling out in prayer (which, as Aristotle says, is neither true nor false), of its link with that which, in all performativity, as in all address and all attestation, appeals to the faith of the other and deploys itself in a pledge of faith.

"One never utters this name," I said. I ought to add an extraordinary characteristic of the Jewish religion, rigorously practiced: one may *write* the name of God, dispose the tetragram YHWH on a support, but one hasn't the right to *utter it*. Hence there exists a name-breath-cutoff that is not spoken, not voiced, save using substitutes, a name whose name is *the name: A Chem*. The Name. I have heard it said that pious Jews will call God by the given- or nickname of Elohim. But even Elohim is held so sacred one would rather not say it. How then not to say it? How to say it and not say it? So one modifies it slightly, one takes a step back, one makes use of a metonymy, a slip of the tongue, one says Elokim, you don't say what you say, you are cunning. You announce and denounce, and here we have the surreptitious beginning of literature in secret.

I shall not speak here of *"religion,"* of *this or that religion,* nor therefore of wars of religion, of the war that shadows all religion, or almost, for even when a religion thinks it is all about peace and love one another, be it Christian Tibetan or Ghandian, it does not escape the fatality of violence. A structural jealousy waits to ambush any proclaimed and elaborated religion. Because it proclaims, privileges, prefers. The minute it elects, and thus, even distantly, announces itself as elect, election gets translated into war. I shall not speak here today of the old struggle, of the inheritance, the identifications, the implacable laws of memory, honor's fidelities, to which for example Jacques Derrida on one side of Judaism, I on the other have always been the indebted, the enrolled, the inheritors . . .

Even though I do not in the least refuse a discussion, later on, from this stage onto which we are all pushed, where religion, as a plurality of dogmas and beliefs, built as it is on fratricide, cannot be separated from politics.

Since my hosts have with their admirable generosity granted me complete freedom, I shall rather speak of the mysterious current that runs for "me" under and between the words *foi* (in French), *faith* in English, *croyance, croire* in French, *belief* in English, I shall speak—as in verity I write—of this living mystery that for you I shall call *faithing*.

[Parenthesis on the words and their resources—idiomatic associations

Croire: is not *"avoir la foi."* To believe is not "to have faith."
Croire (to believe) *gives credit, croire /to believe* is the auxiliary of doubt, its disguise, in the expression—
Croire croise croix (all the word-plays on *croire, cru,* JD).
Believe, Belief. And in English
The secret = to love. To believe loves. To believe loves to believe. Believe *aime aimer* . . .
Another calculation therefore. Make believe = *faire aimer /to make love*]
Allow me to tell you two "stories" I've never got out of my mind.

PROSOPOPOEIA

"'Faith' is not something you *have,* faith is not a credit note, you can however lose faith, hence you had something to lose, faith is not a kind of knowledge, faith does not know, faith doesn't have faith itself, you don't know you don't have it, I thought I had it, I was sure of it, but what does sure mean? Faith was granted me, faith was taken away." This is what was going through Moses' mind as he huddled behind the rock at Meribah. In the space between Numbers 20:13 and Numbers 20:14, the water gushed forth, the rod which had set off the fateful tremor lay at his feet, unmoving, still as if nothing had happened. "Nobody pushed me, nobody tricked me, neither serpent, nor woman, nor inflammation of the senses. I trembled myself," Moses thought. "A trembling overcame me, a fluttering of faith's eyelash, a spasm, night in a billionth of a second.

Somebody trembled, I can't say who without trembling, who, if it's me *I*, Moses, who trembled, maybe me, or my brother within me, Aaron, who trembled me, one of me, you can't not tremble when you are about to speak to a rock, it's the least you can do, tremble in fear or awe, tremble with humility or hope, tremble without knowing and because of not knowing, is what Moses was trying to tremblethink since, he was thinking, I think therefore I tremble, between Abraham who thinks not a word and Moses on the telephone forever being called up by God and calling him up, there's a tremor of a difference, in the olden times on Mount Moriah when the man, me, the two of us all alone with the ass, it was our duty not to tremble, God said, first we do then we listen, no space between, today it's all become so complicated, the self is plural without end, I tremble, my tongue stammers, Aaron speaks in my place, *it seems* Jacques Derrida states, that *it is necessary* to tremble, *qu'il faille trembler,* you have to accept *the fault, the flaw,* he says, I who am split, I who cannot be dissociated from an Aaron who translates me and dissociates me, I who am not one, who am heterogeneous to myself, I who am more than one and less than one, I the contemporary of Balaam and not Abraham, I with my staff beating me, I with my staff like the Jew Gross and the Jew Klein meeting for the Conversation recorded by Celan, each with his more than and less than a self trembling itself and trembling the other, a heterotrembling self, I who cannot not tremble I mean not think, I mean find myself subject to the law of the other, heterologically." Moses thought—

"I didn't even have time. You don't see it coming. An accident. Not even a struggle. No explanation. The cause: is finitude." Moses beamed. Don't believe he felt sad. Faith was up and running again. "It's incredible," thought Moses. "All is lost. Nothing is lost." "To think I had to turn a hundred to discover what faith is: believing the unbelievable. The great believers are unbelievers who believe. Believe and not believe '*in a split second.'* Believe and not believe mingled in the chink of a second. A space so fine that the opposition of contraries can't slip in, without room for opposition, contraries touch, illuminate each other, annul each other, annulluminate. I don't ask myself why, the conflagration of the beyond begins 'there,' in the blaze, unimaginable uninhabitable save in dream, where I believe I believe that I believe what I don't believe but nobody to counterbelieve me, where I don't see I don't see but my she-ass sees and so what. Oh Balaam, in vain, three times in vain does the she or the he who has borne you forever see what lies ahead. The animal, male or female, Jacques Derrida called the-animal-that-(therefore) I am, the animal Jacques Derrida will have followed, that went ahead of him, whom he will have been, simultaneously going ahead of and coming after himself, in the apocalyptic instant, when I am dazzled by the revelation, is the animal-that-I-worse-luck-am-not. In the flash of this darkness I lose faith, I lose the world.

It happens in a flash. Everything happens in faith's *split second.* In the tremor, in the pulse beat of faith, in the fissure that sets fideism in action, in the *faithlure* where you experience the exposure of faith to time to the intemperance of human time. Anything can happen, at any section of a second, I mean any and every event can cut the thread of a second which can in each second of a second start to breathe again. *"And no one knows how to keep on* (Nelly Sachs) there where my life leans out beyond the limits our skin imposes on us."

You keep on, faith keeps on, once (*une fois*) interrupted faith keeps on, who knows how.

I was ten years old. I was reading Numbers 20. Moses struck the rock twice. The water came forth abundantly. The people drank, the animals drank. Then God said:

> Because ye believed me not, to sanctify me in the eyes of the children of Israel, therefore ye shall not bring this congregation into the land which I have given them.

I didn't understand God, naturally, God is not made to be understood. In my view, Moses believed in spite of the unbelieving, he lost faith for a billionth of a second between the two blows of the rod, and then it sprang forth abundantly. If there hadn't been a cut, it would never have been given a second time, it wouldn't have had any taste, it wouldn't have shone through the drops of water. There is no faith, I told myself, save more than once faith (*Il n'y a pas foi . . . que plus d'une fois*). In French.

That's why God in punishing Moses (and Aaron) rewards him equally. Paradoxically, God *keeps* his *promise*, keeps it *promise*. Promised promise. Moses will enter and will not enter the Land kept promised: as his people, called "congregation," he will enter, he will be in the Land, he will *not see* the Land from afar, from the top of the mountain, the people will *possess* the Land fully. As Aaron's brother, it is granted to Moses to see and not to see, that is, another kind of possession, possession-desire that keeps desire desiring, some people would call this the experience of mourning, but mourning has its sources of joy, there must be mourning for there to remain something to be desired, Moses does not renounce waiting for that which he will not attain, what he loses (has lost) is given back to him in another way, I told myself.

I had just lost my father. How to keep on? I began again to wait for him, with the other side of my skin. By dint of waiting, from time to time I obtained permission to see him coming from afar.

Man kann doch nicht nicht leben, says Kafka. One has to live—and well, French says: in French this means you must bring yourself to accept life as a *pulse-beat*. A rhythm through which death comes.

Now I shall tell you the story of the dispute that brought us together, Jacques Derrida and I, for forty years, the "singular dispute" is what he called it in 1998, you will find it evoked at length in *H.C. For Life, That Is To Say*. A magical dispute, he says, around the question of *believing*, and whose Derridean leitmotif is the phrase, the wish, the sigh: *"Puissé-je la croire"* ("If only I could believe her"— "Would that I might believe her").

For forty years we thought of death of life of death of death of life after that of death then of life, after death of death after death of life of going away then coming back, we get away from it, the further away we get the closer we are we run to every window for forty years it's the same storm, each time we get away from it we think of death, we are giving life to death, I would say we're putting death to death my friend would say, let's stop talking about it he would say, we're giving life to death, each time we talk about it we won't talk about it anymore my friend would say, we don't talk about it anymore, enough of that.

We don't talk about it anymore. I think about it all the time. Everything I say everything I think takes this road narrow as the crest of a dune, we slither down one side down the other, we don't talk about it anymore, the minute you think you're not talking about it any more you think more and more about not thinking about it and we have to start all over again J.D. would say may we forever be having to start again he'd say, first go, not so fast, go further more slowly, slow down, I'm always behind, he would say, always calling you back, reminding you of death he would say, in the end I'm forever having to remind you that on my side we die too fast, while you on your side live too fast, he would tell me, you don't recall, up to three times a week, he would call to remind me, you don't believe me, you know, and don't see, he used to say into the phone, he called me back he sent his voice out into the dark, you don't recall he would say, no no I would say, I don't recall up to two or three times, over the years

Over the years, I tell myself, I ended up surrendering completely to the strange evidence of the essence of our friendship. We never stop talking of God who doesn't exist stopping and starting, stopping beginning starting up again without ever stopping starting to end as late as possible, of his craft and his art of my craft and my art whose subject according to me is living and in the end you die—and according to my friend it's thinking living and thinking of the end and thinking in the end we die, too fast and thinking the too-fast doing all you can to slow down thinking what the too fast means. Such was the theme of all our times and for years

thinking "that we die too fast" which makes us live and think, too fast I told myself too fast perhaps to be able to ask myself in the bottom of my soul what I could do about this too fast that my friend kept repeating

in the end I reminded myself we'd forever be having to start all over again him telling me on the phone remember, on my side we die, in the end, too fast, me on my side telling him *I don't think so,* are you sure? do you recall, yes I recall I don't believe it, over the years I was starting to start to believe that I really didn't believe that in the end, we die, too fast, on his side, the years pleaded, my friend pleaded, every time he called finally I saw that he was pleading *against* what he believed, with his voice he reached out to touch my voice so as to reassure himself it wasn't trembling when I said I don't think so, I began to understand that I would be forever having to start over not believing what I knew, the main thing is not knowing it is knowing not to believe it, I'd ended up thinking that the closer you got the less you'd need to believe the more I'd have to remind myself not to believe, over time I'd come to wonder if he wanted to call me back to his side or did he want me to call him back to my side, that is, to the side where he believed I didn't believe that in the end we die, too fast, calling me back two or three times in a row to remind me that I on my side still didn't believe whereas he on his side believed too quickly, that in the end we die, whereupon believing that I saw that my friend did not want to convince me but on the contrary to convince himself he hadn't convinced me, in spite of unstinting efforts to remind me that on his side, we die too fast and despite the great authority he always had over me, and above all despite his constant wielding of this authority, having begun to think over time that my friend was once again making sure that he hadn't been able to shake my conviction, despite not having spared his saliva, his anxiety, his authority, going so far as to call me fifty or more times a year on the topic of his wretched belief and my pig-headed contrariness

and whereas, contrary to what my friend believed I believed, I'd always been racked by fear, anguish, apprehension, whereas I'd had to struggle my whole life against the malediction that strikes me the instant I love, casting an aura of fatality over any person I have the good fortune therefore worse luck to love, whereas in my view I have always known—which my friend knew—starting with the brutal and catastrophic death of my father therefore from the age of ten, that too soon does the hour of separation come, and having already lived through death more than once I have never been for life save against death, having always known, I have never therefore been able to do otherwise, for the simple sake of survival, than be content to live from life to life day to day, astonishment to astonishment, finding life so much longer than what death gave me to think from the very first dawn, I was forever having to start all over finding life longer than expected so as not to die of fear several times each week, and because if I started knowing what I know and believing what I believe I'd have already crossed to the other side, that is to the side of my friend, that is I'd have passed on, ages ago

by dint of reminding myself that life is longer than I believe it to be on my side whereas he on his side was forever calling me back to the phone to remind me what he on his side thought: we die in the end too fast, in the end I'd started to believe I might believe what I on my side was supposed to believe, so that on his side he might believe what he couldn't keep from believing and that he couldn't believe without putting his powers of reason and perhaps even his life in considerable danger and being sure that I on my side believed the contrary, however, that which on my side had come to constitute, in the long run, by dint of beginning and re-beginning our *singular dispute* on the telephone, a choice of sorts, mandated by the violent pressure of circumstances, hence a decision but taken who knows when who knows at what depth, in which murmurous back corner of the mind, to stick to a belief opposed to his, this was never as simple as all that, in one way allowed him to tell himself: "if only I might believe her" or "oh! if I could only believe her, if . . ." with the result that this slender *if* was like a wire to which he could cling in order to drift on the tenebrous tide of his belief that death in the end comes too fast, putting some minimal limit to the risk of drowning; but on the other hand I was thinking if he tells himself I'm right and he's wrong, he thereby lets himself float on the black tide of his unreason. However in the end this debate had for me an unforeseen consequence: eventually it became impossible for me to express the least un-steadfastness of conviction without endangering the whole lifeboat, along with its frail and meticulous arrangements, which made it out of the question for me to let myself be shaken either by myself or by him and hence to risk expressing the least shadow of a doubt without wreaking havoc beyond calculation.

Eventually, first by dint of thinking I didn't for a moment believe what he kept reminding me of: "we die in the end, too fast" at first on the telephone, once or more a week for years (which goes to prove the struggle, the difficulty, the necessity) then in writing—as if it were necessary to add to prophetic speech the gravity, the authority that paper's publicity confers upon the word—as if he took the world as witness to our *two faiths (fois), the in good faith and bad,* and by dint of tracing magic circles in time in whose center the dispute might begin once again, I took to imitating faith in this not-believing what he had transformed into a lesson of thought then into a philosophy. In the beginning I imitated it out of the discreet computation dictated by tenderness and respect, so as to limit the anguish, even using a subterfuge, such as friendship requires, during the first ten or fifteen years I countered the assault of those few words, so terrifying so terrified so authoritative so

anxious to be contradicted and de-authorized but one must not say or
do so, with responses that were frankly neither here nor there, modu-
lated by "not always-es," "save exceptions-es," "except in your case-s,"
I first took a step toward him, then in a trice I backed off, I made a
credible show of faith which is to say firm but shakable but victorious
over doubt, in which in the beginning I myself in my heart of hearts
did not for a second believe but which seemed nonetheless not totally
lacking in sense. So that, had I myself not been already so wounded
and terrified I might have known how to believe this truly. Therefore
I wasn't lying. I was doing my job. I shilly-shallied but secretly. And I
had the fortitude as champion of the king of death to seem rebellious
in the eye of his speech. But fortitude to seem is already fortitude to be
and this fortitude to have the fortitude to seem I had. What gave it me,
I must say, was him, that is, it was the solicitude which his need to be at
one and the same time approved and contradicted naturally aroused in
the camp of friendship as a force good for him inasmuch as it joined up
with his own life forces against his own death forces. Nevertheless the
equilibrium of the measure had each and every time to be recalibrated,
for to oppose too much resistance to his forces of death would naturally
have merely reinforced them. I compromised. For years at every phone
call I adjusted, I tossed in a pinch of light or semi-dark pragmatically,
letting myself be guided by the thickness, the variation of rhythm, of
the slowness—speed of the timber of the brightness and vice versa of
his second voice as highly precise indicator of the state of his soul. Naturally I trusted to his second voice in my supersensitive groping, the way
you tune a musical instrument better with your eyes closed, for years,
I never stopped tuning I mean tuning *and* un-tuning several times each
month the tone and tension of the arguments I added to the dispute,
relying on indications of which I took note at top speed, on the spot,
as soon as I detected the first notes of the second voice, the telephone
voice. The same thing in person at the same moment in the same room,
study, living room, would have been another body of voices, would
have been the voice with hands, the voice dressed up. But always I
let myself be guided by the voice he called "defenseless," the second,
the voice to which distance allows repose and disarmament. "Between
voices you hear one another better than when you can see each other."
"Entre voix on s'entend mieux que lorsque l'on se voit." Montaigne was

right. Just as Montaigne and La Boetie telephoned one another, without which they wouldn't have reached so absolutely and simultaneously the heart of hearts, and all the knots and ties, later designated by the vocables beginning with co-, would never have come to be. The telephone was installed in the Tower between the first little room the one with the starry sky, on whose wall St George small on his horse is painted in the likeness of La Boetie arriving at a gallop at the call of Montaigne who is in the box hollowed out of the stone one floor up, where for ease of conversation they set a chair no bigger than a prie-dieu, for the phone box is narrow. The acoustics are excellent. Stone carries. Let your heart murmur, the other hears perfectly. The décor of the two scenes in which the call takes place means that wherever you may be in heaven or under the heavens the other on earth or underneath the suit of armor, neither iron nor stone will ever cut the connection. To be together without either losing his solitude, to remain alone each on her side without the whole breaking, this is what the miracle contrives.

The whole time I worked for him, I had to work against him, I worked against him for his sake, I did his job, which job I don't know, when it was necessary to disobey I obeyed: I disobeyed. At the moment of disobeying I obeyed. I can see clearly that I let myself be guided by his second voice down the path where he was waiting for me to guide him, but without hope, right up to his front door. Thus: I followed on his heels a fraction of a second behind. I carried out the order so fast it was as if I were ahead, so that when he rang, I was there to let him in.

This is neither impossible nor unique, even if it is at the same time both unique and impossible. I receive the SOSs of my cats before the messages are sent and vice versa. I write this sentence, you notice, as he would have written it and as he wrote it otherwise.

Today I recall only the broad lines of this work which knew no rest, forever on its way without a terminus airborne without a landing, en route without arriving right up to the day I heard myself saying loud and clear on the phone, in a rapid, convinced voice, that I on my side absolutely did not believe that on his side "we die in the end, too fast." That was the early 90's. I could find the date in my notebooks. Suddenly the evidence was blinding. Suddenly I saw that I truly didn't believe what he wanted me to believe and also wanted me not to believe. As if *I had begged the question* and it had been granted. Now I really was on my team, on my side. I had won myself over, I'd won over my father's daughter within me. That day I felt the invincible little body of my mother stir within me. I might have expected a little of the German graininess of my mother's voice to mix with my voice. Luckily this didn't happen. Being on my side just as my friend had always imagined and thought, I naturally and effortlessly became his ally against himself on his side therefore against his own deadly forces. Now I had my mother inside me just as she keeps within herself, and not only at the end of her arm, her umbrella.

He was at it again. "It's starting up again. Starting up again." I quote him. His version of the endless dispute was published once in 1998 and then in 2002 and in 2003. And the starting again was him. And the starting again was me. Twice.

"I, he would say to whomever would listen, I'm forever having to remind her that on my side, we die in the end, too fast." Tacking on: "I'm forever having to begin all over again." You should have heard him. You would have to hear him, him, and the sentence as well. *"Moi," disait-il, et il me montre,* lui, *de la voix, moi, de mon côté dans la phrase je sui 'lui'* . . . Me" he would say, and he points to me, *lui,* with his voice, on my side of the sentence I am *"lui."* Me, as you are my witness, he would say, first with one voice then with another voice and then he wrote it and he has written and published it in a book, which then gave and henceforth gives I know not what weight to the declaration that he reread and signed and in which he addresses some persons, an audience, the public, so as to inform them of the existence of the *interminable dispute* he says and give them an idea of the singular nature of the dispute, that is, give to whomever may wish to listen his version and his feelings about that extraordinary dispute.

Puissé-je la croire (if only I might believe her), he would say to himself, in French, drawing on the resources of *puisse en francais,* on the glimmer of the *puissance (might),* even if he had thereby expressed an *untranslatable* hope, and in this case the sacred language, the magical one, in which he himself addressed himself, was French.

Here I should open a vast chapter on the experience of translating which preoccupied him, on the translation an untranslatable original calls for, an experience of faithless fidelity—but time is short, *il faut* (untranslatable) the time we do not have.

What is a prayer? "If only I might believe her." He would pray to himself. To himself in whom he didn't believe he addressed a prayer of *puisser* (*of mightiness*) beyond the lack of the power to believe. What is it, to pray for belief? What is praying? What is it to pray without belief? Can one then *not* not pray? Yes, there's something about prayer that one doesn't comprehend. One doesn't oneself comprehend. One still prays. One prays on the off-chance. One prays in case. One prays (*prie*): one wagers (*parie*) (Pascal). One prays to a pseudonym of G-D called Just In Case. One prays in a language of which often one doesn't understand "a damn word"—"un traître mot"—as we say in French. Thus the Jew prays in a Hebrew he doesn't understand. The Catholic in foreign Latin. That's what praying is. That's where sacrality starts: where the signifier is cut off from what's signified, where the I prays *in the other language*. Even if one understands the idiom, one gets to grips with the idiomatic only when it estranges and *keeps us at arm's length*.

—Why did Jacques Derrida pray *himself* to believe Hélène Cixous? To believe Hélène Cixous believed, thus enacting a sort of casting: he to play doubt, she faith? Meaning disjunction-contamination of doubt by faith. And vice versa?—I here propose one *response,* among others. *Perhaps* because Hélène Cixous is a dreamer, a seer of apparitions and *incredible* ghosts. Give me a night and right away I *see* things, beings, that one ought no longer to see that one *can/may no longer* see

the dreamer I am, the dreamer, dreamster, dreamdirector, nightfilmmaker, without me being the least bit aware of it *may* see what one *no longer can see.* There is a time behind time, a day that comes after the days, when all those whom I have lost come back, without my being able to do anything about it, without my *doing* anything, without my wishing, without my being able to foresee, count on, in the inexplicable, incalculable occurrence of the miracle. Without believing I believe, without asking I receive, I am visited, without bestirring myself. I am a stretch of land, I am a stage, without a clock. Extra-temporally, it happens that those who no longer are, are all the same, that death grants them what I call *special leaves* from death, the right to spend time, time that neither denies nor forgets death, in life. When I spoke of these incredible visits to him he believed in them. What he didn't believe, in my case he could believe, when I bore witness to them.

—Crois-tu qu'on sera encore là dans dix ans? dit-il.

Crois-tu qu'on sera encore là? Après? dit-il. Il me demande une réponse.

—De toute façon, moi je ne croit pas. Dit-il. Mais je voudrais que cela m'arrive et croire autrement dit-il.

—Do you think we'll still be around in ten years? he says.

Do you think we'll still be around? Afterwards? he says. He waits for my response.

—I, in any case, don't think so. He says. But I wish it could happen, I wish I could believe differently he says.

One day he gives a seminar on bearing witness, in the course of which he discusses at length the themes of the miraculous, the prodigious, or the extraordinary, favorite topics of testimonial experience, he speaks of the unbelievable in which he doesn't believe he believes but still there is always an invisible perhaps, passionately he speaks of *Hamlet*, the play of witness-bearing, the character who saw and says he saw his father assassinated *and* here-present.

Faith, like language, like a house, like the self, the thou-me, does not exist before the something which opens it, before the flexion of the relationship to the self which opens the possibility that it be open/closed, that it open or close itself. Someone from outside acts as threshold, door, possibility, limits the impossibility.

He demands an answer. And I give him the answer he wants. I lend my voice to his response. That's what he waits for: a voice for his response.

"Everything must remain secret, miraculous, oracular he says. The miracle, the miraculous (which is the supernatural within the realm of the visible, of what is seen), the miracle can't be dissociated from the oracle, the miraculous from the oracular. A true testifying as veritable, authentic testimony, in accordance with its witness-bearing vocation, is not only astonishing and miraculous, it is always oracular. This may be discreet, all but unapparent in manner, murmured, on the edge of silence, confidential, but this confidentiality in no way excludes the properly oracular dimension of all witnessing.

Rather than *croire* in French, he would perhaps have liked "Croire" in English, I believe. I believe that he really liked to believe, by the other language, the other in him thinking believe now in French now in English, both of them. For *croire*, I recall is not *believe; croire*, credere, *credo: posits*, whereas *believe lieves, it holds dear,* likes.

Je voudrais bien croire (I'd as lief believe), he thought, I'd like to, I'd like to believe you, he would say in his idiom, in his Derridean French. In the conditional of *I would like, I wish,* you cannot distinguish between the potential and the unreal of the present. *J'aimerais aimer* says the other language, that is, I would like to like.

TOWARD THE CONVERSION

Toward the end of the year I'd stopped sleeping, over and over I repeated to myself a phrase my friend had said to me around the 15th of July of the previous year, I remember having noted it down but I didn't remember where in which of my dozens of notebooks, some mornings I could spend hours hunting for it, which made my life sick, time and states making me dizzy with their mingling, I couldn't find it, abruptly I called a halt to my frenzy, I told myself the sentence again such as it seemed to me I had heard it, we spoke of "courage" and of "two sides" I think I remember. Then the phrase had said: "I ought perhaps to convert." I said the phrase over to myself. Perhaps it was "I will perhaps have to convert." But sometimes I thought I remembered he'd said "I believe I must convert without delay." The variations were killing me. Over and over I repeated the word I had right away flinched at. As soon as he'd said the word *conversion* I'd been clutched by a spasm of doubt. As if the hearing faculty had blacked out. The word *conversion,* I am absolutely certain of it, this was the word upon which my presence of mind had failed me, instead of following the conversation, I went after the word *conversion,* which had instantly joined up with that other mighty word, the word "instructions." Names of things my friend had constantly in mind, and that I experienced like the words of a dream fading, gleaming afar on the black waves, toward which one heads guided by the conviction that they have the explanation, unstable glowworms flickering, shifting, seductive to which we trust, for in all likelihood they have the secret. I remember having felt the brief expiration of the enigma on my brow. An inflexion of urgency in my friend's voice. Perhaps I could have asked him what he meant, but this I believe was impossible. He didn't say this sentence to me, I tell myself. He said it to himself just as on the phone you talk to yourself through the other.

I went quiet. Maybe I was wrong. It seems to me he was in a rush. As if he said, "Perhaps I should go right now and convert." "We'll talk about this again," he'd said. For me that meant both that he would speak to me about it, and wouldn't speak to me about it, or that he believed he'd spoken to me about it and would speak to me, both, what it meant was: wait for me here I'll be back.

Right away I wondered what *conversion* meant. I could think up thousands of interpretations. In every version of the word I could perceive the difference of one or the other "conversion" with itself, there is no word as convertible as the word *conversion* in every sense of the word, each with its own divergence from itself, with its true and its false, which are not true or false. I could also imagine thousands of hypotheses within the difference itself. Naturally I didn't ask him when we would talk "about this" again. Naturally never afterward did I ask him if he'd converted in one way or the other. What was at stake was *a conversion*. Which one? I wondered. I'll get back to you on this, says he. And never again did the subject come up naturally.

I may have thought it had slipped his mind. I may have thought the time would come. I may have thought I'd invented the phrase. I may have thought I'd dreamed it, this was plausible, it does happen. I no longer know whether certain events happened in reality or in a dream. What might have made me think all this happened in a dream was the extraordinary intensity and the extraordinary uncertainty that emanated from the words, a supernatural synthesis of uncertainty of intensity, a red-hot combination of the two. Over time the phrase acquired the intensity of The Word. Eventually, what with the natural impossibility and the natural possibility of questioning my friend about it rubbing together, I take to thinking about his phrase by the hour.

"How could I not have asked him? How could I have renounced his answer, how could I have lost it?" I asked myself. And immediately I pushed the question aside, hard as I could, I saw it as a hydra, I wanted to close the door. I could have given myself hundreds of answers, none of which would have calmed the immensity of the regret that roared in my breast each time I told myself I should have asked him. Whereas each time he'd uttered this or that enigmatic phrase in my hearing, talking to himself through me, I naturally began by telling myself that I should above all not ask what he meant. I know perfectly well that he deliberately left there one of those kaleidoscopic propositions, I would tell myself. He himself might have a preference for one or another interpretation, maybe he has no preference whatsoever, he would let me choose or not, he leaves me to choose, he lets me choose or not choose or not, such is his vital flexibility. Whereupon I thought quite the contrary. Perhaps he hid a key. And I don't see it. But at that point I could tell myself that he knew *or* on the other hand didn't know I didn't see. Since I said nothing. I wondered what he would have said, I mean what he would say, if I were to tell him in just what internal labyrinth I had embarked, and I knew exactly. He would have told me: all you need to do is ask *me*. I knew it. Not to be able to ask the question it is permitted to ask, this impotence I could not get into my head. It is and it cannot be. It makes me ill. I dreamed of it.

In a totally unexpected manner my friend had at long last dropped by to say that having an appointment in Paris he couldn't stay but he would be back. He couldn't tell me when exactly. When it's over he says. I begin to wait. A strange bliss whose other heart is pain. This time I tell myself. This time I'm going to ask him. It's all I can think of. Little by little time catches fire. Each hour goes by. This means, I tell myself, that he is busy.

Unfortunately my conviction that he would be back "when it's over" has slowly been eaten up by an anguish of doubt seeping under the skin.

In the meantime I am invaded by gloomy thoughts *intus et in cute*. I am burning to talk to him. I need to tell him there is a crush of questions I didn't manage to ask. Unfortunately among needs I am at odds with myself. I must not fail to ask him my questions this time, but the idea of satisfying this need horrifies me. I argue with myself without end. When he finally turns up, I choke with concern. He'll go away in the end, I tell myself, and everything will be over for eternity, including eternity. All the same I am madly conscious of the luck I have in the midst of my misery. I wanted urgently to ask: was the fact that he is alive maybe proof of the famous *conversion?* Could and should I think I was face to face with a "conversion" success story? I wanted to ask him: should I think of you as a convert to dreams? Was this the sort of conversion his phrase had hinted at? I trembled with terror at the thought that he was not converted, just a dream. Were this the case, best that I, in my eagerness, not disturb the illusion. Finally I said that if I could, I should like to ask. Immediately appalled at the thought of the consequences, I start to say to you that if it were possible maybe you might tell me where you had been, and what you'd been doing, though I wouldn't, above all, wish this to deprive you of the least bit of freedom, of lightness, I was wretched, for wasn't I committing the irreparable blunder, maybe the best thing since he was alive at that moment was not to make any allusion at all to what at that moment was not, but on the other hand I feared it would offend him if I seemed to forget where he came from, and to act as if the unconceivable were not the gaping maw behind the door. Unfortunately I had no experience at all, no opinion. And I writhed in anguish at the very moment I found myself nonetheless in the world truer than truth with my friend. No, I tell myself, I must not yield to my absolute need to know. I don't know whether I want to know, I don't know whether I ought to know, I twist in pain at the thought of not knowing, and I feel sure this anguish risks offending him and producing the small deadly shock to the dream. In the end I say: I am glad to see you. Me too, he says.

So long as he is alive, I tell myself, the dream is a blessing. We know not what dreaming means.

Eternity on Leave

When *all is lost*, I say to my brother, and only then, when you're really done for, that's when there's a hope of salvation, I say to my brother, for this, I say, two things are necessary: (1) that I know in my soul and conscience that not only *have* I nothing left to hope for, but further that I no longer hope; (2) that there be some kind of salvation on this earth or hereabouts, which is unlikely and naturally uncertain. An *event* had occurred, which I was beginning to think—without being able to predict or calculate—should it not fade away, promised perhaps to become as powerful, as enabling, as serious, as consequential, as revolutionary, as the meteoric event of the discovery of literature as reality in the Guermantes courtyard, or of the reality of literature, an event of such fantastic power that the striking of a heel against a bump in the pavement had forever changed all literature, an event comparable to that, also involving a slab of stone, of the reading of the tablets of the law, at a time when all was lost for the narrator on Mount Sinai. I still had the taste of the event on my tongue. If this is not an illusion, I was thinking, then it's the answer at last to death, it's the road to happiness *in* suffering, I have found it. If

I've found it—what I saw as a series of acts of grace and gifts was nebulous, astronomical, I saw nothing clearly and I've got time, I tell myself.

I speak the facts: I've just seen my friend J.D. again last Thursday, I say. He was on leave, I tell my brother. I should have stuck to that. Last Thursday, I thought. Last, Thursday! But I got carried away. I took a chance.—Do you think there could be leaves? I say.—There are weekend leaves for patients with chronic illnesses. It's legal within a structure. "Outside the structure?" I say. That's beyond my allopathic competence, says my brother.

It is a *special leave,* that it be *special,* that my friend be let out of hospital for a *special leave* we are not for an instant permitted to doubt. Reeling from the shock of such an *unbelievable* event, as if the bolt from the blue in its descent had flipped the hourglass over to believable, I flung on my clothes, not a second to lose, and ran to the designated address. What was wonderful and painful in those hours, nearly a day, is that they were part of day-to-day-life, whereas the special leave had been granted by the beyond, with the result that the two vital worlds were mingled in a bewildering synthesis of the extraordinary with the commonplace. Nothing solemn. Each of us however was aware of the cruelly precious value of each moment, each of us in our own way did all we could to ensure that each drop of blood, each breath, each word be distilled to the essential.

So there may be leaves! I murmured the phrase over and over. Dreams—I've had lots of dreams since the line was cut, I could write a book. But this time it was a *special leave,* this is different from a dream. We were conscious of reality, of its laws, of history, of time, of duration, and we'd accepted, without a word, without putting our heads together, him having advised me that he was on leave, this finite infinity that left to my own devices I'd never have let myself hope for, since all the work would be for him: the travel, the going through customs and immigration, the security checks coming back to this side, but above all, horrific moment I'd no wish to think about and which we never discussed, it would have been mad, the return to a beyond that he'd named, as a euphemism and alluding to his world-renowned writings on hospitality: the hospital. In a flash we'd figured out how it worked, the structure. *Everything* we did and exchanged in our day-to-day-life we did and exchanged, without exception, but condensed into ultra-quick, apocalyptic summaries, for example, a book: just as we used to, seeing it coming, one or the other of us, this time he's the one who does the writing, me the correcting, I correct in a flash. He had other ideas as well for the future and on condition, of course. All this we did with the same lightness and felicity and without letting ourselves be cast down by the brevity of the program, though I for my part was nervous. I was curt with people who'd have wasted my time, telling myself that he would scold me for this, but he didn't notice, so I did the right thing, everything happened during these hours. This is what was so admirable: all the genres but in a paroxysm, some grotesque as well, but above all the wisdom of a kind of felicity of which I would never have believed us capable in times of peace. The dream as well in which we were on leave and which was called *A Leave*, we each lived—dreamed it in our own usual different manner—me from within, him more from without. I'm the one who told him the name of the dream, which had a name like a city-name, and he as usual was part-skeptical part-mystical. "As usual I am skeptimystic," my friend said, a little excited both that the thing should come to pass with a name and maybe by the name, going after the name, and that all this should be possible, the worst having happened—which we never mentioned by name, out of anxiety, but also because the thing hasn't any name—. And we were thinking. As thinking beings, we were ultra-quick, especially him. Millions of thoughts, torrents of them. "I wish I could believe you, as we used to say," he thought, and at the same time believing, sadly believing, sad-believing, because, as he thought, "This can be happening only if the worst has come to pass, but the worst is not this; it's that if the worst seems to have happened, it means the worst hasn't yet happened." And I could see him thinking, but from another side.

So there may be leaves, I told myself, and I tried to keep in step with him despite the contradiction, which almost brought me to a halt, unthinkable, of the worst yet to come and the being-on-leave. And the proof is that what was granted was withdrawn *at the same time,* which was more or less what he felt, but which didn't keep us from enjoying the brief happiness. *There may be leaves!* I told myself. But you're the one who's dreaming this, he thought. Obviously, that's the condition of a leave, to be only a leave, I thought back. But on the other side, yours, you're the one who gave me the idea of an incomprehensible but very real leave, I thought. We thought. To save time, we were reading our thoughts at supernatural speed. What we had in common was this headlong rush. We never stopped thinking for even a fraction of a tenth of a second. Super-speed made possible by the rubbing together of our two brains over decades, faster than the speed of light.

"Dream or no dream, it's" I thought. And he agreed. Not reality, a reality truer than reality, and finally he thought "the Veridical." That's what we'll call it. I laughed. It was his *Ver* coming back. The *Ver à Soie (Silkworm)*. *Veridical*, I thought: a word I have never in my life to date employed.

Something not in the least like a dream. "The resurrection."

The Resurrection is what one doesn't believe in. If one believes in it, there isn't one; if one doesn't believe in it, there isn't one. It's a total absolute complete limited resurrection. The only limit to the resurrection is its leave status. I'm not going to complain about this. It is not the resurrection of the past. Not at all. It's the resurrection of the present. The friend who comes is not who he used to be, he's who he is now today such as he emerges from the wreck. I've never seen him in this state. This brings on an exaltation of worry and chagrin, but an awful happiness breaks out, infinite and condemned. Nearly a day. A few hours, all the forces of life after death gathered together to substantiate a return to reality will keep you going for a few hours. Then this provisional life, having *utterly* exhausted its energy reserves, stops. The final moments of the leave are awful. You feel yourself losing the last drops of time, and all of a sudden, as if a call had rung out, nothing audible though, but a bell in a locatable part of the brain, you are warned that it will soon be over. Half an hour left, so everything gets written shorthand, in broad strokes, so little time, there he goes, sentences shorter and shorter. One of you says: may I? the other: yes. Then all of a sudden he has to go, you have to let him go, it went so fast, no adieu.

So all is not lost I tell myself and hence nothing being completely lost, nothing at all is lost. I felt a kind of courage to be happy and, though alive, the sensation of being brought to life. Since leaves may be granted, all it will take is a revolution in our habits, thought uninterruptedly working on itself so as to throw itself beyond itself, use its imagination to drag itself in the direction it doesn't know how to go to, but this isn't much to ask.

It's not that we were "freed from the order of time" during the leave. Quite the contrary. We were freed from the order of death, I tell myself, that's why time's order had never been so omnipresent and authoritative. So late do I discover the different "orders." For the first time I was discovering the complexities and the resources of "the order of death" of which I'd been ignorant. Hence I had only just learned that after the knife falls, the great separator, after the final words of the Essay of Friendship ceased to echo, there could be another realm not totally closed-and-nothingness, a realm of retention not totally cut off in a neverness, but with suspensions, remissions, hesitations, leaves, brief liftings of the latch. Every now and then one could *restore the lines of communication that nourish friendship.* Some kind of reestablishment of the line, such as I hadn't had the joy to work out with my father, for we hadn't had time to think together and to talk to each other for so long and so often on the telephone and maybe even never. That which we experience as death-sickness is to be located in the complete and utter impotence to which I saw myself yield on my side as pale imitation of the impotence-other on my friend's side. I had even lacked strength recently to meditate on the malevolence of the kidnapping that had taken place, which, from the feebleness of my soul and my force of representation, I'd had all the difficulty in the world to fight against, helpless as I was to reflect upon the ghastly mystery that struck the ghost of my friend during the period that preceded his leave: I noticed without comprehending it, without managing to analyze the dust of a butterfly wing substance of his presence, is it presence is it absence is absence not absence but feeble presence, a light too light presence of my friend? And this was my fault, as if the ghost who ought logically and naturally to be exactly the same, whether he's off on a trip or on the Long Voyage, was of a different species.

As if the ghost of ordinary absence were nourished and kept breathing by the certainty of return, hence by a spiritual act due to my belief. And as if, him gone on what I believed to be the Long Voyage, a nourishment and substantiality that ensure the charm of the ghost in his absence, were no longer dispensed, resulting in a wasting away of the ghost, a scattering of the absent person's body, which I naturally reckoned was caused by the harshness of the kidnapping, by an inexorable debilitation of the person of his presence, a chastisement that brutally struck out at those of his near and dear who were pretending to act as if the irreversible had not occurred. But I was completely wrong. He hadn't wasted away, I had wasted him. Because I didn't *actively* believe he would be back, I, without being cognizant of the danger I was opening the door to, had undernourished the image, which grew thin and pale for want of regular insufflations of patient waiting, of a familiar and gentle projection of return that safeguards the thickness of our friends when they are off on a trip. Everything possible in the case of an absence (help, hope, waiting, patience, correspondence, calculation, the right to prayer and supplication) being null and void in the case of a Long Voyage, I had allowed myself to be stripped of my rights and powers of invocation and to be myself annulled.

The great surprise was the annulment of the annulment. I'd just wakened. And as if during the night I'd forgotten not to believe or to believe, as if I'd forgotten about the wall, as in a dream I'd sprung up to answer the telephone, and where there'd been a wall there hadn't been a wall, I'd slipped through to the other side. And right away the leave began.

What the leave left me on deposit after the moment of grace expired: a crazy sad feeling of exaltation, sad and exciting both. A wretched happiness, yet another affect I'd never have suspected I'd be able to feel, happiness in tears, relieved, raked by claws, at the discovery that death lets pass, that it may unclench, that it makes exceptions. As if one *could do* everything one is capable of imagining, all of us the living dead dying life death and other beings-subjects to laws so harsh but open to interpretation, natural phenomena. What it is, is an extra-mortal joy that keeps death in mind. No disclaimers. I don't deny the sentence, its execution, its frightful consequences, the solitude, the enfeeblement, the ruination of beauties, the carnages of skies, global chlorosis, anxiety, that flatten us, the butchery of living moments, the uprooting of the heart of things and beings. But it was clear to me, on that day, that we had found: the answer. It was *Leave*. It will suffice.

The rest is patience, process, search for new modes of existence in the inner lining of life.

Not that the death in my life became a matter of indifference to me, nor that the *insoluble difficulties* lost all their importance and virulence, nor that I as if by magic were suddenly reconciled with destiny, nor that the ablation of my friend that began anew each day as soon as I opened my eyes and thus the wound were stopped up, and not that it lost its power of suppressing the beauty of beautiful days, of poisoning each meal and every page; but the synthesis of vivisection and nothingness, which stretched its infinite nothingness out from the window sill, out from the edge of my lips, the abyss-nothingness that had taken up all the space in the world, but the hole had become something. A horror but with pauses. It was no longer that perpetual nothing nothingness that forces us to renounce. I even had an inkling of a surprising advantage to the hard work that awaits me: there could be no mourning, no getting used to it. Above all, one could *keep* everything: the suffering to the quick and its whims, the sticky shadows, the somber viscosity of the veil stretched over cities; everything could be tolerated, since it was not out of the question that legal outings a few hours long might take place, I told myself. Of course, I thought, no use pretending one wasn't dead. But on the other hand, rather than let oneself yield to the maneuvers of the conservation instinct, strategies that convince us to flee the inner pain by hiding from ourselves within ourselves from whom we flee, its poppies, its hypnotic operations which the strong currents of daily life reinforce with a thousand vulgar, pressing duties, turning us from our heart

on the contrary, I thought, do what you can to resist the ingenious proposals of the compromises, hold on to the suffering, fan the dread, for the monsters are also the benevolent guardians of the presence of the survivor within me.

We were dying of death, one is dying for a long time, still we might meet up again,

so life could come and go, come back from going, I told myself, its warm flux flood everything that was dead dying from the death of my friend, my animals, my trees my books my dreams. All I needed I told myself was to sum up some superhuman strength I prepared for huge unfamiliar kinds of anguish I know me I say I am no good at waiting doubt can plant its hooks in me suddenly, but on the other hand I start to believe again fast

"I'll see to this" I thought, "first thing tomorrow." "Do what you need to," he was thinking. "You can count on me," I thought back. Nothing being cut off. Besides, I can also count on the genius of my friend, I say, the sort of genius that has always involved leaping further than any other being in the world on the scent of the spirit and especially leaping beyond the place he himself imagined he could reach. What will make the wait so airless naturally, I thought is not to have any definite date even a far-off one to hook your heart to, to hoist it over the abyss. It is at the mercy of all the bedevilments of waiting with which I am all too familiar (patience wearing out, discouragement getting out of hand, wilting of all the sublimating faculties, desertion of the passions . . . abandoning your post, giving in to resentment). But underneath I tell myself the tiny glow worm of the Leave event will be blinking. My job's to rise about the trial; it all depends on my will, impotent, tenacious, powerless, dogged, inflamed with a taste for honor, I tell myself. I know me. Not that I'm the strongest as my friend used to pretend, but I've always had the strength, weakness maybe, to believe that if "in the end we die, too fast," as he puts it, later on, as sequel, there's a chance that someone-I-don't-know-who—or who-knows-what—may come back. You can't keep from dying. Afterward there's no longer *anything* at all keeps you from returning.

I then felt a joy not sharp deep and a little crazy, the slight drunkenness of appeasement after too long a pain when having suffered the horrors of drowning, the worst of human anguishes, the gulf with its claws spits us up, air arrows into the lungs. So this life would not always be the glacial lifeless life into which I'd sunk alive lately, I tell myself. Once a year it will get its colors back. Starting tomorrow, I'd thought. *Do what you need,* he'd thought.

I'll do whatever it takes, powerlessly, I tell myself, in a burst of sadness. My mission: submit to the absence without resisting, without counting all the way to discouragement. Then sink, sink into discouragement right to the limit of discouragement. After that there's a desert. In the desert, let yourself be vanquished.

Nothing is more mysterious than belief, except for death. Believe, die, something clicks. No one knows why, there comes a moment, you believe, you die. Suddenly you find yourself on the other side without having seen the least trace of a way to the door on time's threshold—no time no door. To believe resembles to die and vice versa to die is to arrest belief.

I took notes of all this as baggage for what might come. I knew life would go back to death looking so much like him you couldn't tell them apart.

I wrote: "there may be leaves" on a rectangular post-it I stuck to the window above my desk. These post-its are tough; they look like nothing and they go on for years.

The post-it will keep me company, I thought; when I stop believing, it will go on believing.

Right to the end of our days I knew we were in the order of death, that from then on I had nothing to wait for but loss after loss, one worse than the next. Often it would be tough to breathe. I knew I'd want to die and that the order of the dead and the living would forbid this, but at least the horror of having to lug a lifeless life around in dead time was limited by the thought of being able to taste again *all life's riches* without exception, a few hours a year, I told myself, to be able to tell myself that in the end everything is rendered us, for just the time it takes to rediscover the lost taste of writing, to smile at the sight of the voices coming to drink in the stairwell, to hear a scrap of meaningless yet archi-signed conversation, exchange a few words with a waitress in a café while listening to the touch of an accent chime in my friend's sentence, to receive the world entirely summed up in the dazzling brevity that shines from him when, rising two thousand meters above the planet in a little plane no bigger than a chair as big as life, the divine prop, for once you are given permission to see everything you are, from above.

The immortal mortals who are us—how utterly beautiful they are seen all together and colored with the shining colors that appear to us only when we are neither within nor without, but between the two. A-few-hours-a-year, I told myself, for already I was counting on a small number of leaves, as human beings will in their childish computations. Two years I tell myself without leave, for the moment I cannot bear it.

I jotted this program and its details down while I was still basking in *the aura of the Leave's enigma.* I hastened to begin the work I knew awaited me. From now on I would have to believe, believe believe believe the unbelievable, in anticipation of lean times when belief dried up.

Only those are granted leaves who *believed* in them before the passage. Or those who *thought* about them without believing. Those who, not believing, would have liked to believe. My friend was never able to believe, but he would greatly have wished to be able to believe had he been able to; he wouldn't have refused *to believe on my side,* even if on his side it had always been refused to him to be able to believe there were leaves; it wasn't his fault he couldn't believe; he'd never had anything against the idea that I might be looking forward to some leaves, simply a sort of incredulity but admiring, light, generous, which always encouraged me on my side to persist in my own way even if he was watching me believe from his shore without even seeing me, like a blind Moses to whom someone describes the other shore, that there is a mountain with a rosy top from whose summit you might catch sight of the promised land.

EIGHT

Concluding Roundtable: Feminism, Sexuality and the Deconstruction of "Religion"

CAPUTO.   It is always a special moment for us when we are able to bring our speakers together to interact and to raise questions back and forth. We think of the theme of this conference, "feminism, sexuality, and the return of religion," as so many sparks that could be fanned into larger flames. We are interested not only in the question of feminism but also in the wider issue of gender and sexuality in all of its ramifications for religion. As Kelly Douglas said in her paper, when we are discussing sexuality, we are discussing who we are, for there is no purifying our being human of our being sexual. The expression the "return of religion" is in the air and not of our own devising. Not unlike the word "postmodernism" itself, I do not invest a lot in it semantically and conceptually, but it is an efficacious way to start a conversation. Still, we had two things in mind in invoking this expression. First, the return of religion in the emergence of a powerful religious right in the United States. Most sociologists who a generation ago thought the United States was undergoing a process of relentless secularization have been sent back to the drawing board. We are having arguments today about teaching evolution, for example, that we could not have even imagined not too many years in the past. Secondly, we also had in mind the renewed interest that intellectuals, indeed, quite secular intellectuals, have shown in religion. The first conference we had at Syracuse two years ago concerned the appropriation of Saint Paul by Alain Badiou, Giorgio Agamben, and Slavoj Zizek, which results in a secularized and politicized Paul. If modernization has meant secularization, the word postmodern, if it means anything, inevitably means "postsecular." Intellectually, Enlightenment critique produces the critique of Enlightenment, and this opens up the door to a renewed reflection upon religion in a post-Enlightenment way.

ALCOFF.   I want to raise a question that will hopefully elicit a conversation among our guests. One way to look at the topic of feminism, sexuality, and the return of religion is that it raises the question of what response feminism and the sexual liberation movement should make to the return of religion. It is very clear that secularism is not a panacea, that secularism is not in all cases the root of liberation for either feminism or sexuality. I think this is a lesson of postmodernism: that any discourse has multiple meanings in different contexts and can be used for different kinds of political ends. There is no uniform political meaning that can be guaranteed if only you get the metaphysics right. When you say something, when you write a text, it goes into the world and takes on a variety of possible meanings, and this includes secularism and even asceticism. The question is, as Sarah Coakley asked yesterday morning, can we think about aligning feminism, sexuality, and religion in a new non-oppressive way, in an egalitarian way, in a liberating way? This is really the question that all of the papers have addressed and have answered in some different ways.

There was a lot of contrast in the papers we heard on this question. Contrast between, on the one hand, the reign of sex, or Dionysian sex, or a discourse of sex, which some people have seen as liberatory, and on the other hand, a very different answer, a Christic sex that involves a silencing, an allowing of silencing, of sacrifice, a kind of pure nothing, God as a kind of nothingness. We also heard a contrast between Christianity and Christendom. We heard a contrast between feminism and the state-sponsored or enforced feminism of imperial modernity. There has also been a contrast between a sort of professed faith, a new articulation of faith, and, on the other hand, Hélène Cixous's articulation of prayer without understanding, a mingling of belief and unbelief, a naming without naming, a kind of fluidity. One of the other main contrasts is between the idea that to make feminism, sexuality, and religion compatible again we need a new articulation that is specific and substantive, a Christ with a body, a Christ with a sexual identity and an ethnic identity, for example. A new paradigm, a new articulation of religion, on the one hand, and then on the other hand, the articulation of a real fluidity, a kind of emptiness or ultimate possibility or pure difference as the way to go, because any new paradigm, any new content, is going to lead to more exclusions, will close down possibilities, and move us away from egalitarianism or liberatory possibilities. I invite our guests to answer this question of how feminism, sexuality, and religion might be aligned or realigned.

COAKLEY. One way of saying what you've just stated so elegantly, Linda, would be to ask if there is anywhere to go beyond repression and libertinism. It's very easy, I think, when trying to describe a way out of repression, constantly to re-embrace new forms of libertinism. Yet if libertinism is the reign of sex, then I think Mark Jordan has rather clearly indicated why this doesn't help our project forward. For my own part, as a Christian theologian, I am interested in reevaluating strands in my tradition that may have critical applicability to the present, especially when one is trying to escape beyond a false dilemma such as this; and I'm also concerned about what may be represented as the "enemy" from the past, lest precisely here lies something that may strangely help us forward. In this regard I would like to take up a point of contention, if I may, with Kelly Douglas. Kelly and I share the responsibility, burden, and joy of being priests in the church, in my case the Church of England, and in her case the Episcopal Church. So I was fascinated, but in some ways very disturbed—and I think this is something that may bring more people into the conversation—to hear her describe the "Platonic" heritage in Christianity as the main *problem* that she sees has to be overcome. For of course the Platonic tradition was fruitfully bound with Christianity from the second or third century onward. Some of the greatest mystical writings in the Christian tradition provide us precisely with the sort of move into what Hélène is also interested in, prayer without understanding. That, in turn, potentially provides some kind of critical riposte to those strands within the Christian tradition that precisely have been "repressive." The acknowledgement of the relation of desire for God and sexual desire, and the ascetical task of bringing these two into some sort of spiritual alignment, is not a project currently very attractive to American cultural mores; but it could just be that here lies a wisdom greatly in need of reconsideration. So I just throw down my gauntlet here. I don't know whether Kelly or others would like to reflect further on the Platonic heritage within Christianity and what its future might be for those who seek to move beyond repression and libertinism?

DOUGLAS.   Obviously, it's a mixed heritage. Let me begin by saying that it seems to me that religion and all that it implies never functions in a social, historical, cultural vacuum. Religion emerges in culture and is a reflection of culture. The frameworks from which we try to see the world are not innocent. They act themselves out in a social, historical, cultural context, and they interact in different ways. I do not deny some positive evaluation of Platonic thought, but even as I do that, I also have to recognize what have not been the positive dimensions of that thought. I suggested that it has projected a kind of dualism that to me is hegemonic and oppositional and has indeed spelled trouble for typically subjugated peoples. So in that regard the negative consequences of the Platonic split are significant enough, particularly as it functions in relationship to those who have been othered. That indeed does need to be called into question. I think the other thing that we have to recognize is how these things function when connected with power and empire in Christianity. In my most recent work, I talked about that and about the implications of these things, about Platonic thought in terms of subjugated bodies, in terms of power, in terms of those who have been othered. I don't know that we're at odds. I can affirm a positive evaluation of Platonic thought and what it has given to Christendom. But even as I do that, its negative impact has been such that this cannot be the framework for the way in which I think about Christianity. I think it has had more a detrimental impact on the way we think about the body, and that stands in contrast with an incarnate religion.

COAKLEY. Perhaps there are two points that might help to open up the discussion further. First, when you talk about "dualism"—about what you see as an "anti-body" quality in Plato (which in one sense no one can deny)—I wonder whether that doesn't then set off the body *against* the spirit in a way that neither alleviates the difficulty we are trying to solve, nor does it do justice, either, to the manifold ways that early Christian writers themselves modified Platonic anti-materialism in the light of the incarnation? I am interested, as you know, in that strand of Platonism that fruitfully combines with the early Greek fathers' perception of Christianity precisely as an incarnational religion. In someone like Gregory of Nyssa, this leads to an extraordinarily rich, ascetical understanding of the body precisely *because of* its marriage of Platonism with Christianity; and it also promotes a contemplative dimension in Christianity, a capacity for transformative silence, which I think alone allows us to listen to "otherness" with true attentiveness. So here is my second point about the value of this "Platonic" heritage within Christianity: there is an awful lot of talk about "otherness" in postmodern ethical and religious discussion; there is rather less talk about what might be the contemplative practices that would allow you actively to listen to the other as opposed to merely talking about it.

KELLER. I want to point out that it's rather marvelous that in this Syracusan home of secular theology and a strongly secular analysis of religion there are three Christian feminist theologians on this one postmodern panel. I think that's excessive and rare and very oddly hospitable; and it allows me to take a mediating position. I hear Kelly not at all in danger of pitting the body against the spirit but occupying a critical, self-critical, and nuanced third position that raises the question of signifying. How can we signify sacrifice and not fall into a repetition of the wrong sort of sacrifice? How do we signify some of these ancient symbols with a difference, with some blues and some irony in them? I hear her sense of the blues and the spiritual voice as a trope of embodiment, as really a third space between what rightly worries Sarah and Mark. Mark, with devastating beauty and subtlety, was unveiling for us a dangerous dance between the totalizing truth of a disembodied God and of the "King Sex" that rises up in defiance in a way that became commodified and even then redistributed oddly on the religious right. So we are involved in a kind of dance between what I call the absolute and the dissolute, between a form of totalism and a form of relativism. Good old God on the side of the absolute, and the satiric libertine tradition that we don't want just to sacrifice on the other. I agree with Sarah and with Kelly that the Platonic tradition is of course not one, that there are multiple folds and auto-critical dynamisms within the Platonic tradition. Like Sarah, I've fallen in love with the apophatic tradition that begins with Gregory of Nyssa; and precisely because of its deconstructive gesture, the whole poststructuralist tradition has also been attracted to it in a careful and suspicious way. It is suspicious precisely because the Neoplatonic Absolute will intrude at any moment, just when you're starting to relax into the marvelous deconstructive radicalism of the Pseudo-Dionysius; just when that luminous darkness begins to unfold and liberate one even from our light supremacism, from the binary of the evil darkness and the white light of the One. At any moment that richly deconstructive mystical tradition may resort to the worst of the Neoplatonic disembodied hierarchy. But one can then read it against itself, over and again.

VATTIMO.   I want to jump in and to start very basically: Is there anybody among us who still believes that God exists? No, we don't believe this. But all the discourses we have heard here more or less—quite aside from the problem of the Platonic tradition in particular—concern some aspect of the problem of metaphysics. Many of these discussions gave me the impression that everyone agrees, God obviously exists, but how do you think him with sex or without sex? With Jesus or without Jesus? Is God a woman? The question is, what are we talking about? I propose this question in a very radical way. For instance, the death of God in Nietzsche seems to me important precisely because there is both a time before and after the death of God. After the death of God, there is history. Can we interpret the sacrifice of Isaac and the sacrifice of Jesus in typological terms, as if one was the figure of the other, without considering what happened in the meantime, without considering the historicity of our idea of God? We reach a situation in which we can deconstruct because deconstruction is not a simple invention of a genial man by the name of Jacques Derrida; it is also something that has historical substance. It is possible today to speak of deconstruction because God is dead. But how did he die? This is also an interesting story. For instance, when we spoke of sacrifice the other day, I was astonished by the absence of René Girard, not just because Girard is very important but because of the absence of any idea of the transformation of the idea of sacrifice. Girard thinks that there was an idea of victimization in the interpretation of sacrifice in the Old Testament, and then after the New Testament something has changed. This could be an interesting way of going back to the sacrifice of Isaac. Girard wants to keep a symbolic form of sacrifice because he believes that this is important for the functioning of humankind, but this is a problem. Shall we keep either a symbolic sacrifice or not? Did Jesus come to the world, if he came, only to show that sacrifice is very difficult? No, he changed something, but what did he change? So the problem of history is the problem of not interpreting the relation between a figure in the Old Testament and in the New Testament in a simply typological way. This is very important to me. I am not familiar with the feminist American discourse, and I apologize for that. But even the formation of a new perspective on feminism depends on the dissolution of metaphysics and the fact that metaphysics has also been the affirmation of natural forces. Man was traditionally stronger in society than woman. The woman had to take care of the children, and man was the authority, which raises the question of metaphysical authority, which we would have to discuss. We cannot simply substitute a feminist metaphysics for a non-feminist metaphysics and say that God was not male but female. I have nothing against that, but I just don't know exactly what we would be saying. I intervene at this point because I do not want to let the discussion go on without raising this question.

CIXOUS. I'll join in from another point of view. First, regarding feminist theology, I'd like to come back to that. There may be a need for feminist theology for those who feel that they belong to the universe of theology so that they have to fight from within the precincts of religions and theologies in order to affirm the rights of women as you do in the political sphere. That's one thing that is undeniable, but it belongs to this theological enclosure. What do we do within theology, when we're within religion? Although this seems to be a semicircle, it is a circle. That is, it is from within that most of these discourses have been held, from within a supposed adaptation of religion or God. Now the Christian tone of the conference is most striking. I accept it, but of course I have to situate myself anthropologically, if I may say so. I do understand and accept the problems that arise in Christianity, in Christendom. But what if you're not within Christianity? I would like simply to play the part of the animal and maybe even of the donkey. I just felt a little left out, even as a Bible reader. I am a Bible reader, I adore reading the Bible, but does it mean that this is a religious attitude? This should be discussed. I want to come back to the sacrifice of Isaac. I've always been interested in those primal scenes that you find in the Bible; they are abundant and there is a wealth of enigmas that we have for millennia dreamt about. How was it that we were caught by the scene of the sacrifice of Isaac? Why did I speak about Moses striking the rock? But when I say that, I draw a limit between where we can refer to those myths and where these don't exist. I mean the other half of the world, which has never heard of any of that. I don't speak of course of the Abrahamic religions, because the Muslims share a regard for Abraham. But if you turn to India or China, what do they have to do with that? So what about religion elsewhere?

Now let me come back to the sacrifice. I can't forget what Derrida has opened and said in a way that is intrepid, not without trembling, and at the same time with utter courage regarding the extreme refinement of his thinking. He has already answered everything that we're talking about. Gianni was part of a fantastic dialogue that they had on the island of Capri a while ago, which addressed all these questions that we are discussing. Jacques Derrida has already opened the way for rigorous but not rigid answers, for ways to be extremely flexible in thinking about the return of religion, faith, belief, knowledge, the Platonic traces in Christianity, Kant, the death of religion. I but follow, as a donkey. I think I entered the Bible through several doors, but one of the doors was the animal door. For instance, Tobias and the angel journey together, and the dog walked behind them. In my version, the dog became a cat: I preferred a cat to follow the angel. Back to the Bible: I looked at Tobias, the fantastic story of Tobias the father, the son, and the angel and the dog, and of course the fish, and I followed.

Back to the donkey. In the sacrifice of Isaac, I always thought, when they start climbing up the mount for the sacrifice, I am the donkey. Who are we when we go up the mount? Are we Abraham? I think Derrida, for instance, when he writes on this incredible moment, sides now and then with Isaac but mostly with Abraham as the one who is sentenced to secrecy. That is very interesting since Derrida was, unconsciously, if I may say so, rather on the side of the son and consciously on the side of the father. I for my part may now and then feel that I am Abramized, but I don't feel I'm Isaac. I always feel that I'm the donkey because I hear everything you say and I am supposed to be mute, whereas of course I have my donkey language. I understand everything that is happening. In French a donkey is *âne*. I suggest you call me *Abrahâne*: a mixture of Abraham and the *âne* because they have the same fate. They share the same terrible tragic and at the same time not tragic secret. Then of course I would follow the path of Kierkegaard and of Derrida rereading Kierkegaard.

We are touched, we are moved, we are set in motion and thinking by all those situations that we find in the Bible, which I think are the works of genius, of the geniuses who wrote the Bible. Clarice Lispector, the great Brazilian writer, speaks of *eles*, "they" in the masculine, *they* (who wrote) the Bible. *Eles dizem tudo, a Bíblia, eles dizem tudo.* So when Gianni asks, "But who believes God exists?" I think that's a question, of course. I won't give an answer because I think that the fact that the word God and the name of God and the names of gods circulate means something for all of us. But I couldn't in any way feel that I have any solution to what is agitating all of us if it were inside religion. I would give up. Religion is like a credit bank for our anguish. I do not privilege one religion or the other. That's why I ask, what do we do with others, other religions, other cultures? I feel very close to the reflections of Buddhism, if it is a religion, but it is more like a philosophy, more dialectical, more open to contradictions. But again, these are our humble answers, inventions that we make up and then subscribe to, in order to try to find ways to confront ourselves with the unnamable, with the unknown, with what is coming, as Derrida would say. That is what we must recognize if we are not inside a religion: that we have to borrow the language that religion has left for all of us. When Derrida, for instance, speaks about messianicity, in order to be understood throughout the world he uses a word that comes to us through Hebrew then through Latin. But again, what if we don't believe in religion, which doesn't mean what if we don't believe? says the donkey. The last donkey, of course, is the she-ass of Balaam, who is the wisest, as you know, and who, being a she is, of course, of interest for a feminist theology. Why is she a she, or is she a she, and how is a donkey a she?

VATTIMO. May I jump in again? I just want to say whether or not I believe in God. Allow me just one sentence: God is the meaning of the word God, but the word God has a story, and this is the only reality of God that we can talk about. So let's reflect upon this.

MAHMOOD. Let me introduce a different note of dissonance here. I also have felt extremely uncomfortable, I must say, with the Judeo-Christian thrust of the discussions for the last two days now. Unfortunately, we are holding the "Roundtable" before some of us have had a chance to speak, so this might make more sense after you have heard my talk. But in any case, let me spell out some of my reservations. My discomfort with the Judeo-Christian thrust of this conference cannot be resolved simply by having more religions represented at the table. To do so, as Judith Butler suggested in her talk yesterday, is to confuse plurality with heterogeneity. Plurality is a liberal gesture that might invite people from different points of view to be represented at the table but does not challenge the assumptions that secure the conceptual supremacy granted to the Judeo-Christian tradition when pondering the question of religion. One of the key problems that attend both academic and public discussions about religion is the assumption that all religions share a commonality of problems that center around issues of belief, cosmology, and metaphysics. As much of recent work on religion argues, this is a very narrow conception of religion, one that no more captures Christianity's premodern history than it encompasses other forms of religion and practice. As an anthropologist of religion, I think the interesting question is not so much whether people believe in religion or god or metaphysics but what the modern notion of religion has done in the world, what kinds of subjectivities it has produced, what forms of hierarchies, what forms of inequalities, what conceptions of justice and freedom has it enabled and foreclosed. I would like us to question the modern category of religion (as if it has an identifiable essence that is locatable across histories, cultures, times and places), and its power to produce normative subjectivities and worldviews.

One very troubling aspect of the study of religion has been the way in which the concept of religion, in the social sciences and the humanities, has come to assume Christianity as the model through which religion is theorized, imagined, debated and discussed. This has had a transformative effect on non-Christian traditions that have been made to measure up against a normative conception of what religion should be. This is a point that has been made by a number of scholars in the field of anthropology, religious studies, and history in the past two decades—such as Talal Asad, Steven Wasserstrom, and Winfred Cantwell-Smith. Yet this perspective has been crucially missing from our discussions in the past couple of days. So the question is, indeed, if our analytical concept of religion is indebted to a particular genealogy and history, then how can we continue to use it without any sort of reflection on whether it really encompasses what it claims to describe? There have been attempts to make the analytical category of religion more copious and robust, but most of these attempts remain inadequate because the conceptual architecture of religion continues to derive from the Christian experience and its universal and normative assumptions. This is not simply a historical problem but a philosophical one as well.

JORDAN. I could not agree more with Saba's critique of the category of religion, which is why the first thing I did in my paper was to dispense with that category. But I want to carry the critique all the way down. There is no religion, there is no Christianity, there is no Roman Catholicism. There is a large, complicated, ever-mutating set of discourses that sometimes speak to each other and sometimes don't, that fight most of all about whether the others deserve the title "Roman Catholic" or "Christian" or "religious." But once one pursues that line of thinking, the difficulty is that one ends up talking only about the rhetorical tensions and tropings of one's own particular community. One can of course draw analogies. One is *compelled* to draw analogies. I share the belief that discourses ought to be in conversation with one another. Hegemonic discourses that have a bloody alliance with imperial power need especially to be checking their own assumption that their discourse is the universal discourse. But I am sensitive to the dangers of facile comparison and also sensitive to the assumption that there is a scientific or pseudoscientific discourse that can attain a universality that somehow escapes from the dangers of universality.

MAHMOOD. I think you're absolutely right that no analytical discussion can proceed if it remains at the level of particularities. But I think that we need to think more carefully about the distinction between universality and particularity, and the way this distinction functions in solidifying the inequalities of power between the West and the non-West, between the North and the Global South. The problem of how to reconcile the particularity of Christianity with its universal and transhistorical claims has long exercised modern European philosophers and historians. This was the preoccupation not only of Christian apologists but of a range of Enlightenment thinkers who acknowledged that Christianity was one among many other religious forms embraced by humanity but who remained convinced nonetheless that it was only Christianity that was capable of transcending its historicity and addressing the human condition. For thinkers as disparate as Locke, Hume, and Kant, what enabled Christianity to rise above its particularity was its singularity, its unique ability to capture and embody universal principles and truths in a manner that other religions could not because they remained mired in their cultural and doctrinal particularities. It might be argued that the disciplines of Religious Studies, Comparative Religions, and History of Religions have overcome this problem, but a quick survey of these fields shows that this is not the case. Tomoko Masuzawa's work shows this quite convincingly and forcefully.

JORDAN. Can I just make sure that we understand each other, because I am not sure whether we are disagreeing or not. Saba, you heard me to say that I don't believe that there is a universality, right? I am not one who is comfortable using the category "religion" or the category "ritual" as a generic category. And so I quite agree with you in what you just said. But I want to add that for me the issue is not universality and particularity. There is no issue about universality, because there is no universality outside of representation.

MAHMOOD. Oh, I think there is, even if we want to challenge it or de-center it. Normative discourse almost always strives to be universalistic.

DOUGLAS. May I interject? First, I agree with this critique. But how can we understand and talk about religion? Religion doesn't manifest itself up there; religion manifests itself down here. Religion is something that human beings do, not something done by the transcendent. Our way of relating to or accessing the transcendent, as I said earlier, doesn't function in a vacuum. Religion functions in human reality, emerges from below, even if what we're talking about is the transcendent and presumably the universal. We can't access it universally. That is one of the dangers of talking about universality, and I agree that certain particularities obliterate other particularities. Christianity lends itself to this sort of imperialistic movement, even if there is a side of it that resists it. But we can't appreciate the universal if we don't appreciate the particularities. There is a danger of obliterating and obscuring the richness of the particularities. It's not that I don't believe in the universal, but I don't know how we access it. I don't know if we can access it, but I do know that we begin with a rich appreciation for what is particular, which is not to suggest that one particularity overcomes another. I think when we talk about and start with universalities we only do so because we define the universal by what is the dominating particular, and I think that's problematic. I don't know how you have religious discourse without an appreciation for a way in which religion and religious discourse emerges.

KELLER.   I would like briefly to incarnate here Tobias's dog. Actually, the word is *cynos*, dog, and my exegetical friends have told me that he is probably in the story to represent the Greek presence. So that dog is a way of indicating already, in that very late scripture, that the notion of religion as anything self-encapsulated would be internally deconstructed by its very presence. Until about the second century, as Daniel Boyarin has helpfully pointed out, the word *religion* has been a Christian invention within the context of the empire that allowed the differentiation of Christianity from Judaism. That was very difficult to accomplish and actually took centuries. Boyarin shows there was tremendous resistance to drawing a clear boundary between the Jews who followed Christ and the Jews who did not follow Christ. So "religion" became an important tool in the development of a Christianity that could travel compactly through the Roman Empire and eventually engulf it. But I have also learned from John Thatamanil, working in comparative theology, of another problem with the notion of religion. It creates a false sense of boundedness that not only will create delusional separations between religious bodies that are actually extremely porous and permeable, but it also occludes the radical heterogeneity within each of the so-called religions. In the present context, having a trinity of feminist Christian theologians may seem like a kind of triumphalist, nearly papal takeover, emitting a Christic force field in the room. I appreciate and repent of that effect. But the communication between each of our three perspectives represents an achievement of the feminist decades that have shaped the three of us, with our heavily historically inflected differences. These contextual differences have required years and years of practiced and conflictual engagement across the discourse of sexuality, race, ethnicity, gender, and at the same time through the negotiation of our deep discomforts with Christianity itself. It's painful for me to be seen as performing a Christocentric theology. I certainly practice a Christology, but one that I imagine is an internal deconstruction of Christocentrism, that decenters Christ radically without erasing the meanings and symbols of the Incarnation, but redistributes them dramatically. That is itself a Christian effort, one that performs a service, and not just for those struggling for a voice within the church. Some of us are only involved in the struggle *within* the church because we think that it's also awfully important for those of you who never want to come near a church that some of us on the inside work to heal the apocalyptically threatening pathologies of Christendom.

VATTIMO.   I want to join the anti-universalists among us. But by the way, I don't want to affirm as a universal truth that there is no universal. I simply take into account that today one speaks of universals only concerning Iraq, magically. It is an impossibility to speak decently of universalism in our situation. I learned from a very important book by the young Heidegger, his *Introduction to the Phenomenology of Religion,* that you cannot speak universally of religion because it is exactly when you speak of religious experience that you realize that it is impossible to speak universally. In this book Heidegger analyzes a letter of Paul because he finds himself within a Christian civilization. This has a lot of consequences. I have always thought as a Christian that there was a sort of progress from the particularism of the Jews to the universality of Christianity. I have some doubts about that now because universal Christianity is parallel to the Constantinian church. I don't know at which point we stop deconstructing Christianity. It also strikes me now that instead of universality we have to introduce Derrida's notion of hospitality, which is the only way to treat other cultures. There is no limit to hospitality, no accepting the other just to this point but no more. I give you the keys to my home and then you come in and of course that's a risk. But that's the only reasonable thing I can do.

COAKLEY.   I think by now the audience can probably tell that there are three different and internally very complicated conversations going on in this roundtable. I am amused to find myself down at the European end of the table, sitting here with Hélène and Gianni. It reminds me that I am going back into a very different sort of discussion from that in North America when I return to Cambridge next year. For there, in "secularized" Europe, it seemingly is often just assumed that God is dead; whereas we all know that God is very much alive in America, and that 90 percent of Americans believe in the existence of "good old God." So we have some mixed signals at this table, and more than one debate in play. First, we have a conversation about the deconstruction of God language, which has dominated European discussion for many years now but is often ignored in religious American circles. Secondly, we have a conversation about how American Christianity can cleanse itself, if you like, of its past sins about sexuality. Thirdly, we have another, and different, conversation, which Saba has pressed upon us, about the study of religion and the extent to which Christian assumptions about religion are hegemonic. These debates are interconnected in rather complicated ways. But I do want to say that I am not racked with guilt (white liberal guilt or any other sort!) about the maintenance and continuation of the language of Christian metaphysics. I would love to have a longer conversation with my immediate partners here at the table about whether such metaphysics has a future. But I think that if we are rightly equipped with a proper understanding of apophatic traditions and practices within Christianity then we can see that the questions raised by Heidegger and others against the whole "metaphysical" tradition are capable of resolution.

Cixous.   I just wanted to reassure my good friend [Keller] who is deconstructing inside Christianity that I don't disagree at all. I don't want to make deconstruction a kind of universal religion replacing the different religions. Deconstruction is a movement, a powerful way of going further into what Derrida calls night light, a light in the night, and a very dangerous one. Of course deconstruction is not abstract; it demands a lot of strength and spiritual, intellectual power. It has to be applied to all situations. I am absolutely sure, having started to read your book, that you are doing it where you are. It is obvious to me that you are doing that. Of course, each time it becomes a strictly personal, subjective question: How far do I go, how far can I tolerate or suffer the suffering of deconstructing to go on? Do I go on infinitely? Do I apply it the way you do, because your personal desire, which I totally respect, is to maintain, to save religion, in a way to better it, improve it, make it more open, indeed responsive to hospitality? You do it with all your might, and I think that's necessary. But then we are all overdetermined. All of us here are speaking from archives that others don't know about. As you [Coakley] said, you are among the Europeans, who themselves are also cast among several influences, texts, languages, although the French and Italian are not very far apart, and they are all quoting the Bible in Greek. This is something that we have to analyze. I feel close to each one here in a very personal way. I appreciate, for instance, when Sarah said "in my tradition." She was cautious. She said "in my home," "there, that's what I think." Of course, she thinks it with the whole world, but it's in her, from her precise place. Each of us has this problem; each of us is a mixture of worlds, spheres, a chaos, and then we start speaking about world issues that we all share, that have very threatening political consequences. Every sentence that we analyze here, if we follow it, can bring us to a war scene. Gianni was right when he said that there is a suspension of concepts when you bomb Iraq. It's true. We can separate our reflections here on religion—what is religion and what is not religion, what is within or without religion—from the other religion, I would say the veiled, surreptitious, very lethal religion that comes around us under the name of politics. We keep quarreling about definitions, about me and you and they, and justifying through God/dog. I heard Gianni say that, but you know in English God is dog the other way round. In French, *Dieu* sounds like *d'yeux*, eyewise, and dog is *chien*, and *chien*'s anagram is *niche* (kennel). So I was thinking, when you were speaking about going to Europe and about the different Gods you will have to work with there, that in some countries God is a refugee.

CAPUTO.   Perhaps we should take this occasion to open the discussion up to the floor.

MARY AQUIN O'NEILL (Director, Mount Saint Agnes Theological Center for Women, Baltimore, Maryland). First, I want to say that this has been a terrific conference and all the more excellent for the courageous pointing out of limitations that you engaged in at this Roundtable. I realize that we have not heard all of the talks yet, but I do want to follow your example by pointing out one thing that I missed in the talks we've heard so far, and that is the presence of the female body. With the exception of the she-ass who was mentioned this morning, and Mary, who was mentioned only in passing, the female body has been remarkably absent. Not only that, but the male body has been feminized. Isaac was feminized, and there was a fleeting reference to Jesus as a lesbian, I think, if I heard it correctly. So I just place that before you. I'm not expecting anybody to respond but I do think that it is something that needs to be said.

DOUGLAS. My whole talk was on the black female body. Were you present for the talk? I hope you weren't suggesting that in my talk black women weren't accepted as such.

GAIL BEDERMAN (University of Notre Dame). This is both a political question and a pastoral question, and I ask it as someone outside the discipline, who doesn't study religion at all. I teach history and history of sexuality. In my class are 20-year-olds who are wrestling with heterosexuality; but I see this also with ordinary middle-school girls. For them the question is really about sex, no matter what their views on religion. And for them, I think it's a question of how to understand the relationship between sexuality and the social. Mark raised some of these issues, but he did it so poetically that it doesn't help me figure out what to tell the kids. They're not the only ones who can't see their own desires in terms of the social, of course. In the United States and especially in conservative areas, we have lost a sense of the social in a variety of ways. Nobody knows why to pay taxes, what holds us together. My young women students, many of whom are Catholic, see sexy heterosexuality as feminist and as empowering. They can't see any difference between second-wave feminism and Hugh Hefner. [Laughter] That not funny: they are constructing themselves as powerful women by watching and adopting attitudes from music videos, and so forth. This gets them back to libertinism of a certain type, which they see as feminist and empowering. They seem to imagine heterosexual sexiness as something that aggrandizes them but cuts off deeper relations with men. They see sex, sexuality, as something you do quickly, often drunk, and move on to somebody else, and they see that kind of alienated exercise of desire and desirability as empowering. Can you give me some advice?

JORDAN. Gail, as you know I have a lot to say—I have said too much—about Notre Dame. I will say nothing more here. But I do want to use the occasion of your powerful question to reinforce a point your made. One of the beauties I appreciated in the gift that Hélène Cixous gave us, an extraordinary gift, was her invocation of her own childhood, because one of the features of the discourse about sexuality is that we tend to begin in it when we are 18. We drop out our childhoods. We also drop out adolescence, which is for many of us a painful memory, but also the time in which when we worked out the narratives and the poetry, the categories and the language, of our own sexuality. Nothing seems more important to me than to be able to talk about the function of various religious discourses in the constitution of childhood and adolescent sexuality. And nothing is more difficult, given our taboos—and, may I add, current federal restrictions on research about sexuality in childhood and adolescence. In order to garner life histories of men and women who were raised in Christian churches and now identify as queer, I had to negotiate with the internal research board at Emory University as if I were conducting experiments with lethal radiation. So I want to underline what you are saying. It's a feature especially of gay male rhetoric that it begins with the assumption that people appear in the world at the age of 18 plus one minute.

CIXOUS. I just want to say a few words, but I feel at the same time that I shouldn't because what you said has really touched me and I feel for you completely. I realize that indeed this is an American predicament, and it's so overdetermined culturally—the worry and the problem— which for me is very telling, that you appear in the world at 18 plus one minute. All these things don't exist in Europe. Sarah was speaking about libertinism, and while the word comes from France, this doesn't exist in France. So I could react and share positions and difficulties with you, but I feel it would be from the possibilities of openness that really are the mainstream in France. My granddaughter, who is 8, who lives in the States, is already caught in this snare which is a kind of second nature: repression of sexuality, the "PC," the "myth" of sexual harassment, which we all know is the plague in all universities and institutions, works against those subtle variations that are totally musical, against what happens with the body, in our body, that does not start at 18 or 8 or 3. It's a huge problem, and it involves the media and the schools. You spoke in terms of heterosexuality. As you know Derrida tended to think (in terms of sexualities that are not identifiable) that there are many sexualities and many sexual differences.

VATTIMO. Just another word from old Europe. I refer to the first sentence of my paper. I start by saying that it seems to me that the central importance of sexuality in life is a sort of vanishing belief which remains the patrimony of priests and psychoanalysts. Let's not laugh too much at that because, as a friend of mine suggested to me, "you are no longer homosexual, you are a veterosexual." Are we not exaggerating? For instance, in education is it possible that there are many feminine and masculine attitudes that are not related to sex? By the way, the late Herbert Marcuse used to say there is a sexuality without sex, love without sex, and sex without love. In this conference we have not spoken of prostitution, but I assume that it is absolutely devaluated, that it is the devil. I don't know. Is it not terribly bourgeois to think that sex and love represent a sort of sacral patrimony to which we are to be faithful? This is just a modern Europe faith. Marriages in the past were guided by families; some people also had sex without being married. There is an uneasiness I sometimes feel when we speak of sexuality and feminism, because it seems to me that there is a sort of prejudice that shares the most banal European bourgeois traditions. Of course, I am also a European bourgeois, but being veterosexual gives me a greater lucidity.

DOUGLAS. That is why I talked about women singing the blues. It is not European, bourgeois, or white. It projects a whole different paradigm of sexuality and the body. I did indeed try to open ways to talk about sexuality and to talk about loving relationships that are not tied to marriage or even to heterosexuality, and to talk about a variety of sexualities. We have to begin to decenter this bourgeois Euro-American way of thinking. I want to add that the repression of sexuality in children in the United States is a reflection of the way in which evangelical Protestantism has shaped the political and social culture in this country.

JORDAN.   Could we listen to the sequence of questions? Each of them is important; some are poignant. But their sequence illustrates the paradoxes in the demands we put upon this type of discourse, in the demands we put upon our own lives. On the one hand, many of us have been involved over years in struggles to reform certain institutions; to develop particular political strategies, whether civic or churchly; to put these into effect; to recruit and retain allies; to keep proposing the reforms year after year when they are voted down, reformulating the rhetoric to present the message anew, more convincingly. This is work in the trenches when fighting on behalf of any number of oppressed groups. At the same time, in the very next question, one is asked to deconstruct the categories that are the currency of effective political action. Now I point this out, not to say that we choose one side or the other, but to note the paradox. Part of our silence here results from the paradoxical demand that we put on ourselves, on our speech.

CHARMAINE PERREIRA (Coordinator, Initiative for Women's Studies, Nigeria).   I've come a long way to be here. In our network we engage in a number of action-rich projects, one of which is related to the theme of this conference, and that is women's empowerment and how one might understand the different notions of empowerment that come from different constituencies in specific contexts. Ours is just one part of the country-based teams working on this project. In relation to women's empowerment, we're interested in sexuality and what religion, contextually understood, different religions, offer particular groups of women in terms of either restricting or providing empowerment. So I was interested here in what I might learn from this conference about the relationship between feminism, sexuality, and the return of religion. I found that phrase quite intriguing and I actually expected more interrogation of what the return of religion means, for whom, by whom, and with what implications. My own interest in this phrase is not so much religious discourse, though I recognize that is an important strategy for addressing the religious right in different countries, Nigeria among them. I am interested in the politics of religion, how religion is used in ways that dominate, that oppress, but for some people offer scope for empowerment, and what they understand by empowerment. So I feel I've learned something and at other times wondered what I was doing here, but I also would have appreciated a greater grappling with the political here.

JANE LUNIN PEREL (Professor of English, Director of the Women's Studies Program, Providence College). I want to thank you all so very much. Everything has been fascinating. As for the return of religion, I was not aware that it had ever gone away. My sense and my feeling are at the same time that these categories of feminism, sexuality, and religion are the little boxes into which I have been placed my whole life. That's probably why I was hired. If I were missing a leg, that would have been even better. But I'm grateful for the opportunity I've had to work with people. I don't want you to think that I'm ungrateful. My question goes back to politics and to what I see as a complete lack of fluidity in so many academic institutions where the aim is plurality. When you get people together there is no understanding of interdisciplinarity; it's just multi-disciplinary, multifaceted groups of people who are not exchanging. And one of the texts very dear to me is Chandra Talpade Mohanty's *Feminism Across Borders* because I feel there the recognition of the particularities that make us up. I really feel that this conference is about identity, and I wonder whether we can think of a way to deconstruct the title of the conference so that we have a sense that we are understanding ourselves better, not because of categorization but against it.

REBECCA MCDONALD (Student, College of St. Catherine, St. Paul, Minnesota). I came here as a capstone event because as an all-women's Catholic college we are faced with the clash of feminism, sexuality, and religion on a daily basis. I came here to find tools to address these issues. One brief example is that the *Vagina Monologues* at my campus was cancelled because of a Catholic watchdog group that is pressuring our college to not have these events on campus. We also were trying to organize a Gender-Blur, which is a drag show that's very inclusive of poetry and of other things that drag shows usually are not. It challenges the idea that gender is a performance, so we've had issues around these two events and I need some advice. How do we deal with these issues, and how do

I explain this to incoming freshman that don't understand the clash of feminism, religion, and sexuality?

MELISSA WILCOX (Religion and Gender Studies, Whitman College). I'd like to blow a little bit on one of the sparks that I think hasn't really caught flame at the Roundtable yet about which I would be curious to hear people's opinions. By training I am rather an academic chimaera, but by practice I am a sociologist of religion. Sociologists of religion are generally quite convinced there is no return of religion because in the United States it has never gone away, whereas in much of Europe it has never come back. So I'd be curious as to your reflections on what the return of religion really means, whether there is one, or whether we are talking more about change?

VATTIMO. I have some idea about the return of religion. This is a phenomenon of the Christian world. I wouldn't say in the Islamic world that there is a return of religion. We speak about the return of religion in our secularized Western culture. I see it in two different ways. On one side, there are oppressing social problems: the exhaustion of planet resources, globalization, trying to cope with the new bioengineering, the manipulation of the embryo, very new problems to which people tend to react by going back to a sort of basis, to a community or church. Then of course we cannot forget that Christianity played a role in the disillusionment with the communist world. Pope John Paul II played a role in that. On the other side, there is the philosophical, postmodernism, which has undermined any compelling theoretical reason to be atheistic vis-à-vis the classic atheistic philosophy of the last century. Scientism held that since God is not a subject of science, God can't exist. Historicism held that religion is something of the past but now we are developed. But now these two great narratives themselves don't hold any longer. In Italy, we had a strong anti-clerical movement—and in Europe generally—as long as the Christian Democrats were in power. Then the Christian Democrats disappeared in all the political parties. So there is much less secular politics in Italy today than twenty years ago, when Christian Democrats were in power. People listen to the Pope, today, with the help of the TV. The Catholic Church today is completely a media phenomenon. But let me tell you a story. Once during the last Jubilee year, in 2000, many hundreds of thousands of young people went to Rome and applauded the Pope, when he was preaching chastity. After this great meeting of young people, held in a large place in Rome, the people cleaning the streets found 300,000 prophylactics, not new but used. So this is what happens with the return of religion.

CIXOUS. What do we do when we have concrete problems? Most of the time the constituted religions align themselves with the authority of political powers. But there are situations when an individual does something different, an individual who stands on a limit. I shall describe this exception with a word that I have to borrow: a "saint." I just wanted to point to something that happens across borders, over borders, or giving up completely on all borders. I must admit that in my life I've met one saint. I met that person in the Cambodian camps while Cambodia was still occupied by Vietnam and I was visiting the refugee camps. The situation was so traumatic that I can't describe it, so you have to imagine. Imagine camps where people who have survived massacres, when whole families have been destroyed, and there is one man there who spends his life trying to help those survivors survive the survival, which is very complicated. He happens to be a Jesuit, and his name is Pierre Ceyrac. He had previously spent forty years of his life in India working anonymously, whereas, on the other side of the road, there was Mother Theresa, who was not anonymous. Why do I say that? Because this was an instance that remains unique in my experience. This man gave a chance to survive to thousands of people who adored him. But he was unknown. If I hadn't been in those camps, this would pass in oblivion totally. I kept wondering about how he was able to *give* all the time, without any reward. But perhaps that's not quite true. This is an example of what Derrida says about giving. The reward of giving is that he believed. So he knew that at least God notices. If not the Cambodians or the French or the Vietnamese or the Americans, if no one noticed, probably he thought God noticed. Not that he wanted to be rewarded by God. He didn't speak, he acted. So I kept that as something precious, a magic stone, a precious stone, with which I question all situations. I knew by experience that it couldn't have been a rabbi, not because a rabbi doesn't have the capacity for sainthood, but because rabbis are pressed by the needs of the community to take care of Jews first. I know that. So this is actually the other side of Catholicism but in a way that is very close to what Derrida would be able to analyze as the gift without poison. But of course the limit of it is that it needs the huge body of Catholicism, the Pope as an emperor with, as Gianni said, a crowd of 300,000 in St. Peter's Square, for one single little Pierre—he's called Pierre, Rock—to do something alone, without return, without the trumpets of the media, gratuitously, as a grace. But it happens.

CAPUTO.   That is a very powerful note on which to conclude this conference, Hélène. Thank you very much, and thank you all for being here.

CONTRIBUTORS

LINDA MARTÍN ALCOFF is Professor of Philosophy at Hunter College/CUNY Graduate Center. Recent books include *Thinking From the Underside of History*, edited with Eduardo Mendieta; *Real Knowing: New Versions of the Coherence Theory of Knowledge; Singing in the Fire: Tales of Women in Philosophy; Visible Identities: Race, Gender and the Self; The Blackwell Guide to Feminist Philosophy*, edited with Eva Feder Kittay; and *Identity Politics Reconsidered*, edited with Michael Hames-Garcia, Satya Mohanty, and Paula Moya.

JOHN D. CAPUTO is the Thomas J. Watson Professor of Religion and Humanities and Professor of Philosophy at Syracuse University. His newest books are *What Would Jesus Deconstruct?* (2007) *After the Death of God* (2007; with Gianni Vattimo, ed. Jeffrey Robbins); *The Weakness of God: A Theology of the Event* (IUP, 2006), winner of the 2007 AAR Book Award, "Constructive-Reflective Studies"; and *Philosophy and Theology* (2006). He has recently co-edited *St. Paul among the Philosophers* (IUP, 2009). He is editor of the Fordham University Press book series "Perspectives in Continental Philosophy" and Chairman of the Board of Editors of *Journal of Cultural and Religious Theory.*

HÉLÈNE CIXOUS, Professor of English Literature, University of Paris–VIII, is an internationally acclaimed feminist theorist, literary critic, novelist, and playwright. Raised in colonial Algeria, like her lifelong friend Jacques Derrida, whom she first met in 1963, she founded and directed the Center for Research on Women's Studies at Vincenne in 1974 where she taught until 2005. Her first book, *Le Prénom de dieu*, was published in 1967. She is the author of several hundred works, including a trilogy *Le Troisième Corps* (1970; *The Third Body*), *Les Commencements* (1970), and *Neutre* (1972); *Prénoms de personne* (1974); *La Jeune née* (1975; *The Newly Born Woman*); *Portrait de Dora* (1976; *Portrait of Dora*); *Le Livre de Promethea* (1983; *The Book of Promethea*); *Jours de l'an* (1990; *First Days of the Year*); *L'Ange au secret* (1991); *OR, les lettres de mon père* (1997); *Rêveries de la femme sauvage* (2000; *Reveries of the Wild Woman*); *Manhattan* (2002); *Hyperrêve* (2006; *Hyperdream*).

SARAH COAKLEY is Norris-Hulse Professor of Divinity at the University of Cambridge, and previously taught at Lancaster, Oxford, and Harvard universities. A systematic theologian and philosopher of religion, she seeks to combine feminist theory with these more classic disciplines. She is the author or editor of a number of books, including *Religion and the Body; Powers and Submisions: Philosophy, Spirituality and Gender; Re-Thinking Gregory of Nyssa; Pain and its Transformations;* and *Re-Thinking Dionysius the Areopagite* (2009). She is at work on a four-part systematic theology, the first volume of which is entitled *God, Sexuality and the Self: An Essay 'On the Trinity'.*

KELLY BROWN DOUGLAS is the Elizabeth Conolly Todd Distinguished Professor of Religion at Goucher College. She is the author *Sexuality and the Black Church; The Black Christ* and *What's Faith Got to Do With it.* She is currently working on *Black and Blues/God-Talk/Body Talk for the Black Church.*

MARK D. JORDAN is R. R. Niebuhr Professor at Harvard Divinity School. He is interested in the creation of ethical subjects, the discipline of religious bodies, and the words that accomplish both. His recent books include *Telling Truths in Church: Scandal, Flesh, and Christian Speech* and *Blessing Same-Sex Unions: The Perils of Queer Romance and the Confusions of Christian Marriage.*

CATHERINE KELLER is Professor of Constructive Theology at the Theological School and the Graduate Division of Religion of Drew University. She is author of, most recently, *On the Mystery: Discerning Divinity in Process; God and Power: Counter-Apocalyptic Explorations; Face of the Deep: A Theology of Becoming; Apocalypse Now & Then: A Feminist Guide to the End of the World;* and *From a Broken Web: Separation, Sexism and Self;* she has co-edited *Process and Difference: Between Cosmological and Poststructuralist Postmodernism,* as well as several "Transdisciplinary Theological Colloquium" volumes, including *Toward a Theology of Eros; Ecospirit;* and *Apophatic Bodies.*

SABA MAHMOOD is associate professor of Anthropology at the University of California, Berkeley. She is the author of *Politics of Piety: The Islamic Revival and the Feminist Subject* (2005) that received the Victoria Schuck award from the American Association of Political Science. She is also the co-author of *Is Critique Secular? Blasphemy, Injury, and Free Speech* (2009). Her work focuses on secularism, religion, gender, Islam, and politics of religious minorities in the Middle East and Europe.

GIANNI VATTIMO, Emeritus Professor of Philosophy at the University of Turin, is a member of the European Parliament and Italy's best-known philosopher. His books in English include *The Responsibility of the Philosopher, Not Being God: A Collaborative Autobiography; Art's Claim to Truth; Dialogue with Nietzsche; After the Death of God* (with John D. Caputo); *The Future of Religion* (with Richard Rorty); *Nihilism and Emancipation; After Christianity; Belief; Beyond Interpretation; The Transparent Society;* and *The End of Modernity.* His forthcoming book, co-authored with Santiago Zabala, is entitled *Hermeneutic Communism.*

INDEX

LINDA MARTÍN ALCOFF is Professor of Philosophy at Hunter College and the City University of New York Graduate Center. She has authored and edited many books, including *Singing in the Fire: Tales of Women in Philosophy; Visible Identities: Race, Gender, and the Self; Identity Politics Reconsidered;* and *The Blackwell Guide to Feminist Philosophy* (with Eva Feder Kittay).

JOHN D. CAPUTO is Thomas J. Watson Professor of Religion and Humanities at Syracuse University. He is the author of many publications, including *The Weakness of God: A Theology of the Event* (IUPress, 2006) and *St. Paul Among the Philosophers* (IUPress, 2007), which he co-edited with Linda Martín Alcoff.